THE ARMY IN THE ROMAN REVOLUTION

The destruction of the Roman republic, irrespective of other factors, came about as a result of civil wars. The nature of the Roman revolutionary army and the manner in which it carried out the work of destroying the state has not always been properly understood. Keaveney believes this has happened because of both a misunderstanding of the nature of the source material and a mistaken approach to the historical problem it poses. This book therefore concerns itself with the intrusion of the army into the political sphere and with the consequences which flowed from it. Contrary to what is often assumed, Keaveney demonstrates that Sulla, and not Marius, created the Roman revolutionary army and that its economic motivation was perhaps less than its political. In essence, the development and changes in the army will be traced over two generations, and it will be demonstrated that what Sulla began, Octavian finished.

Arthur Keaveney is Reader in Ancient History at the University of Kent.

THE ARMY IN THE ROMAN REVOLUTION

Arthur Keaveney

Routledge
Taylor & Francis Group

LONDON AND NEW YORK

First published 2007
by Routledge
2 Park Square, Milton Park, Abingdon, Oxon OX14 4RN

Simultaneously published in the USA and Canada
by Routledge
270 Madison Ave, New York, NY 10016

Routledge is an imprint of the Taylor & Francis Group, an informa business

Typeset in Garamond by
Saxon Graphics Ltd, Derby
Printed and bound in Great Britain by
MPG Books Ltd, Bodmin

British Library Cataloguing in Publication Data
A catalogue record for this book is available from the British Library

Library of Congress Cataloging in Publication Data
Keaveney, Arthur.
The army in the Roman revolution / Arthur Keaveney.
p. cm.
Includes bibliographical references and index.
1. Rome—History—Republic, 265–30 B.C. 2. Rome—History,
Military—265–30 B.C. 3. Rome—Army—Political activity. 4. Sulla,
Lucius Cornelius—Influence. 5. Rome—Politics and government—
265–30 B.C.
I. Title.
DG254.2.K43 2007
937'.05—dc22
2006035121

ISBN10: 0-415-39486-4 (hbk)
ISBN10: 0-415-39487-2 (pbk)
ISBN10: 0-203-96131-5 (ebk)

ISBN13: 978-0-415-39486-4 (hbk)
ISBN13: 978-0-415-39487-1 (pbk)
ISBN13: 978-0-203-96131-5 (ebk)

ONCE MORE FOR
JENNY

CONTENTS

PREFACE

Scholars in the humanities rarely agree on anything much. There is, however, one matter about which there is, so far as I am aware, no debate. Irrespective of other factors, the destruction of the Roman republic came about as the result of a series of civil wars. I do not dissent from this view, but study of the period over a number of years has convinced me that the nature of the Roman army as a revolutionary force and the manner in which it destroyed the republic have not always been fully understood by modern historians. There is, therefore, I believe, room for a new examination of this self-evidently important topic. Thus this book represents a fresh attempt at analysing the role of the legions in the last century BC in the ruin of the republic and the introduction of empire.

The genesis of the work can be traced back to a paper entitled 'Sulla the Warlord and Other Mythical Beasts' which I gave at the Sixth International Conference of the International Plutarch Society in Nijmegen / Castle Hernen in May 2002. It was subsequently published in L. De Blois, J. Bons, T. Kessels and D. M. Schenkeveld, *The Statesman in Plutarch's Works* (Leiden, 2005, vol. 2, pp. 297–302). By kind permission of Professor De Blois it is, with some modifications, incorporated in section 1(b) of the present work. The title of this book does not, as might perhaps be supposed, derive from a recent work by Fergus Millar but rather from George Rudé's *The Crowd in the French Revolution*. Mine is, of course, a different kind of book from his but I like to think that my title, while it adequately describes the contents, also conveys in some way the sense of inspiration I derived from reading Rudé's work long ago as an undergraduate.

At a crucial stage (Michaelmas 2004) I was granted a Visiting Research Fellowship by the National University of Ireland, Galway. I am grateful for the opportunity to pass that term there in uninterrupted research. My own university then generously gave me study leave for the Lent term (2005) which allowed me to continue what I had begun in Galway.

Once again Robin Seager has kindly read a manuscript of mine and made comments. Louise Earnshaw-Brown has also had something to say about some of it. Their advice has been of profit to me but neither must be held to have any responsibility whatsoever for anything I have written.

Now I must for the third time record my good fortune in having Aisling Halligan prepare my text. As on previous occasions, she has shown skill, despatch and patience. Go bhfága Dia an tsláinte aici.

Finally I thank my wife Jenny for help with reading the typescript and the proofs.

Arthur Keaveney
University of Kent
July 2006

1

INTRODUCTION

The aim of this work may be stated succinctly. It proposes to study the part the Roman army played in the destruction of the Roman republic in the last century before Christ and to make a significant contribution to its understanding.

In its essentials then this book will be concerned with the intrusion of the army into the political sphere and with the consequences which flowed from it. In this introductory chapter therefore we shall be concerned first of all with sketching the historical background into which our study of the army and its actions must be inserted. Then we shall set forth what we believe to be the problems attendant on a study such as this and the proposed method of approaching them.

(a) The historical background

The Greek historian Appian of Alexandria, one of our chief sources, says that Rome was first ruled by kings. Then when the Romans got rid of them they established what he calls a *demokratia*. Eventually, however, with the dictatorship of Sulla regal rule resumed.[1] Modern scholars might, I suspect, dispute some of this. There has been a debate as to just how democratic the Roman republic was[2] and most people would equate what Appian calls the resumption of kingly rule not with Sulla but with the disguised autocracy of Augustus.[3] Yet there is no doubt that, in the essentials, Appian has got it right.[4] He is describing what we call the Roman revolution, or that change in her system of government from a republic to an empire.[5] The rule of an oligarchy gave way to that of one man. In the republic an aristocracy filled the offices of state and effectively controlled the executive, electoral and legislative business.[6] Now those who shared in the rule of the emperor did so by his leave.[7]

The causes of this great change[8] have naturally been a subject for discussion and debate. Whatever disagreement there may be on points of detail, most scholars would agree, I suspect, that the problems of the republic which ultimately led to its destruction came about because of the failure both of its rulers and of its institutions to adapt to the acquisition of an empire.[9] Save for the discussion of one pertinent issue, namely the change which came about in the composition of the army,[10] we shall not be entering into this debate. The reason is simple. By the time the army begins to play its part, the changes, however we try to account for their origin, have already begun to work through and make themselves manifest. Our concern, thus, is with the army's reaction to or shaping of contemporary events.

This means that we can begin our survey at the point most others do: the year 133. Then, for the first time, it became clear something was wrong. The tribune Tiberius Gracchus was murdered and, as had never happened before in Roman history, a political question was settled by recourse to violence. For the next fifty years or so murders of this sort were to recur at irregular intervals. Tiberius' brother Caius went the same way as he a few years later. Then in 100 it was the turn of Saturninus and Glaucia. Some ten years after, Livius Drusus perished, and he was followed in 88 by his imitator P. Sulpicius.

These violent clashes are usually characterised as a struggle between *populares* and *optimates*.[11] A *popularis* was one who claimed to be acting on behalf of the people, while those who closed ranks against the perceived threat posed by him styled themselves *optimates*. Despite their intensity these engagements were intermittent and had actually been occurring for some fifty years before the army intervened in public life.[12]

On a sanguine view this could be taken as indicating that the state was, despite its troubles, still essentially stable.[13] Such optimism should be tempered by one consideration. The Romans were becoming habituated to violence and it was beginning to be regarded as a natural way to solve political issues both domestic and foreign. For instance, in 88, when the tribune Sulpicius was planning controversial legislation, he accepted as a matter of course that his opponents would use force and so he enrolled a bodyguard. A few years before, the Romans as a whole had been presented with a demand for enfranchisement by the Italians. Their resolute refusal obviously owes something to their being a proud and warlike people but we can also attribute it to a propensity for violence regardless of what the consequences might be.

Eventually the struggle between *populares* and *optimates* did bring the army into public life but in a way some find hard to believe: by accident.[14] In 88 Sulla found himself in danger just as Tiberius Gracchus had once been. But where Tiberius turned to the people, Sulla turned to the army and invited them, as citizens, to take sides in a political issue. They responded positively.

But Sulla did not march on Rome in 88 just to chastise his enemies. He had already pondered the problems which beset Rome and he now brought in laws to remedy them. Events, though, swept them away, but he was back in 81 with a more comprehensive programme, which however was not destined to last either.[15] It could very well be claimed that this constitution of Sulla's failed because the ills it was intended to remedy were by now too deep-rooted to admit of a cure. It looks, however, as if the Romans would not have agreed.

Comprehensive legislation, swiftly enacted, seems to have been deemed sufficient to put matters to right. That, at least, is the impression both Caius Gracchus and Livius Drusus give with their proposed laws brought in during their tribunates. Sulla himself fits this pattern.[16] In 88, in the midst of all his troubles, he found time to bring in some necessary laws which he seemed to think would endure. He soon found out they would not, but in 81, when he devised a more far-reaching programme, proclaiming it as marking the start of a new age for Rome, he still found time to pursue the siege of an Italian town.[17] But it is surely the Liberators who furnish the most grotesque example of a simplistic approach to Rome's problems. As is well known, they thought that all that was required to restore the republic was to murder Caesar.

Sulla's constitution was, in fact, the last large-scale attempt to shore up the republic.[18] It was, however, a failure as we said. That failure, I believe, can be put down to two circumstances. First of all, unlike Augustus, Sulla did not live long after its promulgation and hence was unable to lend his authority to those who sought to come to its defence.[19] Secondly, those to whom he entrusted it proved incapable of making it work. There were ardent supporters of his system such as Lucullus and equally enthusiastic opponents like Caesar, but the vast majority displayed a stodgy indifference. So long as their basic position was not threatened then they could tolerate the chipping away, in the 70s, of what they regarded as peripheral.[20] One suspects they knew what really needed to be done but were happy for others to do it.[21]

But, however we explain the failure, we cannot escape the fact that laws designed to bring concord and harmony did not, so that by the 50s Rome was in a state of virtual anarchy. Clodius with his antics illustrates what a tribune, freed once more from constraint, could do. But the percipient will have seen the even greater danger to come as they observed how Caesar, displaying utter contempt for the institutions of the republic, pushed through his consular legislation (59), by violence.[22]

Yet all of this, though serious, had nothing to do with the second intervention by the army in politics. When it came, it resembled the first in many ways.[23] Like Sulla, Caesar was in danger. His enemies proposed to recall him from Gaul and launch a prosecution for what he had done in 59, before he could achieve immunity by assuming a second consulship. Caesar's *dignitas* was wounded and so, like Sulla, he led his army on Rome. Like Sulla, however, he found few friends in a hostile senate.[24] But there the resemblances end. It was given to Sulla to march a second time on Rome, and then as a champion of the senate with a majority of the fathers backing him. And there was another great difference. From the start Sulla had a clear notion of what he wanted to accomplish in the political sphere. Hence his legislation to strengthen the republic after both his marches. Caesar, on the other hand, does not seem to have clearly formulated any plan for the future of Rome.[25]

From this there follows an important consequence. Once its task was done in 82, Sulla dismissed his army and, as we saw, set about what was essentially a work of repair. Caesar, in spite of the bulk of his legislation, seems to have had no definite concept of what he wanted and at the time of his assassination had already put the problem to one side in order to make an expedition against Parthia.

Having effectively destroyed the republic,[26] he left a threefold legacy: a state which was no more than a shell; quarrelling heirs; and troops ready to assist those heirs in pursuing their quarrels.

These heirs eventually established themselves as the Triumvirate.[27] This was no more than an alliance of convenience, and the last years of the republic's shadowy existence down to the battle of Actium are the story of how these men sought to gain an advantage over each other. Octavian emerged the eventual winner and transformed himself from a gangster into Augustus the wise and benign.[28]

Thus we can see that the army played its part twice in the Roman revolution, once in the age of Sulla and again in the time of Caesar and the Triumvirs. Our task therefore now is not merely to describe the characteristics of this army and chronicle its actions but also to explain them.

So we now turn to confront the problem this poses.

(b) The nature of the problem

The problem confronting the student of the revolutionary army may be illustrated by reference to a passage of Plutarch and modern scholarly reaction to it. The passage in question is Plutarch *Sulla* 12. It forms part of the narrative of the First Mithridatic War. We are in late 87, the Pontic forces have invaded Greece and Sulla has been sent to deal with them. He is currently besieging Athens. However, being denied supplies from home he is obliged to levy monies from the shrines of Greece.[29] Plutarch was indignant at this, as he tells us how those who were taking the treasures from Delphi were upset:

> So the treasures were sent away and certainly most of the Greeks did not know what was happening. But the silver jar, the last of the royal gifts still in existence, was too large and heavy for the baggage animals to carry and the Amphictyons were compelled to cut it into pieces. As they did so they called to mind the names of Titus Flamininus and Manius Acilius and Aemilius Paulus too. One of these had driven Antiochus out of Greece and the others had conquered the Kings of Macedonia. And these men had not only kept their hands off the temples of the Greeks, but had endowed them and honoured them and done much to add to the general respect in which they were held. But these, they reflected, were the lawfully constituted commanders of disciplined troops who had learnt to obey orders without a murmur; they were kingly in soul, but moderate in their personal outlay, keeping their expenditure to the ordinary fixed allowances of the time; and they thought that to show subservience to their own soldiers was more disgraceful than to show fear in the face of the enemy. But now the generals of this later period were men who had risen to the top by violence rather than merit: they needed armies to fight against one another rather than against the public enemy: and so they were forced to combine the arts of the politician with the

authority of the general. They spent money on making life easy for their soldiers and then, after purchasing their labour in this way, failed to observe that they had made their whole country a thing for sale and had put themselves in a position where they had to be slaves of the worst sort of people in order to become masters of the better. This is what caused the exile of Marius and this is what brought him back against Sulla. This is what made Cinna's party murder Octavius and Fimbria's party murder Flaccus. And here it was Sulla more than anyone else who set the example. In order to corrupt and win over to himself the soldiers of other generals, he gave his own troops a good time and spent money lavishly on them. He was thus at the same time encouraging the evils of both treachery and debauchery. All this required much money and especially was it required for this siege.[30]

Now, all this appears plausible and coherent and, in fact, has been accepted as such even by those who have set out to present profound and critical analyses of our period.[31] Sulla is behaving in the way textbooks teach us Roman army commanders behave in the late republic.[32] In short he is a warlord.[33]

When we probe it, however, Plutarch's account is found to be false in every particular. I pass over his failure to mention that Greeks had already done this kind of thing and that Sulla had repaid what he had taken.[34] I want instead to concentrate on his position and actions as a Roman.

To begin with, while we may acknowledge that Sulla was a figure of controversy, he was, nevertheless, a properly constituted consul and proconsul, and attempts to deprive him of his command were violent and unlawful. Certainly Sulla never saw himself as anything but the duly appointed servant of the Roman state and went to extreme lengths to emphasise it. The facts of Sulla's career are well known and amply refute the charge that he had risen by violence rather than merit. Ultimately, of course, Sulla did fight a civil war over the issue of legitimacy but it is straining credulity to say he was nourishing his troops in order to turn them against the state. Plutarch's own text shows him using them to fight an enemy of Rome. It is certainly true Sulla saw to it that his troops were well rewarded – at the expense of the people of Asia. We must realise, however, that this was not the attempt to buy their loyalty which we might infer from reading Plutarch. Rather, he was punishing the Asiatics for their disloyalty and providing his men with what every Roman soldier regarded as his due, booty. Sulla feared that, upon returning home, his men would follow custom and disperse to their homes. This is sufficient, I think, to dispose of the notion that he had for some time been indulging them in order to use them in an assault on Rome. Since Sulla had not, as Plutarch claims, made himself a prisoner of his troops by purchasing their allegiance it will come as no surprise to learn that their discipline, at all times, was exemplary.[35]

So it looks as though Plutarch has got it wrong, but the most telling observation is yet to come. After castigating Sulla for his lawlessness and his robberies, in order to bribe his troops whom he is going to lead against his country, Plutarch calmly announces that the Roman commander is actually collecting the money to prosecute the siege of Rome's enemies in Athens.

I cannot pretend to be able to say where Plutarch ultimately derived his erroneous view of Sulla from.[36] So far as we are concerned, it may not anyway be a matter of great moment. It is far more important that we see clearly its exact nature. That comes from a comparison with Appian BC.5.17:

> The majority of the commanders were unelected, as happens in Civil War, and their armies were recruited neither from the register according to ancestral custom, nor to meet any need for their country. Instead of serving the common interest, they served only the man who had enlisted them, and even so not under compulsion of the law, but by private inducements. Nor did they fight against enemies of the state, but against private enemies, nor against foreigners, but against Romans who were their equals in status. All these factors undermined their fear of military discipline. They felt they were not so much serving in the army as lending assistance from personal goodwill and by their own choice, and that their commanders were forced to rely on them to attain their private ends. Desertion, formerly an unpardonable offence for a Roman, was at that time rewarded by gifts, and it was practised by armies en masse and by some prominent men, because they considered that changing like for like was not desertion. All parties were alike and none of them had been officially condemned as public enemies. The common pretext of the generals, that they were all assisting the interests of their own country, made men readier to change sides since they were assisting their country wherever they were. The generals understood this and tolerated this, knowing that they ruled, not by law, but by bribes.[37]

The broad general similarity of this passage to the Plutarch needs no emphasis. But there is a difference. Appian is not speaking of the 80s but of the Triumviral period and, as will be demonstrated in this work, what he says is true. Thus we are driven to the conclusion that Plutarch has inaccurately described Sulla as a Triumvir or something very like it.

In this episode and its interpretation we have set before us the nature of our problem. An ancient author has viewed matters from a false perspective and in consequence has achieved a kind of concertina effect or a foreshortening of events. What belongs in one period finds itself in another. In this he has been followed by modern scholars who have opted for a static view of the revolutionary army. By this last I mean they assume that once Marius, by his reforms in recruiting in 107, supposedly created a professional or revolutionary army then its characteristics were set and not to be altered. So Sulla's role is that of a man who saw what Marius could not, the potential of the new model army, and he was somebody who sought to use it for political advantage. Caesar simply followed Sulla's example, but from different motives and to more deadly effect.

6

But if we approach the history of the late republic from this viewpoint we miss one simple fact which is yet of the highest importance. If we accept as most do that the revolutionary period lasts from those reforms of Marius in 107 until the battle of Actium in 31 then we are dealing with roughly two and a half generations. At the very least it can be conceded that there may have been some kind of change and development in that period. We are, I hold, entitled to wonder if Sulla was really Caesar or a Triumvir and if they all commanded the same kind of troops.

This point may be underlined and emphasised by reflecting on a period of modern French history. In 1783 France was ruled by a king and nobles, and the system of government was feudal. Following the approach of ancient historians, we would have to assume that in 1793 things were pretty much the same. But we know that by then the king had been executed, feudalism and nobility abolished, and France was ruled by a national Convention elected by male adult suffrage.[38] It is my contention that, while events in the late Roman republic did not move with the rapidity of revolutionary France, we have, nevertheless, a substantial body of source material which allows us to demonstrate that over a century the Roman army, too, underwent many changes.

I propose to do this by examining this army under a number of broad headings. We start, naturally, at the top and say something about the commanders. Then follow two sections dealing with the economic status of the soldiers and the discernible characteristics they show. We next look at the ties which bound the commander and his soldiers. Great importance, I believe, attaches to the political consciousness of the soldier, and this is examined in depth. Others have argued in the past that the desire for land played in motivating soldiers and so this too will be put under close scrutiny. Finally we shall be looking at the somewhat neglected topics of mutiny and desertion. With these studies I hope to establish that the question of Rome's revolutionary army is more intricate than has sometimes been thought.[39] My final chapter will bring together the results of the earlier ones and present a rounded picture of the part played by the soldiers in the great events which led to the downfall of the republic.[40]

2

THE LEADERS AND THE LED

Any consideration of the role the Roman army played in the downfall of the republic must inevitably begin with some preliminary remarks on that army and those who led it. Later in this work we shall have a good deal to say about the commander as a political figure.[1] Here though we shall begin by concentrating on that commander as a military man and on how he became a success in his role. As regards the soldiers themselves there has long been a belief that, throughout the second century, the number of peasants who could meet the property qualification necessary for service was slowly declining. Recently this view has been questioned but I shall try to show that it is, in its essentials, correct. However I shall then go on to demonstrate in the course of a discussion of the nature and composition of the late republican armies that the admission of the landless to the legions did not have the far-reaching consequences which are sometimes supposed. Finally we shall close this chapter with a consideration of how commander and troops functioned as a unit.

(a) The character of the leaders

At all times, the good commander was expected to share the life of his men and experience what they experienced. It was believed he should undergo the same labours, dangers and hardships as those he aspired to lead.[2]

This was held to begin in the city with those exercises which preceded the departure on campaign. So Pompey was much praised and admired when, although fifty-eight years of age, he showed great skill on joining in those exercises prior to the Second Civil War.[3] Some sixty years previously, just before the First Mithridatic War whose command he coveted, Marius drew a mixed reception when he likewise exercised on the Campus Martius. Some expressed admiration for the performance of this seventy year old but others – Marius had many enemies – merely derided him for his untimely ambition.[4] In the days of the Cimbric invasion his fitness had also been remarked upon and we may assume nobody scoffed then.[5]

Once in the field, those who gave orders are attested, in prominent cases, as sharing in the life of those they led. This is illustrated beautifully in the Jugurthine

9

War. When Marius went out as Metellus' legate he rapidly became popular with the men, sharing their rations and their labours. Then Sulla, as quaestor to Marius, ingratiated himself with the men, sharing their duties and hardships. In one respect, however, the two differed. Sulla not only lent money to the troops but spoke fair words and made jests with them.[6] Caesar, too, was remarkable for his endurance even though his health was often said to be uncertain.[7] He even went so far as to call his soldiers 'comrades'.[8]

The danger here is obvious. Over-familiarity could lead to a slackening of discipline.[9] Getting this right is, I would suggest, more of an intuitive art than an intellectual skill. This is exemplified in the case of Caesar. He insisted on the strictest discipline when faced with the enemy. On other occasions he was prepared to indulge his troops and once remarked he did not care if a soldier stank of perfume so long as he could fight.[10] Sulla was another noted disciplinarian. When he could, he would impose his authority with the traditional *fustuarium* or cudgel. But he knew when to relax discipline, as at the siege of Athens for instance.[11] Lucullus, on the other hand, was plainly somewhat deficient in these arts.[12] For most of the Third Mithridatic War his men obeyed him, but he inspired no love or affection. Rightly or wrongly they resented his haughty manners, his way of distributing booty and his prevention of the looting of Greek cities. This for a time had no consequences, but then Lucullus found himself making an exceptional demand. When Sulla and Caesar did this their men responded positively. Lucullus' men refused.[13] If we employ the well-worn metaphor of drawing the line, we may say that Sulla and Caesar were better at drawing it than Lucullus.

As we might predict, the commander was expected to share in the hazards of the battlefield. We often hear of Roman generals who led from the front. This is what Marius is said to have done at Aquae Sextiae.[14] And this too was what Lucullus did on the day of Tigranocerta.[15] A leader thus positioned in the thick of the fight was in a position to direct affairs and bring aid to where it was needed.

Twice, once at Chaeronea and once at the Colline Gate, we hear of how Sulla was able to cross from his right wing to his left when he discovered it was in trouble.[16] Sertorius is said to have carried out a similar manoeuvre at Sucro.[17] A commander in the midst of the fray was an inspiration to his troops. With his eye upon them they would fight all the better, and Caesar has recorded for us several instances where this happened.[18] In such a position the general might retrieve the day by showing conspicuous gallantry. Many displays of this sort centred round the standard. So when he could not rally his troops in any other way at Orchomenus, Sulla grabbed a standard and ran between the opposing armies shouting at his men that if they were asked where they had left their chief in the lurch they should say it was at Orchomenus.[19] Caesar behaved in a like fashion in the Second Civil War at Dyrrachium, and earlier, in battle against the Nervi, he grabbed a shield before pushing forward through the ranks.[20] Sometimes, though, if you could not grab the standard you grabbed the standard bearer. This is what Caesar did at Thapsus. He seized a standard bearer, twirled him round and pointed him in the direction of the enemy.[21]

Conversely we have pictures of generals who lose their nerve. Perhaps the most pitiable is that of Pompey at Pharsalus. Seeing he was losing the day, he withdrew to his tent and sat there speechless – like Ajax, as our source says. He only roused himself from his stupor when the arrival of Caesar's men made flight imperative.[22] Likewise at Carrhae, Crassus acted indecisively when news came that his son was in danger. But when word of the latter's death spread fear in the ranks, he put his private grief to one side and attempted to rally his men.[23]

It hardly needs saying that for a general to operate in the thick of things is to put himself in considerable danger.[24] This would be increased by conspicuous appearance and garb. Many of the leading figures of the late republic are described as having striking looks, which must mean that, in a civil war, people who had seen them in civilian life would remember them on the field of battle.[25] I would venture to suggest that anybody who reads Plutarch's description of Sulla's appearance will readily appreciate it was unlikely to be forgotten.[26] Antony probably carried less impact, but was nevertheless said to have had 'a bold and masculine look'.[27] While only Pompey could claim to look like Alexander the Great, he, Lucullus and Caesar were all said to be tall.[28] A commander could also be picked out by his attire. All eyes must have been on Lucullus on the day of Tigranocerta for 'he wore a steel breast plate of glittering scales, and a tassled cloak, and at once, let his sword flash forth from its scabbard'.[29] There were many too who saw Crassus don an ill-omened black cloak instead of the usual purple. Realising his mistake he changed, but too late. The coming disaster at Carrhae had been presaged.[30] Another cloak with a dubious history was that worn by Caesar in the Alexandrine War. It was captured by the enemy and hung up as a trophy.[31] As we read the account of this war we may perhaps be excused for thinking its owner was lucky not to be inside it.[32]

Distinguishing clothing would serve to pick out the general not only for Roman foes but also foreign. Although it is not specifically mentioned, we may suspect Pompey's garb marked him out when he made war on the Albanians. At any rate their leader Cosis knew his target when he made straight for Pompey and tried to kill him.[33] Something the same had happened in the war against Sertorius except that in this instance we hear of the well decorated horse rather than his rider.[34]

Indeed the general often operated from the vantage point of horseback and we have specific testimony to the fact that some had begun their careers with the cavalry. Sulla, for instance, began his soldiering in this way with Marius in North Africa.[35] Pompey, for his part, when he set out to join Sulla in the First Civil War, did so at the head of a company of horse.[36] Often the horses mentioned are special. Caesar had one with remarkable hooves which would obey only his commands.[37] At the Colline Gate Sulla rode a magnificent white beast which attracted the attention of the enemy. Two spears were thrown at it, but a quick-witted groom gave it a touch of the lash so that it sped out of range.[38]

We turn now to something which is of the greatest importance but which somewhat surprisingly has been rather neglected by modern scholars. I refer to the religious dimension.[39] Whatever the religious beliefs of the commanders I do not think they would neglect to carry out the formal ceremonies attendant on battle and on campaign in general.[40] The troops would expect them to be performed.[41] The infrequent mention of such ceremonies means, I believe, that they were carried out as a matter of course and required no especial comment.[42] Where we do find allusion to them is precisely where we would expect to: occasions where they had a special significance.

Although Sulla was a supremely religious man there is no mention in our literary sources of his taking the auspices.[43] But his coins almost certainly indicate that he did. These depict trophies and augural symbols. The trophies refer to the victories at Orchomenus and Chaeronea. From this we are to infer that when Sulla entered on office and took the auspices his *imperium* had been declared *iustum*. Then when he repeated them in the field the signs had been favourable and victory had been given.[44]

The ancient texts are more explicit about sacrifice at crucial moments in Sulla's career. For instance there was one made as he crossed the river Cephisus before Chaeronea, as well as on both of the occasions he marched on Rome.[45] In the latter instance the liver looked like a garland of laurel. This reminds us of what happened to the considerably less successful Crassus. As he was crossing the Euphrates he made sacrifice too, only to drop the entrails.[46] We actually hear too of the *lustratio* or purification by a Caesarian army in Africa.[47] Another preceded a more famous battle. Both sides purified themselves before Philippi.[48]

Omens, it need hardly be said, were usually taken seriously. Once more we can turn to Crassus, whose Parthian campaign provides a ready source of signs which boded ill.[49] From among many we may mention that thunder and lightning greeted the passage of the Euphrates, and once over, lentils and salt, usually considered offerings for the dead, were distributed to the men. Then, on the day of the battle itself there came the donning of the ill-omened cloak we mentioned a little earlier.[50] By way of contrast we may cite the behaviour of the Euphrates when Lucullus arrived at its banks some years before. He found the river in full flood, but towards the evening it began to fall and next day became fordable, so it was said the river-god had lowered the water for him.[51] Perhaps it is worth mentioning also that even the most fortunate of men is said on one occasion to have received a bad sign. Near Dyrrachium, as he prepared to cross over into Italy after the First Mithridatic War, something which resembled a satyr was captured and presented to Sulla. His horrified reaction showed he believed it presaged ill, and it is not perhaps too fanciful to suggest that the doubts about his soldiers' loyalty which he subsequently recorded may owe something to this unpleasant encounter.[52]

'Turning' an omen was very important for a general, and we can realise just how important when we find Frontinus devoting a long section of his *Stratagems* (1.12) to examples, both Greek and Roman, of generals who successfully carried out the procedure. By 'turning' we mean making favourable a sign which at first sight seems unfavourable. Even Crassus tried it. When he dropped the entrails (see above) he exclaimed that no weapon would fall from his hands. Caesar, on landing in Africa, stumbled, but grabbed the ground shouting that Africa was in his grasp.[53] When the shields of his men and the breasts of his horses showed signs of what looked like blood Sertorius said this foretold victory. These were the places which would be spattered with the blood of the enemy.[54] It was in this spirit, I believe, that Lucullus acted on the day of Tigranocerta. Being told that this was an unlucky day because it was the anniversary of the great Roman defeat at Arausio (105) he, confident in the auspices he had received, declared they would make of it a lucky day with their victory.[55]

We may, I think, characterise as routine the religious actions we have been describing this far. They are what all generals will have done and there is nothing in them peculiar to any one individual. But we now discover that many of the leading military men of the late republic had a further religious dimension all of their own. They will have acquired an extra weight and authority because they were able to claim that the gods took an especial interest in them and manifested this in signal ways.

The first figure we know of who made such claims to divine favour was Scipio Africanus, the conqueror of Hannibal, but he is essentially an isolated figure.[56] Arguably it is with Marius that a long line of the especially divinely favoured begins.

Marius carted around with him a Syrian prophetess called Martha to whom he had been introduced by his wife. She travelled in a litter and he made sacrifice as she directed. Some sources say she actually foretold the outcome of battles.[57] His great enemy Sulla laid claim to a far greater and wider divine interest. He saw himself as a man of *virtus* (or quality). Because of this the gods sent him *bona fortuna* (good fortune) which brought prosperity to his enterprises and to the enterprises of those who consorted with him. The resulting state was one of *felicitas* (felicity) and Sulla himself took the title Felix.[58] So we hear of a constant stream of favourable messages from the gods conveyed in various ways,[59] and a career crowned with many successes.

One of the prominent features of Sulla's belief was the conviction that certain deities took an especial interest in him. One of these was Venus. His wayward disciple Pompey also acknowledged Venus as a patron and may even have attempted to upstage his old chief with his displays in coin and building. In the 50s he erected a shrine to Felicitas.[60] How long he had believed himself to be in possession of this quality we cannot say, but we do know that at the time of the passing of the Manilian law Cicero was most anxious that his audience believe he had it.[61] He compared Pompey to the generals of old who had this quality.[62] With it he had achieved great success and would continue to do so.[63] This would be of the greatest benefit to the state.

In many ways, what we know of Sulla's more faithful disciple Lucullus mirrors closely the master. Sulla believed the most trustworthy communications came from the gods in dreams, and Lucullus won one of his victories at Cyzicus after being counselled in a dream. No text explicitly states he possessed *felicitas* but strong circumstantial evidence suggests that he did. Nature could bend in favour of him and those around him. The Euphrates sank for him, and when both he and the Cyziceans required an animal for sacrifice on two separate occasions it presented itself to them. But most telling of all is the decision to fight on the day of Arausio. Only a man confident of his *felicitas* would have done this, bringing to mind for us another great proconsul who helped himself to the temple treasures of Greece in the belief this was what the gods wanted.[64]

Caesar presents a more difficult case. There are those who give up and simply declare his beliefs are unfathomable.[65] Those who are prepared to hazard an opinion veer between lukewarm belief in the gods and outright atheism.[66] Personally I would say that no belief in the divine could equal Caesar's faith in Caesar. However, the most securely and publicly attested higher power he acknowledged was Fortuna. This it was that blessed his enterprises and gave them success.[67]

The modern reader who comes upon the instances of omen turning which we mentioned above could be excused for thinking there was something a little deceitful or fraudulent about them. Good signs were needed so good signs would be got. Such a view must, however, be rejected. To act in this way was perfectly consonant with Roman religious beliefs and practices.[68] Where there is occasional room for some suspicion is in the claim of especial personal divine favour.

To my mind Sertorius presents us with an excellent example of this. In Spain he acquired as a present a pet fawn. He put it about that it had been bestowed by Diana and that it revealed secrets to him. Military intelligence, gleaned by normal means, was regularly attributed to the fawn so that Sertorius acquired the name of being the favourite of the gods among his Spanish following. The majority of our ancient sources declare this was a mere contrivance to exploit the superstitions of barbarians.[69]

Up to a point one has to agree.[70] But one also has to remember that in exploiting beliefs about a fawn Sertorius may have been playing, not on superstition, but on genuine religious belief.[71] At any rate Roman soldiers were not immune from such cynical treatment when it suited a commander. There are a number of instances recorded of Caesar's contempt for omens.[72] Yet when, in 47, he was setting out for Africa, he came upon a prophecy which said a Scipio would always win there. Since his opponent was a Scipio he acquired one of his own. A useless and degenerate scion of the family was dug out.[73] Perhaps in the light of the aforementioned contempt for omens, this might be just a joke.[74] But equally I would maintain it was a necessary accommodation to the views and sensibilities of those he commanded. Any discussions of the religious dimensions of the Roman commander would not be complete without acknowledging that he – from our point of view anyway – could go too far and indulge in human sacrifice.[75] We may start with Mark Antony. After Philippi he had Q. Hortensius put to death because he held him ultimately responsible for his brother's death at the hands of Decimus Brutus. The execution took the form of Hortensius being offered as an expiatory sacrifice to the shade of the departed at his tomb.[76] Less well known is the similar fate of Marius Gratidianus at the end of the First Civil War. He was responsible for the death of Q. Lutatius Catulus (cos.102), and this man's son took his revenge in the Sullan proscription, hauling his father's murderer to his tomb and there sacrificing him to the paternal spirit. Interestingly he seems to have lacked the courage to do the deed himself and got Catiline to do it.[77]

We also have an obscure reference to some kind of sacrifice of soldiers Caesar is supposed to have carried out in 46. Less puzzling is the story that Sextus Pompey made a human sacrifice to Neptune. That would be fitting for a lord of the sea.[78] Most intriguing of all to contemplate is the very real possibility that Octavian, soon to become Augustus, indulged in the practice at least once. After the fall of Perusia some reports say he sacrificed three hundred men of senatorial and equestrian rank at the altar of the deified Julius. The day was the Ides of March and self-evidently the ghost was being appeased.[79] Some doubt this story.[80] I suspect this is so because it sits ill with the picture of a cold and calculating man who was to rule for forty years. But one telling observation argues strongly for authenticity.[81] What is said of Octavian has been said of other members of his class. He fits into an established pattern of behaviour which may be illustrated by a number of examples.

So we have sketched, after a generic fashion, the salient characteristics of the Roman general. Should he be successful then he would acquire a great name.[82] Being renowned as a general meant the enemy feared you the more, while your own men were more confident and men would flock to your side when you called. In a passage relating to Caesar in Africa we hear of just such a demoralised enemy, while the name and repute which brought this about encouraged Caesar's own forces.[83] Of course an appeal to one's name could be for good or ill. When Pompey, in the year before Civil War, said he could call up the men of Italy by stamping his foot, there is some justification for seeing him as a representative of legitimate government.[84] But I doubt if any such plea could be made for Marius when he landed in Etruria in 87. He used the glamour of his name to recruit to do a great mischief.[85] A name could be inherited. Before his premature end the younger Marius showed some signs of ability but we may suspect his consulship in 82 at the age of 27 was largely due to the fact that his name would draw in recruits for a cause which was beginning to look ever more desperate.[86] Altogether more fortunate was Octavian, who launched his career by assuming the name of his adoptive father Julius Caesar.[87] Adoption reminds us that if you did not have a glorious name of your own you could borrow or steal one. When Milo attempted – unsuccessfully as it turned out – to recruit in the Thurine territory at the start of the Second Civil War he evidently thought it would help matters if he claimed he was working for Pompey.[88]

Now if we wanted to sum up the successful Roman general in one word it would be 'empathy', but in the broadest sense.[89] In effect we find, over and over again, that the commander must share to the full, on campaign, the life and experiences of his men, be it in preparation, on the march or in the battle. But doing this still leaves us with two tasks to which we drew attention at the outset. We must say something about the type of troops these men led and then on the ways in which both related to each other in the unit which is the army.

(b) The origin of the soldiers

If we use the word 'origin' in its geographical sense then we encounter little in the way of difficulty. Roman soldiers in the republican period were usually of rural origin. Only in exceptional circumstances, in the Social War for instance, did the Romans call upon men from the city.[90] However, should we wish to divine their social status then we immediately become embroiled in a scholarly debate.

Learned opinion has long held that in earlier Rome warfare was seasonal and that the short campaigns enabled the peasant to return home to look after his farm. However when, with the growth of empire, campaigns became longer, this was obviously not possible and the consequences were grave. Neglected farms fell into ruin and the peasant lost his competence. In his place there gradually came large estates which were worked by slaves. This uprooting of the peasantry naturally meant there were fewer men available for service in the legions, and by about the middle of the second century some at Rome had begun to worry about this.[91]

This particular process is usually held to have started around 200, or maybe a little earlier at the beginning of the Hannibalic War. Now, however, N. Rosenstein has convincingly demonstrated that the yearlong campaign becomes a feature of Roman warfare about a century before the Second Punic War.[92] I do not believe, however, that we have then to accept his further contention that we have to give an explanation for the mid-second-century crisis other than that usually entered. Rosenstein's belief that what ultimately resulted was 'too many people attempting to start out in life with too little land' does not convince.[93] The traditional picture of the deracination of the peasantry is still valid even when we assign an earlier start to the processes which led to it.

Our case will be presented in two parts. We will begin from the premise that the uprooting of the small farmer was not a sudden and cataclysmic event but something which extended over time and was not universal in its working in that it will have affected some places more than others. I shall then proceed to defend that ancient source tradition which shows that, when the Romans became aware that they had a problem, they recognised it was a shortage of manpower, and they were right about this.[94]

I believe, in fact, that we can isolate certain factors which would ensure that the erosion of the small proprietor would be a long drawn out phenomenon. The first of these was one whose importance Rosenstein emphasised, and rightly.[95] Recruitment did not necessarily mean ruin. When a man went to war he will often have left family members behind. Irrespective of whether they were male or female, they could work the farm and ensure its survival. And if a soldier did return from the wars it was often with booty. With this he could repair damage done or, if his holding was lost altogether, purchase a new one.[96] Again Rosenstein points out that the prescient are likely to have bought jewellery or cattle to be sold in the day of dearth and will also have further provided against that day by storing food.[97] Rosenstein offers no examples, but in fact archaeology has unearthed objects of value on quite small farms.[98] We do know, however, that storage is not always a safeguard against spoilage and subsequent want. Our records of famines speak of the city of Rome but it would be rash to suggest they did not occur in the countryside also. We also have to remember that where a situation fell short of actual famine there will have been periods of shortage. Here the experience of the France of the *Ancien Régime* invites comparison. In the time of Richelieu and Louis XIV there had been famines. In the eighteenth century these had ceased, but there still continued to be periods of great want.[99]

Self-evidently the Roman colonisation programme which lasted down to 173 will have done something to repair the damage done to rural life by this new type of warfare in that it provided new farms for the ruined. Rosenstein however counsels caution, arguing that the number of settlers deployed between the outbreak of the Third Samnite War and the beginning of the Second Punic will not justify this view, especially as many of them will not have been veterans anyway.[100] It may immediately be remarked that the figures Rosenstein uses are controversial and conjectural.[101] Furthermore one suspects soldiers would have priority here. These colonies were the *propugnacula imperii* (defences of empire)[102] and men of proven loyalty to Rome were what was required.[103]

Further I believe Rosenstein may have misconceived the significance of colonisation for the peasant, whether as an incentive to fulfil his obligation to serve in the army or as a means of bettering himself. Rosenstein would not accept that a man would inflict want upon his family for the sake of a farm which would be his only some years hence.[104] Ultimately this is grounded, I hold, in a view both of the levy and of the peasant's capacity to endure, which is not tenable. I shall return to these topics in due season. What is important here is to recognise that booty was what chiefly motivated the peasant. It was to the proceeds from this that he could reasonably look forward.[105] On the other hand, a colonisation programme very definitely depended on the will of others, and such programmes were not regularly implemented. And, as we shall see, this was a situation which persisted well into the first century. People took what their betters handed down to them and were no doubt duly grateful.[106] The interests of those in whose power it lay to give were not the same as the interests of those who were to receive. We can remind ourselves again that these colonies were *propugnacula imperii*.[107] For all its willingness to plant,[108] the senate's primary interest was plainly not centred on those it ruled over.

From this I believe it follows that Rosenstein's theories as to why the colonial programme ceased are unacceptable. He thought this happened because emigration to the capital and a series of epidemics meant 'the senate was running out of potential recipients' just as 'the supply of land to allot was drying up'.[109] Whatever view we take about the epidemics, the figures Rosenstein deploys for emigration are insecure, resting largely in hypothesis and disputed calculation.[110] More important, the reasons advanced by Salmon are more plausible because they are in a harmony with the picture we have just seen of a Roman ruling class acting in its own self-interest.[111] The primary reason for the establishment of colonies had disappeared. With no military need, *propugnacula* were not wanted. Further, there was anyway the likelihood of quarrels over who would be founding commissioner and there seems to have been a desire to avoid such confrontations. Finally, the elite now preferred to exploit the *ager publicus* either for the state or for its own profit rather than assign it to settlers.

We shall return to this last point shortly, but here I want to draw attention to what I believe may have been one of the most important reasons which ensured the peasant was only slowly deracinated: his innate tenacity. We should never forget his capacity to endure much and be content with very little.

The average peasant holding, although it could sometimes be larger, usually varied between 2 and 10 *iugera*, which is generally held to allow for a bare existence and not much more.[112] This basic plot could be supplemented in two ways. The *ager publicus* was open for exploitation, and this was made more attractive because the *vectigal* which was levied was not always collected.[113] We can also accept, I think, that sharecropping was practised. Surplus labour would be made available to a landowner in return for a part of a crop.[114]

For the modern historian there is always a risk of not fully appreciating what the peasant might have to endure. Thus Rosenstein suggests that peasants will have produced a variety of crops in order to avoid monotony in diet. This seeking after variety is, I would suggest, more modern American than ancient Italian.[115] In the past people often had to eat whatever they could get. For instance, in early nineteenth-century Ireland, a large proportion of the population subsisted on potatoes and little else.[116]

The case of Spurius Ligustinus is often cited in this context, even if it is with qualifications or even doubts about its historicity.[117] This man is depicted in our source as successfully pursuing a military career and retaining a very small farm. He inherited one *iugerum* of land and a hut.[118] Having married he produced eight children. Much of the rest of his time and energy was taken up with soldiering, and in all he spent twenty-two years on various campaigns. It is self-evident what, apart from answering the call of the levy, drove him to the soldier's life in the first place. It was poverty.[119] Equally self-evident is that the family left behind managed to survive and indeed flourish, for we can see Spurius was able to make trips home in between campaigns. He may have continued to live in his ancestral hut, but rewards from his commanders must have brought some kind of enrichment and the chance to add to that one *iugerum*.[120] Despite scholarly qualms, one thing seems certain. Spurius may be fictional but his story shows us that the Romans found it easy to envisage a situation where a man of little property might take to soldiering and yet be able to preserve or possibly augment that property.

We alluded earlier to conditions in pre-revolutionary France. A return to this theme will prove instructive. When in the summer of 1789 the French peasantry set out to destroy the manorial registers, they were turning not against a system newly devised but rather against one that had long oppressed them.[121] The first lesson to be drawn here is an easy one. If the French peasant could endure, so, we may maintain, could his ancient Italian counterpart.

The second lesson is neither simple nor obvious. We do not hear in Italy of the outbreaks of violence or *jacqueries* which punctuate the history of eighteenth-century France.[122] There are, of course, records of rural violence, but there is nothing on the scale of the *jacqueries*, although interestingly we do have some documented instances of what some historians regard as the standard pattern of behaviour at the time. The strong use their power to dispossess the weak.[123] We would be mistaken however if we assumed there was merely quiescence.[124] Rather we have to reckon with discontent assuming a Roman rather than a French form. A prime characteristic of the Roman citizen is that he reacts more than he initiates. In assembly he assents or dissents to bills put before him and elects to office candidates from the upper classes.[125] In consequence no revolutionary ideas or leaders emerge from the citizen body and we shall see in due course that that is largely true of the army too.[126] The Roman citizen will follow where others lead. So the one real protest at agrarian conditions which we hear of at this time comes from 232, when discontent was orchestrated by a tribune of the plebs, C. Flaminius, who marshalled public support for a measure to distribute land in the Ager Gallicus.[127] Here we catch a precious glimpse of peasant discontent which is normally denied us, for these peasants cannot articulate if they do not find a champion from the elite.

Such, then, are what would seem to be the main reasons for the slow erosion of the peasantry.[128] Recent scholarship in fact draws attention to the long drawn out nature of the process and its consequences. A slave-based agricultural economy, the natural outcome of deracination, developed as early as the late fourth century but, as we know, it did not start to be critical until the second.[129] The most natural conclusion to draw here is that the forces at work took some time to grow and develop and do damage. This view is reinforced by the activities of the Gracchan commission. When the commissioners set out to uproot from the *ager publicus* those who had unlawfully encroached upon it, they discovered that many of those who were there had put down deep roots indeed. The abuse, which would have fatal consequences for the peasant in that it would deprive him of pasturage, was long standing.[130]

Thus far, then, we have seen that the ruin of the peasant is most likely to have occurred over a period of time. We now proceed to examine that evidence which claims it eventually caused a manpower shortage.

If we wished, we might like to suggest that the first sign of trouble came as early as 171. The basis for this is a fragment of a speech by the elder Cato where he seems to be urging the recruitment of *capite censi*. However, in view of the brevity of the quote and uncertainties about its exact context, this evidence must be treated with caution.[131] A generation or so ago better evidence seemed to be available in an anomaly in our sources. It was observed that we have different amounts attested for the property qualification of the *assidui*. These amounts, it was held, represented successive lowering of that property qualification in order to meet a shortfall in the number of recruits. More recent scholarship has questioned this attractive interpretation. The matter cannot be regarded as settled, but such is the

19

state of the debate that it is judged best to leave this evidence to one side also.[132] Instead we may turn to the unequivocal.

We know of three reformers, or would be reformers, who clearly identified the same problem and thought of the same solution: C. Laelius, Tiberus Gracchus and M. Marcus Philippus.[133] It is well known that, possibly in a tribunate held in 151, Laelius brought in a bill which anticipated that of Tiberius, but withdrew it when it provoked opposition.[134] It is less well known perhaps that Philippus when tribune probably in 104 also introduced a bill, after the manner of Tiberius, but failed to pass it into law.[135] All three were concerned with the disappearance of the peasant and with his re-establishment on the land. Only for Tiberius, however, do we have a detailed account of what this entailed and, it would seem, in something approximating to his own words[136]:

> 'The wild beasts that roam over Italy', he would tell his listeners, 'have their dens and holes to lurk in, but the men who fight and die for our country enjoy the common air and light and nothing else. It is their lot to wander with their wives and children, houseless and homeless, over the face of the earth. And when our generals appeal to their soldiers before a battle to defend their ancestors' tombs and their temples against the enemy, their words are a lie and a mockery, for not a man in their audience possesses a family altar; not one out of all those Romans owns an ancestral tomb. The truth is that they fight and die to protect the wealth and luxury of others. They are called the masters of the world, but they do not possess a single clod of earth which is truly their own.'

These words need no gloss. There have, however, been attempts to discredit Tiberius on the part of scholars who share Rosenstein's view that there actually was at this time a population increase.[137] Morley (2001) is one of those. Approaching it from the standpoint of the demographer, he comes to the conclusion, based on his own calculations, that Tiberius has got it wrong.[138] I believe we may have here a fundamental difference of approach. Morley's calculations can sometimes seem complex, but this is because essentially they are mathematical exercises and cannot have anything more than a hypothetical value.[139] Recognising this, I believe, unlike Morley, that when offered a choice between a clear-cut unequivocal ancient source and a fragile modern construct we must surely choose our source.

Archaeological data, too, are often deployed against Tiberius. What we discover in the ground, it is asserted, simply contradicts his picture of depopulation.[140] Again here we may have a difference of approach. To assume, as seems to be the case, the automatic superiority of the archaeological over the written record is dangerous. For instance we would know little of Caesar's invasions of Britain if we decided we should only accept what archaeology tells us.[141] Further, this view seems to make little allowance for difficulty or controversy in interpretation. Evidence for the survival of the peasant in one area does not necessarily mean he survived elsewhere.[142] We should remember too, as Rosenstein points out, that we simply cannot be sure always of the status of some of those who have left their physical remains behind.[143] But above all we should keep in mind that archaeology is as vulnerable to revisionism as is history and may be now offering support to Gracchus.[144]

Rosenstein is altogether more complex and subtle. Recognising the strength of the literary tradition which speaks of a population shortage, he does not seek to overthrow it and put something else in its place.[145] Instead he argues that Tiberius misunderstood the nature of the problem he was facing. This, he says, would not be an unusual occurrence in the primitive conditions of a pre-industrial society. By way of analogy he cites the case of pre-revolutionary France, where savants thought the population was falling when it was actually rising.[146] This is doubly unfortunate. The true extent of the population was known because, like Tiberius Gracchus, people had a good reason for finding out. In this instance it was either social reform or taxation.[147] Citing this French example reminds us of another instance where people knew the nature of the problem they were dealing with because it was incumbent on them to find out. During the *Ancien Régime*, reformers were perfectly well aware of the true nature of the problems posed by the dreadful state of the finances and knew what was necessary to achieve reform.[148]

Thus, *prima facie*, I can see no reason why Tiberius should necessarily have to be mistaken in what he was about. It is perfectly plausible to argue that he knew what he had to do because he had before him the evidence of the census and the levy.[149] Between 164 and 136 the numbers of citizens showed a steady decline.[150] Rosenstein attempts to get around this, arguing that it is misleading for us and ultimately Tiberius because the figures come about as a result of the censors failing to do their job properly.[151] This should not be accepted, since it is not established fact but simply an unproven hypothesis advanced by Brunt.[152] But even if it could be proven, it would not then follow Tiberius was led astray. When Roman magistrates botched the job and kept imperfect records people soon got to hear of it.[153]

It can, of course, be maintained that the quality of the official did not much matter. In this primitive society people could absent themselves from the census and the *dilectus*, and the magistrate could do little to corral and coerce.[154] Achaemenid Persia, I believe, teaches us to be cautious here. The empire was vast, with extended communications, yet the Great King was able to get his levy out and, thanks to a simple system of numbering, knew how many men he had. We hear of people who tried to evade their obligations and they came to an unpleasant end.[155] Returning to Rome we find here too records of magistrates who visit suitable punishments on those unwilling to serve.[156] Yet this is, perhaps, not the most interesting point of resemblance. One would have thought that if you wanted to escape service in Persia you would simply flee to some remote corner of the vast empire. Instead people came in person before the king to ask for permission to absent themselves. In the same way, at Rome there are plainly many who do not elect to vanish but when the levy is held turn up and appeal to tribunes and the senate.[157] Thus reluctance to serve might not always mean failure to attend the levy.[158]

21

There is, though, no difficulty in believing the Roman soldier could be choosy at this time about what wars he fought. He had lost none of his native belligerence and ferocity but was reluctant to serve on campaigns which promised great labours and small reward. As has often been pointed out, the wars in Spain illustrate this point perfectly.[159]

However, it is, in my view, simply absurd to suggest that, looking at falling census returns and disturbances in the levy, Tiberius failed to see, as modern scholars have claimed to have done, the true and only reason for these occurrences. If the real single cause was, as the aforementioned scholars maintain, reluctance to serve in Spain then we should have to presume Tiberius did not know what the rest of Rome must have known, and that further he was incapable of drawing the correct conclusion, which was that the problem was not a shortfall in manpower but the unwillingness of some of its citizens to come forward and do their duty. There is, I believe, no way of evading the natural corollary to this argument. If Tiberius knew – as he surely did – the crisis had not arisen out of the Spanish War, then he must have divined that it had another and more serious cause. The issue was not that potential soldiers were lurking in the background but that they were not there at all.[160]

This naturally takes us back to the fragment of Tiberius' speech we quoted a little earlier. It has often been remarked that there must have been a certain element of exaggeration in these words.[161] I see no reason to quarrel with this view. Radical reformers do not usually deal in understatement.[162] On the other hand I cannot envisage a speech such as this being delivered to a well-fed, well-clothed audience who would then retire to their comfortable homes.

But who were these homeless men who had no place to call their own? Rosenstein is not altogether satisfactory here. In one place[163] he declares this description cannot be taken literally. These men are vagabonds, wanderers without substance, and, as he reminds us, a property qualification was still imposed on those entering the army. So they cannot be men liable for military service. In another[164] he appears however to accept their existence and suggests they were people forced to live as day labourers.

I believe the most elegant solution is to take Tiberius' words as evidence that even now the property qualification was being evaded.[165] It looks as if *capite censi* were making their way into the army at this time. This hypothesis becomes easier to accept if we remember another rule was being broken now. People under the age of seventeen were being admitted to the ranks.[166] Plainly commanders could not or would not enforce the regulations.[167] I am not, of course, arguing that the Roman army was now completely composed of lacklands and wanderers on the face of the earth. But the suggestion that anyway the amount of property which in the second century could make of you an *assiduus* was small indeed is attractive.[168] Tiberius was exaggerating, but not by much.

Plainly Tiberius was concerned with the loss of men who would join the legions, but there was another problem attendant upon deracination which now forced itself upon the attention of the Romans: the slaves who were replacing the peasants showed a tendency to revolt. Here again we return to the question we touched on earlier: how well informed could people in a pre-industrial society be about a contemporary issue? To what has already been said we may add the observation that the problem was perhaps not so much ignorance in itself but the speed with which it was dispelled. It is well known, for instance, that in Achaemenid Persia the king, for a time, might not know of certain events taking place in his lands. But only for a time. News would eventually reach him.[169] In the case of the Romans we have the specific instances of the colonies of Sipontium and Buxentum. Their abandonment seems to have escaped notice for a time, but eventually it was discovered.[170]

Prior to the time of Tiberius, the Romans had received warnings of what could happen. Apart from some relatively minor disturbances, there had been one particularly serious slave revolt in Apulia in 185.[171] In 140, further disturbances began among the slaves in Sicily. These bore a close resemblance to what had happened in Apulia, in that they too were set afoot by herdsmen on great estates. For five years they terrified the island with their brigandage until in 135 the first slave war broke out.[172] It was during this time of brigandage, probably in 138, that Tiberius made his famous journey through Etruria, where he found the land being worked by foreign slaves.[173] I find it difficult to escape the conclusion that he now realised that, just as in Apulia some years before and in Sicily now, such a situation harboured the potential for trouble, and that the same would be true wherever else slave cultivators would be found.[174] Support for the notion of such an epiphany, such a sudden realisation of the true state of affairs in Italy, will be found in the report of another speech made by Gracchus in his tribunate. In this one he castigated slaves as militarily useless, disloyal and the cause of the war which had now been going on for three years.[175]

My conclusion would be as follows. There is no reason to doubt that the Romans of Tiberius' generation feared that they could suffer violence at the hands of the slaves who worked the land of Italy. But that is not our main concern here.[176] Rather it is with the circumstances which had created this situation: the steady erosion of the free peasantry and the consequent reduction in the numbers qualified to serve in the legions. We have just seen Tiberius' attempt to remedy the situation. In our next section we shall find that others, faced with shortage, sought the more immediate solution of abolishing the property qualification altogether. But, as I will argue, this did not have the consequences it is often assumed it did. We shall be trying to characterise the armies of the revolutionary period and, in so doing, we shall acknowledge the presence of the landless, while pointing out that they are not always easy to detect and they do not constitute a section or grouping with their own especial interests to promote.

(c) The army: composition and characteristics

In the previous section we saw that the Roman soldier was primarily of rural origin but that numbers seemed to be falling. Further, we noted that some believe the actual amount of property which rendered a man liable for service was, in effect, very small by now. We also saw that some people may have evaded the qualification altogether, possibly with the connivance of generals who needed to fill their ranks.

If there was indeed subterfuge, then it was brought to an end in 107. Marius, about to set off to make war on Jugurtha in Africa and having difficulty in getting the necessary numbers, simply abolished the property qualification and admitted *capite censi*.[177] There is another tradition that Marius first recruited them not for Africa but for the German War, but this is usually rejected by modern historians.[178] This would not, of course, rule out their presence in that army for, as can be appreciated, there would then, too, be a call for numbers.[179]

At any rate, when we consider the African army we have to remember that it was not just composed of *capite censi*. Marius had recruited men of property also.[180] Furthermore he had taken over troops who had come out under Metellus and had been raised in the traditional fashion.[181] Indeed some modern scholars have gone so far as to suggest that the numbers of *capite censi* involved here were quite small, perhaps no more than about five thousand.[182]

Upon his return, Marius was given the task of fighting the Germanic tribes.[183] He indicated, however, that he did not wish to use his African troops but preferred those raised by Rutilius Rufus (cos.105) because they were better disciplined.[184] Possibly all of Marius' troops were involved, but it might be wiser to press Frontinus' words *sub Metello* and take it we are chiefly speaking of Metellus' veterans.[185] Badian thought that unwillingness to fight might explain this ill discipline.[186] If that is so, then we might venture a little further with Badian and suggest that they were reluctant to serve further because their time was expired and they wanted their discharge. In the course of this work we will certainly meet with instances of this.[187]

Here the question of timing is also important. It seems reasonable to assume that, given the situation, Marius would discharge his veterans early in the year, the better to be able to devote time to training the new recruits.[188] Evans thought the *capite censi* remained with the colours and made the further plausible suggestion that they then served in Gaul.[189] Those who were propertied would, as we have earlier suggested, at this point have gone home. Then, when the time came for a division of land both *assidui* and *proeletarii* would have received something.[190] However there are two further factors to which Evans does not, perhaps, give due weight. Early discharge and a period of waiting is attested elsewhere.[191] In the case of *assidui*, they would be able to maintain themselves on land they already owned as they waited for something more.[192] The landless could subsist on donatives and booty.[193]

Thus far, then, I think it is fair to say that it is very difficult to separate the landed from the landless in Marius' African army. We encounter similar problems when we look at the army with which he had fought the Germans. Saturninus' land bill of 100 aimed to give land to the soldiers from that army.[194] When the city populace showed itself actively hostile Saturninus carried the legislation by force.[195] In doing this he was able to call upon the support of Marius' troops. Many of them had dispersed to their homes, but some now returned to Rome to do battle in defence of their interests.[196]

Undoubtedly many of these men were eligible to serve under a property qualification but, as we know, there may have been, in this hour of need, *capite censi* among them. If that is so, then the situation we suggested existed in the African army may have prevailed here too. Those who had land awaited more or better, while those who had none subsisted on booty.[197] To divine the exact proportions of both types is impossible, since they were united in what they demanded. Moreover with the downfall of Saturninus and the eclipse of Marius we hear no more of them. They lacked a leader to promote their cause and the proposed settlements were never carried out.[198] The difficulties we have experienced in delineating the economic status of Marius' armies will be found again when we examine those other armies which came after him. If we look for the *capite censi* in an effort to weigh up their revolutionary significance we find they form no discernible interest group or lobby. They are not a band apart, with special characteristics which would mark them off from other troops. In sum their actions and aspirations do not differ from those of their fellow legionaries.

When Marius abandoned the property qualification it is difficult to believe he acted in any doctrinaire fashion. He sought to establish no precedent and did not aim for far-reaching changes in the methods of recruiting. Rather, faced with an immediate problem he devised an immediate solution.[199] Thus, as scholars agree, the *dilectus* and the attendant conscription continued after him.[200] The obvious inference to draw is that a property qualification continued to be imposed and that there were sufficient numbers to meet it. The state of our sources, to which I have alluded above, makes it difficult to divine when *capite censi* were next recruited in any number. Recourse must be had to reasoned speculation, and in this I am inclined to agree with Rich, who thinks this would be in the Social War and the First Civil War when there was a desperate need for manpower.[201]

As the Social War drew to a close and the First Mithridatic War began, there occurred the first revolutionary act by a Roman army: Sulla's march on Rome. Some believe that the willingness of his men to join in his enterprise is directly related to the fact that they were landless and desirous of reward from their general.[202] Later in the work, I shall be setting forth what I believe to be the true motivation of these men and I shall be arguing that their economic standing is irrelevant.[203] Here I want to draw attention to the modern misconceptions which may arise from such a view of the role of the *capite censi*. The most extreme example comes from the normally careful Keppie[204]:

> Later historians looked back on his action as an awesome precedent, and indicative of the new attitude of the grasping soldiery, for which Marius took much of the blame. More probably Sulla's legions, bound for Asia, contained many ne'er-do-wells from both sides in the Social War, with little affection for Rome or the Senate, and with the prospect of

restoring their fortunes by the campaign in Asia uppermost in their minds, as Sulla knew well enough.

None of this will be found in our ancient authorities. To suggest, however, as others besides Keppie have,[205] that Sulla will have recruited among Social War veterans is perfectly reasonable. There was the most ready contemporary source of manpower. But to call them 'ne'er-do-wells' is hasty and unwarranted. After two years in the Social War 'battle hardened veterans' might meet the case better and the subsequent behaviour of Sulla's troops in the First Mithridatic War lends some support to this deduction. Of their economic status we know nothing, but it seems fair to suggest they consisted of a mix of propertied and unpropertied. Certainly there was nothing especially 'grasping' about them. Like their predecessors, they desired to profit from war but there is no evidence to support the notion this especially motivated one section among them. I cannot pretend to say if some or any of these soldiers had already served under Sulla in the Social War.[206] However we should not forget that when trouble began the army destined to fight Mithridates was still occupied in besieging the Italian stronghold of Nola.[207]

Yet it is not just modern historiography which misrepresents Sulla's army. As we have already seen, Plutarch's portrayal of it as Triumviral provided the starting point for this study.[208] We now find that Sallust levelled similar changes (*Cat.*11.5–7)[209]:

> Besides all this, Lucius Sulla, in order to secure the loyalty of the army which he led into Asia, had allowed it a luxury and licence foreign to the manners of our forefathers; and in the intervals of leisure those charming and voluptuous lands had easily demoralised the warlike spirit of his soldiers. There it was that an army of the Roman people first learned to indulge in women and drink; to admire statues, paintings, and chased vases, to steal them from private houses and public places, to pillage shrines, and to desecrate everything, both sacred and profane. These soldiers, therefore, after they had won the victory, left nothing to the vanquished.

This, I hold, demonstrates that Sallust could write arrant nonsense in the most elegant Latin.[210] One supposes it is just possible Sulla's soldiers became art connoisseurs but there is something surrealistic about the assertion that it was only now they became acquainted with women and drink. Moreover Sallust does not explain how this supposedly degenerate army managed to go on to win Rome's First Civil War.[211] For the rest it remains only to point out here again that this was a highly disciplined force.[212]

Once more I find myself in agreement with Rich. With the Civil War over, the demand for numbers fell and with it the recruitment of *capite censi*.[213] With the outbreak of the Second Civil War, this naturally changed and recruiting once more became extensive.[214] But yet again it is difficult to say much about the standing of the citizens in these armies. Detecting non-Romans and even slaves who had been recruited by the Pompeians as the war turned against them does not take us very far in our quest to discover the economic status of those who were citizens.[215] The core of Caesar's forces was composed of his Gallic legions, to which of course he added once the war began, but only in one place can I detect a possible division between those who had land and those who had not. When Caesar was faced with a mutiny he was obliged to accede to his troops' demands and distribute land. He began this distribution with those who had some experience of [216] It is a reasonable, but not inevitable, conclusion that some of Caesar's

e they had never had land of their own.[217]

ive to consider if the property qualification was no thought it was, argued this was done about wever, such evidence as we have relevant to the period and thus it is logical to consider it at this

e Triumviral forces, 'their armies were recruited ing to ancestral custom nor to meet any need of ted this to mean the armies these men led were no *lui*. Rich countered by arguing that this seemed a ng to the economic status of the troops and sug-rregular procedures.[220]

take the matter to its natural conclusion – this pas-gether with the famous section *BJ*.86 where Sallust he property qualification in 107. At the beginning Marius had recourse to this method of recruiting for the Jugurthine War. Sallust however also says *ibitionem*.[221] In this he broadly resembles the generals

that Appian speaks of. him they have to defer to those they ostensibly command. The difference is one of degree. Marius recruited on a small scale, the Triumvirs on a great. Marius' aims were moderate and constrained by the conditions of the time in which he lived.[222] The Triumvirs pursued greater and more destructive goals. Probing a little further, we discover that both Sallust and Appian say specifically what Marius and his successors did when they recruited: they abandoned ancestral custom. Since Sallust spells out that this means ignoring the property qualification it is but common sense to assume that is what Appian means too.

Some further observations will not, I believe, be out of place. It is generally accepted that when Sallust comments on the poor man's readiness to do anything for pay since having no property himself he honours none, he is not being doctrinaire. He is not claiming Marius acted thus but is reflecting on the experiences of his own day.[223] So here again I think we can say that Appian, like Sallust, sets forth the same consequence arising from the setting aside of the property qualification: the rise of a mercenary spirit and a weakening of loyalty.[224] However, there is one relevant passage of Appian which seems to have been neglected in scholarly discussion.[225] Talking of the armies which fought at Philippi, he says that here too the normal levy had not been applied because the leaders wanted men for their excellence. Prowess not property was sought.

In conclusion then we can see there is no essential contradiction between the two passages of Appian, nor do they clash with the evidence of Sallust. We can add also that there is nothing here to support the contention that the property qualification had been formally abolished. Rather the Triumvirs seem to have been doing what we think their predecessors were doing. They were ignoring it. This need not cause surprise. The Triumvirs, as Appian says, may, at base, have ruled unlawfully, but they still took care to clothe themselves with some kind of legitimacy.[226] Keeping the form of the levy while abandoning its substance would be in harmony with such behaviour.

If we bear steadily in mind that, despite occasional facile assumptions to the contrary, Appian is speaking only of the armies of the Triumviral period, then I think we can make a tentative deduction. The number of landless in the army may have been greater now than at any time before. Appian's insight has been justly praised and his characterisation of the leaders and the led in this period shows that an almost total disregard for traditional methods of recruiting most likely led to such a result.[227]

But further than speaking of a probable increase we cannot go. We simply do not know the proportion of landed who still remained. In the same way, we know that slaves were sometimes recruited or that men summoned their clients, but we cannot say what percentage of the armies was drawn from this source.[228] And all of this has a bearing on the question of the unruliness and indiscipline which the contemporary Cornelius Nepos commented on and about which Appian is so eloquent.[229]

As on previous occasions when we have examined the army's composition we have been unable to detect any group which had special interests. What is new here is that widespread and prolonged disobedience which is a Triumviral phenomenon.[230] But that disobedience is carried out *en masse*, and those things desired *en masse* before are still the things desired now. What has really changed is that the troops have the means to get what they want. As Appian pointed out, the position of those who commanded at this time was such that it meant they had no choice but to yield.[231]

So we may conclude with the following observations. Marius, recruiting on however modest a scale, waived the property qualification. He did not establish a precedent to be followed by every man who raised an army, but common sense dictates that we accept his example was followed in times of great national emergency. Yet when we scrutinise the armies of the revolutionary period we find these men almost impossible to detect or quantify. For the modern historian they blend with those around them. They desire what their comrades desire, when those comrades are quiescent they are quiescent; when they are turbulent, the landless are turbulent with them.[232] In other words, the commonly held view that landlessness of itself predisposed the legionary towards revolution is false.

(d) Commanders and soldiers

For any army to function at all, let alone be successful, a system of discipline is essential. When the commander commands he must be sure his officers and men will obey. This, it scarcely needs to be said, was true of the Roman army. Patriotic sentiment, a strongly inculcated sense of duty and, we may add, fear of ferocious punishment, all ensured obedience.[233] From this, one consequence relevant to our study comes. In the course of this work we shall discover circumstances which gave rise to mutiny and desertion in a body, but we shall also find that *esprit de corps* was still preserved. Those who reject authority rarely dissolve into an inchoate mass. They remain an ordered body ready to serve the next master. The innate sense of discipline remains strong.[234]

However it is not enough just to speak of formal discipline when we consider the ways in which a general could evoke the loyalty of those whom he led. These may not have been set down in a code but they were none the less real for all that. We can conveniently consider officers and rankers separately.

The officers in a Roman army consisted of the tribunes, prefects, quaestors and legates.[235] Some among these were appointed by the state, but in the late republic the general appointed many himself, often after they had been recommended by another.[236] Initially obliged in this way to the commander, the subordinate would in the camaraderie of the camp often have the opportunity to achieve a close personal acquaintance with him.[237] The quaestor especially often had just such a personal relationship with his commander.[238]

Plainly, in what we may dub normal times, such ties as we have just been mentioning would serve merely to reinforce discipline. Their presence or absence would have no bearing on a man's obligation to do his duty. But in times of civil war it is easy to envisage a situation where somebody might elect to continue to obey a rebellious commander, in part, at least, because of the connections he had formed with him. Our evidence in this area shows that this could sometimes, but not always, be the case, for other motives can be found.

Thus in the numerous instances of officers switching sides which may be found in the Sullan, Caesarian and Triumviral periods it is very easy to point to motives of a political or self-preservative nature.[239] If we wish to see the personal intertwine with the political then we can do no better, I think, than look at what happened to Sulla in 88 and Caesar in 49. Both were followed by their armies when they turned against the state. But outside of those armies they enjoyed little support. So far as their officers were concerned, though, Sulla and Caesar met with two very different reactions. With the exception of his quaestor Lucullus, Sulla's officers, in harmony with the rest of society, abandoned him. Caesar's officers, on the other hand, remained loyal but for one legate, Labienus.[240]

The contrast in behaviour between the two bodies of officers has often been remarked upon.[241] If we wanted to indulge in generalities we could point towards a coarsening of sensibility detectable after the lapse of a generation which simply made it easier to do something dubious in 49 than it had been in 88. But we can also draw attention to certain specific features which would account for the change. In the first place Sulla had more or less sprung his proposal on his army. He had acted without giving much warning. Caesar's troubles, on the other hand, had long been known and people had time to ponder them. Not only would his officers be able to reflect on the merits of their chief's case but they could reflect, too, that success encourages success. Crossing the Rubicon might be a risky business but Sulla had twice shown that such an enterprise could be crowned with success. Hesitancy need not have been as great in 49 as it was in 88, especially as the social standing of Caesar's officers was not particularly high.[242] This will have made it easier for them to act than it did for the supposedly more elevated officers in 88.[243]

But if there is change, there is one constant, the motives of the dissenters from the majority on both occasions. Lucullus and Labienus acted from roughly the same mix of motives. Lucullus' motives are not explicitly stated but they may be divined with almost complete certainty. His subsequent career shows very clearly that his political stance was virtually the same as that of Sulla so that he will have had no difficulty following the consul now. Further his close personal friendship with Sulla is well attested and must have played its part in helping him make up his mind.[244]

This mixture of motives is even more explicitly set out in our sources for Labienus. First of all, we hear of ruptured personal relations between him and Caesar. The subordinate was said to be getting above himself and so irritating Caesar, who began to act coldly towards him.[245] I see no incompatibility between this report and the claim by the contemporary Cicero that Labienus had switched sides because he found Caesar's assault on the republic unacceptable.[246] It is easy to see how the personal and the political would easily complement each other in such a situation.[247]

So much for the commander and his officers. Plainly the kind of personal relation we have just been considering could not exist between the general and a large body of troops. Other ties must exist. Some have thought that clientage may have been among them.

So we turn now to consider clientage. The client–patron relationship was a feature of Roman society. In its essence it involved an inferior, the client, placing himself under the protection of a superior or patron to whom he would then render services in return for that protection. There is disagreement, however, over the degree to which Roman life was permeated by these arrangements.[248] It is no part of our business to enter into this debate but we do have to address a related issue. To what extent is the system we have just sketched found to be operating in the Roman army?[249]

It is not at all unusual to find both in the textbook and in the more ambitious study a statement to the effect that the generals of the late republic stood in the relation of patrons to their soldiers, who were their clients. Commanders could call upon their men to support them in their (often foul) designs. The troops, in return, would expect suitable material reward for the services so rendered. Though widely diffused, this view is doubtful.[250] A soldier did not have to be a client to be assured of his booty. Only the reckless or a Lucullus would deny him what was his by customary right. However we view the question of the land grant, it has to be conceded that demand for it was curiously muted for a lot of the century, while the generals' largesse was sporadic. Further, when a commander rallies his troops it is around some great issue of the day. We never hear of men being urged to fight and die because they are clients and have been called upon to do so by their patron.[251] The ever possible accusation of deploying an *argumentum ex silentio*[252] cannot be sustained here, for the simple reason that we do indeed hear of a client and patron relationship in a military context but it is not the context generally supposed. Where we actually come upon it is in accounts of the raising of private armies and irregular forces.

The first army to which the term 'private' may be applied would seem to be that raised among the Hirpini by Minatius Magius to fight on the Roman side in the Social War. Unfortunately we know nothing of the status of his following and cannot say whether or not he was able to invoke some kind of formal tie.[253] In the next instance, that of Marius and Etruria in 87, he seems to have had to rely on other means to gain support.[254]

With Pompey there is no doubt. His clientage is well attested and often cited. In 83, from among the clientage his father Pompey Strabo had established in Picenum, he raised an army to fight on the side of Sulla.[255] And we hear again of these clients.[256] When Clodius began to make difficulties Pompey summoned them to his aid.[257] He planned to do this again with the outbreak of the Second Civil War but Caesar proved too fast in advance and Picenum fell to him before Pompey could recruit.[258]

Others besides Pompey began to bestir themselves when it became clear Sulla intended to make war upon the Cinnans. Metellus Pius and Crassus, who both had their own quarrels with the Cinnans, put together armies in the provinces and it seems reasonable to suppose some of those recruited were clients.[259] On the other side, when Marius Jr became consul in 82 men flocked to his side. The glamour of his father's name must have drawn some, but here again it would probably be rash to deny he was able to draw upon clients inherited from his father as Pompey did.[260] Equally Octavian must have been able to rely on his father's name as well as drawing upon inherited clientage. It may well be too that his fellow Triumvirs also drew on a clientage, as did Cn. Pompey.[261]

We can see that the recruitment I have been describing took place in time of civil war. I risk being accused of stating the obvious because I wish to refute a notion based on a saying of Crassus, that commanders of the later republic regarded all their armies as private possessions.[262] Crassus remarked that you could not call yourself rich or be a leading man in the state unless you could maintain an army out of your own resources.[263] There is no need to apply this to the maintenance of a private army once we recognise a more plausible alternative. It was not unknown in the late republic for regular armies to be starved of funds. Monies for pay and regular expenses would fail and the commander would sometimes make up the deficit from his own resources.[264] Twice in his career Crassus may have encountered such a situation. It may very well be, as some think, that because of contemporary economic difficulties he himself had to maintain the troops impressed for service against Spartacus.[265] But there is also the intriguing possibility that someone else's difficulties provoked the remark. Pompey was one of those who ran out of money. At the start of 74 he wrote from Spain to say he had been deprived of supplies and forced to call upon his own resources and credit, which were now exhausted. I find it difficult to believe that Crassus, who hated Pompey and lost no opportunity to belittle him, would have missed a chance like this, hence the wounding remark.[266]

But whichever occasion provoked Crassus' remark we can see there is no need to connect it with the incidents we are considering. Broadly speaking these fall into two types. We encounter those who are without *imperium* and raise forces on their own initiative. The young Pompey and Minatius exemplify this and they made haste to join a man with *imperium* to regularise their position.[267] Marius did exactly the opposite to prove a point. When he joined Cinna he refused *imperium*. The squalid old man had been declared a *hostis* by the Roman people and he made it clear he would accept no office or honour until the declaration was rescinded and he was once more a citizen.[268] Others, like the older Pompey and the Triumvirs who had *imperium*, seem to have sought to supplement the normal levy by calling out clients. Appian, in fact, twice accuses the Triumvirs of recruiting in an irregular fashion.[269]

But it was not just among clients that troops were sought in these times. Lepidus (cos.78), for instance, seems to be unique in adding to his ranks the rebellious Etrurians he had been sent to crush.[270] Though separated by a generation, Marius in 87 and Milo in 48 recruited among herdsmen. Milo, too, in his ill-fated private rebellion in the Thurine country, also tried to woo debtors. And herdsmen showed up at Pharsalus brought to Pompey by one of his sons.[271] Others seem to have preferred to call up their tenants. At least that is what Catiline in 63 and Domitius Ahenobarbus in 49 are said to have done.[272] This has provoked a good deal of scholarly debate about how Catiline and Domitius enticed these people into their armies. It has been suggested they were clients as well as being tenants and in debt to their patrons; others hold that to be a tenant was to be effectively in a state of dependence.[273] Such speculation is probably unnecessary and a simple explanation is to be preferred. In the case of Catiline, desperation is surely enough to account for these men joining him. Domitius had something more to offer. Land would be provided from the break up of his extensive estates.[274]

As might be expected, a number of foreigners made their way into the legions with few questions asked, and no side was blameless in the matter.[275] We also hear a great deal about the calling up of slaves. In 88, as he struggled with Sulla, Marius twice offered freedom to any slave who would join him, an offer Cinna repeated when he found himself in trouble in the next year. Neither offer drew an enthusiastic response, largely owing to the desperate case of those who made them.[276] Things improved for Marius when he got back to Italy, and he seems to have been able to add a number of slaves to his herdsmen.[277] Milo, who we saw resembled Marius in some ways, also tried to get slaves into his ranks.[278] The evidence on Caesar is equivocal but, on balance, it is likely that, as with Sulla, he had small need of them thanks to the excellent army he commanded.[279] His opponents in the Civil War who were not so fortunate did not hesitate to take slaves into their ranks.[280] Nor did the Triumvirs or Sextus Pompey.[281]

Scholars have occasionally wondered if all these stories are true.[282] The opprobrium which attaches to encouraging the slaves to revolt is such that one would almost automatically hurl it at one's opponent. This is nicely illustrated in the case of Catiline. As a Roman gentleman he would not have slaves in his army; as a hate figure he would be accused of so doing.[283] Two considerations, in fact, need to be borne in mind. First there is habitude. By the 50s Romans were used to seeing violent slave gangs operating on the streets of Rome.[284] It was just a short step from here to seeing them in the field. We should remember too that necessity dulls scruple. When every man counted, nobody asked where he came from.[285]

The picture of swaggering patrons at the head of vast armies of clients has disappeared. Patrons do call clients to arms but it is not habitual or ambiguous. We find it in times of great emergency, but the recognition that it is but one of a number of means of recruitment available counsels against attributing excessive importance to it.

From clientage we turn now to something which resided in the person, or perhaps more accurately the personality, of the commander: charisma. Every soldier will naturally have hoped to serve under a successful general.[286] In (a) above we saw what were the qualities required of a man in order to achieve such success. Charisma, I believe we may safely say, is the additional possession, but not the invariable possession, of such successful men. To divine what it is about a man that ensured he had such a gift is not easy.[287] But if we accept a dictionary definition we can at least see quite easily who were the men of the late republic who possessed it. Charisma has been defined as 'a capacity to inspire devotion and enthusiasm'.[288] In the light of this we can claim the following as having this somewhat elusive characteristic: Marius, Sulla, Pompey, Caesar and Octavian.[289] Conversely Lucullus provides a convenient point of comparison as one who for a time was successful but clearly did not have this gift.

Exercising charisma is obviously a help when one wishes to assert one's authority. However, some scholars who have nothing to say about charisma as such believe that in our period the authority of the commander anyway becomes paramount. The authority of the state fades away and the soldiers become, in effect, the personal retainers of the general. This thesis was propounded in the 1930s by H. Drexler and has been influential ever since.[290] Drexler rested his case especially on analysis of *Bell.Hisp.*17. Here Tullius parleys with Caesar, saying he wishes he had fought on his side rather than Cn. Pompey's. Now he and his colleagues are public enemies, abandoned by Pompey and beaten by Caesar. They ask for mercy from Caesar, which they will receive.

Here, it is claimed, Tullius is not speaking in the capacity of a fighter for the *respublica* but simply as a soldier of Cn. Pompey.[291] A number of objections, however, can be made to this interpretation.

To start with there is the question of historical context. In the civil wars parleys of various types were common and dealt with diverse issues.[292] In the situation as depicted here it is hardly surprising that Tullius' plea took the shape it did. He is attempting to transfer from a failed commander to a successful one in the field. In the circumstances discussion of other issues might well be secondary to immediate military concerns.[293] Nevertheless such issues are to be found. Tullius invokes his own standing as a Roman citizen and the state of the fatherland.[294] But more than anything else, I believe Drexler has failed to take account of the position of Caesar and his opponent Pompey. Both represented two sides in a civil war and as such will naturally have assumed that authority and right lay with them. Tullius is in no doubt about this. He and his friends are now public enemies because of the disaster which has come upon their country. In other words because of the cause for which he fought, his country, not Cn. Pompey.[295]

Speaking generally, we have therefore to reject Drexler's thesis. There is, however, one well-documented period when generals ruled by their own authority. This was the Triumviral period in which App.*BC*.5.17 says, 'the majority of commanders were unelected ... all parties were alike, and none of them had been officially condemned as public enemies ... the common pretext of the generals, that they were all assisting the interest of their country'.[296]

All of this bears a certain resemblance to a description taken from modern Africa: 'he is a former officer, an ex-minister ... desiring power and money, ruthless and without scruples, who, taking advantage of the disintegration of the state (to which he contributed and continues to contribute) wants to carve out for himself his own informal mini state, over which he can hold dictatorial sway ... [He] will always proclaim that [he is] leading a national movement or party.'[297]

We need not waste time expressing amazement at how little has changed in two thousand years. Instead we can claim that the obvious resemblances justify our adopting Kapuściński's terminology. He calls his subjects 'warlords', and we may do the same with the Triumvirs for theirs was a period when men of dubious legality ruled by their own authority and no other.

So our survey has taken us through a number of gradations. We have glanced at traditional customary discipline and then gone on to see how it may be supplemented by personal relations and charisma. Two notions we have rejected, that as a matter of course the general's authority was habitually greater than that of the state or that his armies were composed of men who were his clients. With regard to the former, however, we do concede it was true in the few years which make up the Triumviral period.

(e) Conclusion

When we look at the Roman army it is natural to begin our investigations at the top and work down. We find that basically those who led these armies were expected to do so from the front or, to put it another way, they had to undergo what their men did. The qualities and traits they were expected to display are easy to divine and explicate. The legions they commanded were largely drawn from men of rural origin. It has long been held that many men of this type were now failing to meet the property qualification necessary for entrance to service. Recent attempts to overthrow this view have not, in my view, been successful. But, at the same time, the traditional belief that the admission of the landless to the ranks was an act of great significance must be given up. The presence of such men is very difficult to detect in the armies of the period, and all we can say is that they articulate the same grievances and aims in both the economic and political spheres as do their more fortunate brethren. In delineating the direct relations between the commander and his men we find that normal military discipline is still important. The further formulated formal tie of clientship in fact seems unlikely, but the less tangible personal quality of charisma and its effects can hardly be rejected. Nor can we deny that in the Triumviral period this notion of a general's personal authority succeeds in producing the warlord.

3

POLITICS AND PROFIT

Did the Roman armies of the revolutionary period have any kind of political motivation? Responses to this question have ranged from a flat negative to a tepid and doubting assent.[1] Making the immediate warning that such a motivation need not always be on the highest level of sophistication,[2] I here propose to set forth my reasons for believing not only that the armies of the late republic manifested a political will but that this will was of the greatest importance. At the same time it was accompanied by a constant in Roman history: the Roman soldier, irrespective of his other motives, expected when he went on campaign to profit thereby from loot and booty.[3]

The politicisation of which we speak was, I hold, introduced by Sulla, and it is with his age we begin.

(a) The age of Sulla

Sulla's march on Rome in 88 was unprecedented. Efforts to explain the behaviour of the troops tend to centre on their supposed status as a result of the reforms of Marius. Hence, I believe, the true nature of what happened here has been obscured. Sulla addressed a *contio* and told the troops of the wrongs that had been done to him. Rome and the senate were in the hands of tyrants. Now, for the Romans *contiones* were of two types, the civil and the military. As can readily be appreciated, the former dealt with political matters, the latter with military. What Sulla did now was quite simply to abolish the difference between the two. He brought civil business before a gathering of soldiers. In so doing he politicised them. He invited them to become involved in the great issues of the day. Their response showed clearly they understood what was involved and their belief they could do something about it. But, although Sulla had called attention to their standing as Roman citizens, these men never forgot they were still soldiers, and among the reasons they elected to follow Sulla was the fear that if Marius took over the command he would enlist other troops and so they would lose the profits of this war.[4]

I believe it is worthwhile lingering over Sulla's position as viewed from the background of that intermittent violence which had characterised Roman public life since the murder of Tiberius Gracchus in 133. Indeed a comparison with Tiberius himself, although I doubt if Sulla would have made it, is instructive. Like Sulla, Tiberius, at the end of his life, stood in great danger. Both turned to the people and, in both cases, the people failed them. For Tiberius this was the end but Sulla went to the soldiers. There, almost by accident, he discovered a political will. Both men went, with their respective cases, to a politically aware group, but in Sulla's instance that group bore arms.

If Tiberius was deserted by most of his aristocratic supporters so was Sulla. With the exception of his quaestor Lucullus, all his senior officers abandoned him when he began his march. The split along class lines is clear enough and one source is quite explicit on the reason. Unlike the rankers, who believed they were being led to right a wrong, Sulla's staff thought they were actually being led in an attack on their country. Other factors may have been at play[5] but here we shall simply gloss what our sources tell us. From at least the time of Tiberius Gracchus we can detect a natural dislike for improper or extreme behaviour among the Roman nobility. This was what cost Tiberius his noble followers, but it is also characterised by the reluctance of the consul of 133 Mucius Scaevola to take pre-cipitate action against him. A remarkable parallel to the split between Sulla's officers and men has gone almost unnoticed. When the Italians took Nola in the Social War they gave the Romans the option of joining with them. The common soldiers accepted but the officers refused and were starved to death. This spirit is illustrated too in Metellus Numidicus' withdrawal from Rome rather than endan-ger his country in a struggle with Saturninus. Sulla found his officers' attitudes soon echoed by Q. Scaevola, who declared to the sullenly hostile senate that he did not propose to be a party to the condemnation of Marius. And finally in 87, when reasons of state would seem to have demanded it, Metellus Pius refused to con-clude an easy peace with the Samnites. In a word, Sulla in 88 held a position akin to a radical tribune. He enjoyed only popular support.[6]

That was soon to change but, more important, we have to realise Sulla had set a precedent. Scholars may squabble over what his legacy to Rome was, but here was one thing we will find repeated again and again. Men of ambition, in order to accomplish their designs, must have a care for the political sensitivities of their troops if they are to succeed in making of them their followers. Sulla had shown the way by discovering, more or less by accident, the latent political power of the army.

There can be no clearer proof of the truth of this proposition than the simple fact that in the very next year the first of Sulla's imitators appeared. The actions of his great enemy Cinna paralleled almost exactly those of Sulla and showed that he had absorbed thoroughly the lessons to be learned from 88.[7] As consul Cinna had championed the cause of Italian redistribution among all the tribes. He was opposed by his colleague Octavius. Rioting then followed and Cinna was forced to flee.[8] As Sulla did, so did Cinna. After an excursion to some of the towns of his natural allies, the Italians, he wound up at Nola where Sulla had left an army to besiege an insurgent force which still held the town. Leaving aside his *fasces* he told the assembled troops what was true: his enemies, once he had left town, had deposed him from the consulship. He then went on to broaden the argument. This was an injury inflicted on him but it was also an injury inflicted on them. They were the sovereign people but their decisions, which should have been binding on all, had been set at nought. The political issue had plainly been brought to the camp and the soldiers were not only being asked where the right lay in the current quarrel but were reminded that their rights as members of the sovereign people were being endangered. To strengthen his case Cinna followed up with a display of histrionics which featured tearing off of clothes and culminated in a good roll in the mud. His audience were impressed. They put him back on his curule seat, restored the *fasces* to him and, hailing him as consul, bade him lead them where he would. Clad once more as a consul, Cinna deposed Appius Claudius Pulcher, the commander Sulla had left behind, and, joining his new army to his Italian recruits, led the lot on Rome.[9]

So far we have spoken only of Cinna's appeal to the political sensibilities of the troops. Now, however, we come to some source material which, at first sight anyway, suggests to some that he applied slightly grubbier means of persuasion. In a word, he dispensed bribes.[10] According to these sources, Cinna corrupted tribunes and centurions and then bought the ranks by hope of future rewards.[11] We might, perhaps, if we were so minded, dismiss this story as black propaganda disseminated by Cinna's enemies, whom we may suspect were numerous, in order to give him an evil name.[12] But, since an earlier story of Cinna disbursing cash seems plausible,[13] it makes more sense to believe these stories, especially as they can be explained in the light of contemporary behaviour.[14]

It will not be forgotten that those whom Cinna attempted to woo had been left behind by Sulla when he went off to fight Mithridates. Hence they must have felt a certain sense first of disappointment and then subsequently of rejoicing when the opportunity for profit presented itself. Convinced as they were of the justice of Cinna's case, they nevertheless, as true Romans, expected to be enriched as they lent him their support. The money disbursed by Cinna now almost certainly came from his Italian allies.[15] Our sources are vague about where the next payment was to come from (*spe largitionis*) and I suspect so was Cinna himself. I doubt if he had promised Italian cities for the sack[16] but the wording suggests a donative at campaign's end, wherever it was to come from.[17]

Two other incidents from roughly the same period show clearly how the soldier acted from political motives. When, a little after this, Marius landed in Etruria to reclaim his lost position he was obliged to put a programme before his potential recruits. He therefore reminded them that he deserved well for his past services to Rome. He also pledged he would support the redistribution of the Italians among all the tribes.[18]

Our other instance is that of Q. Flavius Fimbria. In 86 the Cinnans had sent out an army to replace or perhaps co-operate with that of Sulla. On the road, however, the commander Valerius Flaccus was murdered by his subordinate Fimbria. The latter won some considerable success in the field but this was not a consideration when he and Sulla finally met.[19] Sulla demanded Fimbria surrender his army since he held it unlawfully.[20] Fimbria, for his part, had an answer to hand. Sulla, he said, did not hold a lawful command.[21] It soon became clear which of the opposing views was destined to prevail. As Sulla's men drew a line of circumvallation around Fimbria's camp the latter's men began to desert. Twice he summoned an assembly but his pleas proved in vain. Prostration before individuals and bribing of the tribunes did no good either, nor did attempts first to assassinate Sulla and then to parley with him. Finally Fimbria killed himself and his army went over to Sulla.

There are a number of interesting points in this account which deserve comment. The first and most obvious is that the Fimbrians have been placed in the same position as those men who listened to Sulla and Cinna. They would have to decide where legitimate authority lay, with their own commander or with Sulla. From the start Fimbria has lost the argument. His troops have no doubt that Sulla holds the valid command. Like Cinna and Sulla he has recourse to the *contio*, but to no avail. Even a display of hysteria, reminiscent of Cinna's, failed to move his audience. Bribing the tribunes is a logical consequence of this for they then tried to sway the assembly.

We can with some accuracy divine why Fimbria's troops made the choice they did. First of all, though no ancient author says so, I would guess self-preservation played its part, as it must have in the subsequent civil war. People naturally like to be on the winning side, and if it came to a fight Sulla, with his superior numbers, was sure to win. Appian also says the Fimbrians were simply unwilling to fight their fellow Romans. Despite the doubts of some, this seems perfectly believable, especially now when the idea of Roman killing Roman was still something of a novelty.[22] There was also the question of persuasion. Sulla's men mingled with their opponents and convinced them of the justice of their cause. This was a technique they applied again in the Civil War when, in similar circumstances, they seduced the army of Scipio Asiagenus (cos.83).[23]

Here, as in the case of Cinna discussed above, the question of money intrudes. We hear of Fimbria's *corrupto exercitu* at the hands of Sulla, and when we come to Scipio we are told it was not just arguments which won their hearts but also bribes. Fimbria himself does not appear to be much better than Sulla in this respect. We have already seen him bribing his tribunes and earlier his subversion of Flaccus' army is also described as *corrupto exercitu*.[24]

In weighing up this evidence we have first to recall that *corripio* can simply mean 'seduce' without any suggestion of bribery being involved.[25] However Flaccus had the reputation of being a mean man so it is not incredible that Fimbria offered a cash bait to those whose loyalty he wished to subvert.[26] It is difficult to see, however, why Sulla should offer a bribe to Fimbria's men since he was in much the stronger position. In the case of Scipio it is marginally easier to accept since at this stage of the war both sides were desperately lobbying for support. The story docs have one suspicious feature however. Other commanders are reported to have used their troops as agents of persuasion in this war but nothing is said about money. This detail may derive from Plutarch's mistaken conception of Sulla as a warlord after the manner of the later Triumvirs.[27]

One other facet of the First Mithridatic War must engage our attention here, the occupation of Asia at its end by Sulla and his troops. There is no doubt they were oppressive to the natives but it is also important to realise what they were about. Sulla's troops were receiving the booty which was their due as victors in the war. The hopes expressed in Appian BC.1.57 were being fulfilled.[28] Some of course want to go further and claim there was something more sinister than a general seeing to it that his men got their just reward. Sulla was buying the loyalty of his troops with a view to their use in the civil war which he was about to launch.[29] Before we embrace this view wholeheartedly we should remember that he himself had no such design in mind, for when he landed in Italy in 83 he feared the troops would, as they were permitted at war's end, leave him for their homes. They did not, but it was not until they had fought a battle that Sulla could feel sure of their support.[30] A new campaign with a new objective was about to begin and, as in 88, Sulla had to discover if his soldiers approved of what he proposed to do.

At base the Civil War was about Sulla's demand that the decree that made him a *hostis* be rescinded and that he and the other exiles be restored to their positions. But it was more than that, for by the time campaigning began Sulla stood at the head of a coalition of diverse interests who were now agreed that lawful authority lay with him and that an end should be made of the Cinnans who were but mere usurpers. Furthermore everybody knew that Sulla, who had tried to play the reformer in 88, would now do so again when victorious.[31]

We catch a glimpse of what Sulla proposed to do in the issues he and Scipio Asiagenus debated when they came to parley[32] but that is not our chief interest in these talks.[33] It will be remembered that Sulla's troops used this occasion to lure Scipio's men away from him. Bribery we know was mentioned, but persuasion was surely just as important. As with Fimbria, Sulla's men, convinced of the rightness of their cause, convinced others.[34] And this was not the only signal display of loyalty these men gave. At the campaign's start they offered Sulla a loan. He refused – a gesture which stands in strong contrast to that of Caesar who, in similar circumstances, accepted on the grounds that when everybody has sunk something into an enterprise they are in consequence more likely to show enthusiasm for it.[35] Caesar's hold over his troops is celebrated but perhaps that of Sulla over his was greater.[36]

With the battle of the Colline Gate, Rome's First Civil War effectively ended. Two further conflicts, however, arose directly from Sulla's victory: the Sertorian War and the rebellion of Lepidus (cos.78). With regard to Sertorius we need only say that scholarly dispute over the support he drew from Spain itself need not concern us. We need only point out that those he led there or later welcomed will have needed no persuading of the justice of the Cinnan cause and will have shared his ambition of returning to Rome some day.[37]

Lepidus and his uprising require a little more detailed treatment.[38] Even before election he had announced a comprehensive anti-Sullan programme. He promised restoration of the powers of the tribunate, recall of the exiles, the rescinding of Sulla's land settlement and the enactment of a corn law.[39] Despite all of this, when a revolt began in Etruria against the Sullan colonists the senate sent Lepidus and his consular colleague with an army to suppress it. There the pair quarrelled and Lepidus threw in his lot with the rebels whose attitude to Sulla's colonial programme was the same as his own. With his mixed force he advanced on Rome, only to be defeated by Pompey, who had been called in by the senate to deal with the situation.[40] What, however, is for us the most important feature is that when a commander calls upon his army for aid in implementing a political programme they respond and even go so far as to make common cause with rebels they are sent to suppress.

Thus we can see very clearly what had been the result of Sulla's actions in 88. Troops as always would seek gain from a campaign, but the objective of such a campaign might be different from what it traditionally had been. Sulla had shown how the Roman army might be politicised. He had demonstrated that a commander might come before his troops with an essentially domestic political issue and persuade them they should help him resolve it by force of arms.

(b) The age of Caesar

The issue which led to the Second Civil War is not in doubt. Caesar desired to proceed immediately from his proconsulship in Gaul, to a second consulship. He wanted to do this in order to avoid prosecution for what he had done in 59 during his first. His enemies at Rome were not prepared to grant him this concession and on the first of January 49 it was decreed he should resign his command by a certain date. This meant he would have to appear in Rome to canvass in person and thus leave himself liable to prosecution.[41]

Once he had marched out of his province,[42] Caesar made haste to put his case before his troops at a *contio* in Ravenna. He told them wrongs had been done him. He complained that the government at Rome had passed the s.c.u. against him. He then portrayed himself as the champion of tribunician rights, pointing out that when the s.c.u. was passed two of the tribunes who supported him felt their inviolability threatened and fled to him for safety. He asked his men to defend his dignity and they responded enthusiastically.[43]

Only a portion of Caesar's army formed the audience when he set forth these grievances but its example was followed by the rest of his troops. It is but common sense to assume that Caesar's army was long acquainted with the issues. After all, the political wrangling had not exactly been of short duration. His men seem to have needed little persuasion. His officers too remained steadfast. Only one, T. Labienus, abandoned him.[44]

Caesar did not, however, confine himself to preaching his message to believers or half-believers.[45] Wherever possible he encouraged his men to fraternise with the enemy with the intention of subverting their allegiance. Two particularly noteworthy instances occurred at Ilerda in Spain and at the river Apsus in

Illyricum.[46] I do not think it rash to suggest the legionaries repeated what Caesar had said to them as he left his province. Certainly he himself says that is what he did when, on his advance in early 49, he encountered one of his opponents, the consul Spinther, and tried to persuade him of the justice of his cause.[47] Of course not everybody was charmed. As he advanced through Italy in the opening days of the war he was opposed by the praetor Minucius Thermus, who then fled before him. The latter's troops, however, showed no inclination to join Caesar and, evidently judging the war to be over as far as they were concerned, went home.[48] He had better luck after defeating his next enemy, Attius Varus. Some of his troops did head for home but others joined themselves to Caesar.[49] By the time he had come to grips with Domitius Ahenobarbus things seemed to have changed. His men were ordered to join Caesar's ranks.[50] Although there are other instances of voluntary changes of side – most notably at Ilerda and again after Pharsalus[51] – we must assume the bulk of Caesar's armies were raised because he exercised his power as consul and held a levy.[52] The numbers involved will admit no other explanation.[53]

Nevertheless Caesar was obviously proud of his attempts to lure and reconcile. So he tells us that when, before Dyrrachium, some Allobroges deserted him this was most unusual. Before this, such traffic had all been in the opposite direction as when men deserted Pompey *en masse*.[54] Just prior to Pharsalus, Appian represents both Caesar and Pompey as holding *contiones*. These are of the normal military type. The general is exhorting his men before battle.[55] Caesar himself says he did indeed hold such a *contio* but adds that he recalled his efforts for peace and the specific occasions on which he had made them.[56]

Yet, however legitimate Caesar felt his grievances and his cause to be, those who opposed him obviously did not share his views and held themselves to be the legitimate government of the Roman republic.[57] That legitimate government enjoyed a senatorial majority when it passed the s.c.u. in order to defend itself against the threatening proconsul.[58] Pompey himself made it clear he was acting on behalf of the state. In a private communication sent to Caesar while the latter was still at Ariminum he declared he was not acting out of personal enmity but on behalf of the state.[59] Perhaps confidence in this viewpoint was shaken after the retreat to Greece. At any rate Pompey addressed a *contio* there in which he defended his strategic withdrawal from Italy and, citing precedents such as the Athenians in the Persian Wars, vowed, like General MacArthur, to return. He then went on to declare they were defending their country from a public enemy who would be punished. For himself he was offering the state, as always, his services as a soldier. This speech, we are told, was greeted with great enthusiasm.[60]

Another reminder of what they were fighting for was given to the troops before Dyrrachium in 48. This time it came from that rather unattractive character, the younger Cato. When the soldiers were responding sluggishly to other commanders Cato made a speech invoking such notions as freedom and virtue and finally called upon the gods as witnesses that they were fighting for their country. Inspired, his listeners rushed into battle.[61]

In the light of these remarks we must assume, I think, that the Romans whom Pompey levied for his armies[62] acknowledged that the right lay with him.[63]

We may leave the last word, or rather, in view of the source, last words, with Dio, who manages in two places to bring out well the confidence both sides felt in the rightness of their respective causes and how, from one perspective, there was essentially nothing to choose between them. Reflecting on Caesar's seizure of the treasury once he had occupied Rome, Dio points out that both Pompey and Caesar called those who fought against them public enemies while proclaiming themselves champions of the republic.[64] Then in his accounts of the *contiones* before Pharsalus, which differ from those of our other sources, he, in essence, makes the same point again.[65] Both sides called the other tyrants and themselves liberators, and their leaders, spurring them on to battle, reminded them of this.

We turn now from the idealistic, if we may so term it, to the question of costs. Here it would seem Pompey and his allies had the advantage when it came to monies, even though he had to do without the contents of the treasury which had been voted him as Caesar had proved too quick and seized them.[66] What could be extracted, however, from the great swathe of territory he controlled more than made up for Pompey's loss. With the eastern half of the empire in his hands he was able to extract money from the provinces and from Rome's client kings. Individuals too were made to contribute, as were the companies of the *publicani*.[67] Inevitably this kind of thing could become oppressive. That, at least, is what Caesar himself says of the activities of the savant Varro in Hither Spain at the start of the war. His exactions in the Pompeian interest were said to have been burdensome and when Caesar came that way he gave relief to those who had been oppressed.[68]

Scipio Nasica, the proconsul of Syria, seems to have been worse and Caesar has left us a vivid account of his extortion in his province.[69] Not that gross behaviour was confined to the Pompeians. Caesar made a very bad choice when he put Q. Cassius Longinus in charge of Further Spain and we have a detailed account of his enormities to prove it.[70]

In contrast to Pompey, Caesar's financial position was, to start with anyway, far less secure.[71] Whatever Caesar's profits from the Gallic War,[72] it is plain they would not be sufficient for this new conflict. At the start of the war centurions agreed to fund the cavalry and the ordinary soldiers to forgo their pay for a time.[73] During the first campaign in Spain he borrowed money from the tribunes and centurions to distribute to the legionaries.[74] Caesar's own way of making war did not help matters since wherever possible he tried to spare both the innocent and the defeated. As a result there was little plunder to be gained from captured cities or defeated armies.[75] Caesar had doubled the pay of the legionary[76] but, in the absence of funds, this was of little use so that pay itself tended to be irregular at times and promised donatives did not appear.[77] The upshot was that Caesar faced mutiny in 49 and 47.[78]

It has not always been appreciated, I believe, that there had been warnings a couple of years before that something like this could happen.[79] One of the things that emerged when the soldiers mutinied was war weariness and the demand for discharge which was now overdue. But we actually hear of such discontent already in the previous year. Early in 50 it was decided that in order to aid Cornelius Balbus in his campaigns against the Parthians, both Caesar and Pompey should contribute a legion each to his army. Pompey designated as his contribution a legion he had lent Caesar in 53 so that the latter would then lose two legions. Those who were sent to collect them reported that Caesar's army was worn out and eager to go home. They would, on their arrival in Italy, desert to Pompey whom they allegedly worshipped. Our sources pour scorn on this, claiming Caesar's troops were well disciplined and loyal. They speculate that those who carried these reports either acted from ignorance of military matters or had simply been bought.[80]

Pompey, too, is castigated for giving ear to these reports. Such an attitude is held to betoken clouded judgement and a further incident to indicate an excess of vanity. He fell dangerously ill at Naples in the summer of that year and prayers were offered throughout Italy for his recovery. When he did recover there were demonstrations of universal rejoicing up and down the peninsula. Moved, Pompey declared that if he wanted troops all he would have to do would be to stamp his foot and they would rise up.[81]

Reflection, though, may lead us to take a less severe view of Pompey. He never really got a chance to stamp his foot. The rapidity of Caesar's initial advance in 49 took him by surprise and robbed him of any real chance to recruit a great army in Italy.[82] Even more difficult to believe is that a soldier of Pompey's experience would have displayed such naivety in 50. The mutiny of the next year is his partial vindication. The reports from Gaul may have been exaggerated but what happened at Placentia showed they were not without foundation.

Part of Caesar's problem lay with the nature of his soldiers. They, of course, wanted their booty and I cannot pretend to say they were especially rapacious. They do, however, seem to have entertained great ambitions. Caesar's *contio* after coming into Italy[83] was one of those unfortunate occasions when communications partially broke down. Caesar's words and gestures were misunderstood by his audience, who assumed they were going to be offered equestrian status and the money to support it.[84]

Though not quickly enough to forestall another mutiny, Caesar's attitude changed after Pharsalus.[85] He now began to treat the enemy as a source of revenue. After he had extricated himself from the troubles in Alexandria in 47 he had headed eastwards and there applied the principle that what areas had raised by way of monies for Pompey was now his and, in addition, some places were required to pay over and above this.[86] Upon returning to Italy he further increased his store by collecting gold crowns and loans.[87] In the next year the victories in Africa led to the fining of the defeated and the confiscation of their property as they were regarded as bearing arms against Rome herself.[88] The final campaign in Spain (45) led too to various exactions.[89] The result was that, when the time came to triumph, Caesar was able to pay his men a lavish donative, the amount received being in proportion to rank.[90]

Caesar's crossing of the Rubicon is something which, throughout the ages, has caught the popular imagination, and rightly. It is one of those moments which are called 'defining'. Yet here we are really concerned not with the far-reaching consequences the act had for Rome and the world but rather with the war which now followed and those who fought in it.[91]

Our first concern must be to acknowledge the strong political element in the situation. Caesar informed his troops of the wrongs done to him and to others and asked them to help him find a remedy. They as Roman citizens gave a positive response. But the remedy involved going to war and war must bring profits. Hence the very marked desire of these troops for material rewards. When they rebelled it was not because they repudiated Caesar's objectives but because their terms of service were not acceptable.[92]

But there are certain disturbing features discernible here. Caesar himself, as we shall see in a moment, spotted them, but it is an open question whether he divined their full import which is perfectly plain to us with our knowledge of what happened after his death.[93] I refer to the more mercenary element which now creeps into the relations between the commander and his troops and for which Caesar himself seems to be responsible. Of his transactions before Ilerda he says that by distributing money to his troops he had bought their allegiance.[94] Dio also records for us a remark he is said to have made to the effect that dominance was maintained by two things: money and soldiers. They were interdependent for without money one could not keep an army.[95] This last must be treated with a certain reserve because, as we know, Dio is perhaps capable of blurring historical distinctions and assimilating Caesar to the Triumvirs who came after him.[96] Much the same might be said of Dio's report that those who mutinied were really practising extortion.[97] This was more the style of the Triumviral armies than the Caesarian. But, if Dio is to be taken at his face value, then what we have here is not a historical anticipation but the first signs of what we shall see in the Triumviral period: commanders becoming the prisoners of their troops.

A certain insecurity in his position, which was, of course, known to his troops, may have helped shape Caesar's attitude.[98] Comparisons are sometimes drawn with Sulla.[99] Both made their attack after laying their grievances before their men and receiving their support. But there were two Sullas, the Sulla of 88 and the Sulla of 83. The Sulla of 88 had only the support of his troops. His officers had deserted him, and senate and people were hostile. In 83, with a loyal army, he stood at the head of a great coalition and was the acknowledged champion of the senate.[100] Caesar in 49 had his officers and army and virtually nobody else. The shakiness of his position made him ever more dependent on those he commanded.

In another important aspect Sulla differed from Caesar. On the two occasions he marched on Rome he did not merely seek a remedy for grievances but looked beyond them to formulate plans for the better governing of Rome. From before his first consulship he had aspired to the role of statesman.[101] About Caesar, however, there is doubt. We certainly know there were people at Rome who had long had suspicions of him and his intentions. As early as his aedileship Catulus had accused him of taking a battering ram to the state.[102] But such a judgement, issuing from a partisan source, must be treated with caution. Thoughts on crossing the Rubicon would be valuable but unfortunately Caesar himself does not mention that crossing. All that we have are the accounts of later writers which depict him as preoccupied with immediate matters, the enormity of the undertaking, the vengeance he would like to take on his enemies and the suffering he might cause.[103]

There would seem to be only one place where Caesar himself revealed his intentions. During the first of his Spanish campaigns he declared that his objective was to secure the tranquillity of Italy, the peace of the provinces and the safety of the empire.[104] We can, I think, agree with Gelzer that he was sincere in this pronouncement.[105] However, I would hesitate to describe it, as he does, as some kind of definite plan of action. It reads rather as a vaguely beneficent expression of goodwill.[106] In fact, it is generally recognised that his planned departure for a Parthian war, which was aborted by his assassination, is a clear enough indication that he had not made up his mind by then as to what system he would impose in the state.[107] From that it is a short step towards concluding he never had any plan to begin with.[108]

A delineation of the position of Caesar's opponents requires less time and space. Some, out of personal enmity, sought his destruction, but as a whole his enemies saw themselves as representing legitimate authority against a rebellious proconsul. From the sources, the troops they commanded appear as less vociferous for loot but they shared one thing with their opponents, awareness of what they were fighting for. They have answered the call to defend the republic just as Caesar's men have answered the appeal for assistance against his enemies.

(c) The Triumviral period

The immediate aftermath of Caesar's murder presents us with a situation confused overall and complex in detail. The senate, the Liberators and Caesar's political heirs engage in a kind of *Totentanz* characterised by shifting and insincere alliances as enemies seek mastery and the destruction of their rivals.[109] Fortunately for the historian of the Roman army there is one theme which is now a constant. The troops are determined that Caesar should be avenged.[110] It should be explained that this is a sentiment which, though often shared by officers, came from the ranks.[111] As we shall now see, the likes of Antony and Octavian might, for whatever reasons, postpone the realisation of this aim but they would be recalled to it by those they commanded.

Thus, when Antony's army mutinied at Brundisium they expressed anger at his failure to avenge Caesar. They offered to join Octavian if he would do this and eventually two legions did actually desert to him.[112] But this restless mood could not always be successfully exploited for selfish advantage. In November of 44 Octavian tried to persuade his troops to turn on Antony but they would have none of it. Antony was now consul but, more important, many of them had served under him and they did not propose to attack their former commander. They were disappointed to learn they had been mistaken because they believed they had been summoned to hear that Octavian and Antony were to unite to pursue Caesar's killers. They then proceeded to drift away under various pretexts and only the promise of a donative and distaste for farming brought them back.[113]

Indeed we twice in this year hear of military tribunes intervening to get Antony and Octavian to moderate their behaviour and become reconciled.[114] Troops, too, could spontaneously advance the cause of their leaders. Octavian's men furnished him with lictors and urged him to assume the title of propraetor. When he said he would refer the matter to the senate they proposed to go there in a body to extract the magistracy from the fathers and it was only with difficulty Octavian made them desist.[115]

However, for all of this political activity, the Roman soldier expected, as he always had, substantial rewards from those who led him.[116] Octavian showed early promise when people feared lest he distribute largesse in the city.[117] The reputation for lavishness thus acquired was soon fulfilled when he wooed Caesar's veterans in Campania with cash and even travelled as far as Ravenna with his moneybags. Later in the year, when he found himself at Alba Fucens, he disbursed further monies and promised even more. Antony, on the other hand, facing a mutiny at Brundisium,[118] earned derision with a promise of 100 denarii. Soon after, outside Rome, probably disconcerted by desertions, he became more generous and gave 500 denarii.[119]

As we pass into 43 we find, unsurprisingly, that Caesar's name continued to exercise men's minds. Cicero, who it should be remembered had a disdain for the ranker's political reputation, explicitly states it was this, and not love of the state, that motivated the Martian and the fourth legion when they deserted Antony.[120] And when Octavian made his way to Rome for the second time and was wrangling with the senate about the consulship, his troops supported him because he was Caesar's son.[121] Octavian himself is said to have made a speech in which he emphasised the dangers faced by Caesar's friends and, in the manner of Sulla and Caesar himself, spoke of the wrongs he and his men had had to endure.[122] Troops, however, did not always need a *contio* of this sort for, as they continued to demonstrate, they were perfectly capable of acting on their own initiative. So, after Mutina, Antony had to change his plans and, at the instance of his troops, make for Pallentia instead of going over the Alps as he originally intended.[123] Octavian's consular bid, to which we referred a moment ago in the context of the potency of the Caesarian name, shows how enthusiasm for that name could inspire the troops to act. They despatched centurions to Rome to demand the office. When the fathers refused, the men told Octavian to lead them on Rome and he, capitalising on the mood, did so.[124] With the formation of the Triumvirate the soldiers played matchmaker, but not in any romantic spirit. In order to cement the alliance they insisted Octavian should marry Claudia, a daughter of Antony's wife Fulvia.[125]

Money, or just as often promises of money, continues to figure prominently in our narrative of 43. Even a loser like Decimus Brutus felt obliged to distribute gold among his men who were dispersing to their homes.[126] His fellow Liberator Cassius got a better return for his outlay. Failing to buy the night watch of Laodicea he purchased instead the centurions on day duty and they betrayed the city to him.[127] When Antony, as he campaigned against D. Brutus, wanted to subvert the loyalties of Pollio's and Plancus' armies he took care to offer acceptable financial inducement.[128]

The story of the fourth and Martian legions, to whom we have made reference already, is long but instructive. The senate voted they should have from the treasury a sum equal to that Octavian had already promised if they were victorious against Antony.[129] When the latter was defeated at Mutina and good report came from Pansa, Cicero confirmed the bounty would be paid and a property tax was established to pay for it. Further the soldiers would have the right to wear an olive crown at festivals.[130] In addition it was decreed that the sons of the fallen should have the rewards that would have gone to their fathers.[131] With some difficulty the money was raised.[132] The senate, however, had shown once again it had no ideological objection to rewarding troops, especially when a desperate situation warranted it.[133] By his reaction Octavian showed he understood this well and was alive to the dangers it posed. Fearing he would lose men, he chased away the column bearing the senatorial cash which met him on the road.[134] Then, as he marched on Rome, the opposition panicked and promised 5,000 denarii not just to the two legions but to all of Octavian's men.[135] This did no good and it was left to Octavian to gather money from the Janiculum and elsewhere with which he paid what Cicero had pledged originally, and then promised the rest would follow.[136]

We have remarked on the strong motivation of the Triumviral troops. They wanted revenge for Caesar's murder. The extent to which the soldiers of Brutus and Cassius shared their enthusiasm for a revived republic must now be considered.[137] As is known, the pair chiefly recruited in the east.[138] Many of those they impressed had served under Caesar and, given what we have said above about the attitude of such veterans, we might have expected them to behave as the fourth and Martian legions who refused to serve under the tyrannicide Decimus Brutus the previous year. Instead they proved perfectly tractable.[139]

It may very well be that some were where they were because they had little choice.[140] However there is good reason to suppose both sides were perfectly well aware of what they were fighting for when matters came to be decided at Philippi. One side sought vengeance for Caesar's murder and then domination, while the other stood for liberty and a free republic.[141] Speeches of exhortation are mentioned as having been made by both sides. Many of these, though, fall into the category of the traditional military *contio* with generals urging their men to perform well.[142] Only Cassius, who is represented earlier as calling the Triumvirs tyrants,[143] is equipped in our sources with an elaborated reconstruction of a speech with a clear political message. The speech is long but the message is straightforward and apt. The murder of Caesar is defended and the restoration of the republic promised.[144] If this in any way represents what Cassius said – and I see no reason why not – then we must take it that his audience shared his sentiments.

Despite this the Liberators did harbour some doubts about the loyalty of their Caesarian legions before battle, and took care to pay them a donative they had previously promised.[145] Then, when he had finished the rousing defence of liberty we have just mentioned, Cassius still judged it best to confirm the loyalty of those he commanded with a bonus.[146] After the first battle of Philippi Brutus complained that the soldiers had been more interested in gathering booty than finishing off the enemy. Nonetheless he, too, had to put on the harness of necessity, promising yet another donative and, it is alleged, pledging that certain Greek cities should be handed over to the troops for the sack.[147] At exactly the same time the Triumvirs were making promises. Each man was to have 5,000 denarii.[148]

The next year, 41, saw a joint revival of the republican ideal in Italy in the Perusine War. This was set afoot by Lucius, Antony's brother, aided and abetted by Fulvia. The pair pursued two chief objectives. The land settlement of the Triumvirs which was then being administered by Octavian was to be modified.[149] Octavian and Lepidus were to be called to account for what they had done as the ancestral constitution was restored.[150] Significantly the troops here intervened in politics once more. On the first occasion the legates of both armies arbitrated between Octavius and Lucius at Teanum but the agreement cobbled together then was never implemented.[151] On the second occasion the troops assembled in Rome[152] arranged a meeting at Gabii which never took place because Lucius, fearing for his safety, never turned up.[153] The boldness of the common soldier was underlined by an incident which occurred about this time in the theatre. Octavian removed a legionary from his seat because he had sat in a place reserved for *equites*. At once soldiers surrounded Octavian and demanded their comrade, fearing lest he had been put to death. The soldier was duly produced and he denied he had been imprisoned. His friends then claimed he had been suborned to tell a lie and asserted he was acting against their common interests.[154]

This assertiveness continued in the year 40. With the Perusine War finished Octavian began to contemplate action against Antony, only to discover his men would not fight against the victor of Philippi even after they were assured he proposed to modify the Triumviral land settlement in order to accommodate Sextus Pompey and his followers. As the year progressed things got no better. Octavian and Agrippa severally made their way towards Brundisium to encounter Antony. On the way they called out veterans from their colonies, only to find these too would not fight against him. The subsequent treaty with Antony, known as the peace of Brundisium, came about, in part, because the soldiers desired it and compelled their commanders to act thus.[155]

Not long afterwards the Triumvirs were forced to compromise with Sextus Pompey and his naval power. The result was an agreement made at Misenum to share the mastery of the world with him.[156] This, we are told, had been greeted with great enthusiasm by the troops who were now war weary.[157] Harmony, however, lasted but a little time and soon Octavian and Sextus were at war again. The upshot was total victory for Octavian in 36.[158] He then turned on Lepidus but employed gentler methods to bring about his neutralisation. Applying his skills in subversion he lured away his army and reduced Lepidus himself to the status of a private citizen.[159]

At this point Appian concludes his narrative of the Civil Wars. Although Actium, with all its consequences for Roman and world history, was yet to come, one cannot help but feel he was justified in this decision by events. Having disposed in different ways of his only rivals in the west, Sextus and Lepidus, Octavius was now master there and when he returned to Rome he was heaped with many honours. He then busied himself with much serving, setting to rights the affairs of the city and bringing order to Italy. On his image he was proclaimed as the bringer of peace on land and sea. We are twice told he explicitly declared civil war at an end. But only civil war. Now he proposed to march against the Illyrians. There would be an end to donatives and handouts, for here the Roman soldiers would as heretofore earn their booty.[160]

Arguably the situation was roughly paralleled in the eastern part of the empire. There was one master too, Antony, and he, like Octavian, engaged in administrative work and made war on Parthia and Armenia.[161] But there is one vital difference. Octavian was able to make good his claim to have brought civil war to an end and successfully present his subsequent campaign against Antony as a war against a foreign foe who sought to dominate Rome.[162] It was unfortunate that the two consuls of 32 and three hundred senators do not seem to have agreed and decamped to Antony, but we may set against that the cohesion and loyalty of his armies. Now there were none of the switches of side of a few years before.[163]

The soldiers of the Triumviral period have an evil name. The charges of unruliness and indiscipline have been laid against them. When the contemporary Cornelius Nepos was writing his life of Eumenes he came upon evidence of indiscipline in the latter's army. This immediately reminded him of the Roman armies of his own day, who would not obey their commanders but issued orders themselves.[164] About the same time Sallust was claiming they would do anything for money.[165] This theme of cupidity bulks large in the later ancient sources. So Plutarch, talking of the events of 44, describes the soldiers as being available for the highest bidder and portrays Antony and Octavian as going around Italy trying to purchase the allegiance of the *evocati*.[166] Appian twice speaks of mercenaries and, in another place, emphasises how thoughts of gain propel men to military service.[167] Dio, in turn, represents the soldiers as extortionists and calls their donatives bribes.[168]

Unsurprisingly, this kind of thing is repeated by modern scholars. Smith, for instance, emphasises the theme of indiscipline.[169] Syme speaks of Octavian's activities in Campania early in his career as bribe giving.[170] I readily admit that the soldiers from the time of Caesar, as we saw, had become more demanding and often exploited the current situation for their own advantage.[171] But I hold they had considerable justification and that a defence of their conduct may be made.

We must bear steadily in mind that the Roman soldier looked for profit from war. This attitude had not changed but the usual sources of booty had virtually dried up since this was a time of Civil War. Between the expedition of D. Brutus against the Alpine tribes in 44 and that of Octavian against the Illyrians in 36 there would seem to be no foreign war waged which would yield booty.[172] A civil war could, of course, on occasion yield booty. We may recall how after the first battle of Philippi M. Brutus upbraided his men because their lust for loot diverted them from the business of killing.[173] But such opportunities were rare and the leaders of the day had to look elsewhere for the money for those they expected to fight and die for them. So we find virtually every means – chiefly illicit – of raising revenue known to mankind was employed. We hear of embezzlement, levying of tribute, illegal appropriation of revenue, confiscation of the fortunes of the proscribed, naked extortion and piracy. One or two leaders are actually said to have borrowed money or spent their own personal fortunes.[174] The monies thus raised were then spent on the troops in order to give them what they had always wanted. It is true, certainly, that the soldier was now more demanding but he had not lost political awareness either.

In addition to the desire for profit the ever-present idealism and a certain rudimentary political consciousness are still discernable. If we look for the idealism it is most obviously to be seen in the armies of the Liberators who we may suppose shared the enthusiasm of their leaders for the republic, and we should not forget that some of these men had once served under Caesar.[175] And it may very well be that we can attribute some kind of idealism also to Lucius Antonius. But the most remarkable feature of the time is that the troops now give directions and formulate policy. Caesar's troops had dared to speak to him of bonuses, land and discharge.[176] Octavian's men did likewise, but all Triumviral armies went further than that.[177] They literally dictated the course of events.

We may discern a number of issues which concerned them. To begin with there was the determination that Caesar should be avenged, and whenever Octavian and Antony seemed to be tardy in pursuing this objective they were sharply reminded where their duty lay. And when the republicans were no more, Octavian found he could not turn on Antony because his men would not fight the victor of Philippi, while at both Perusia and Brundisium he also had to yield to the wishes of the troops. However frustrating this may have been, Octavian can hardly have been displeased when his soldiers made it clear he should have the praetorship and the consulship, even if he also had to enter on a political marriage at their behest.

As I have stated, this kind of behaviour along with the frequent calls for money is a development of what had gone on even under Caesar. It takes its rise from the position of the Triumvirs themselves. The Triumvirate was established by due legal process but it was a process carried out in a truncated form and under press of arms.[178] A title so conferred must always be open to question and it may be said it does not bring with it the kind of authority Sulla or Caesar held by virtue of their offices. Indeed the command of the sea granted to Sextus Pompey shortly after Caesar's assassination and never relinquished has as much legitimacy as, and maybe more than, the Triumvirate.[179]

Much of the behaviour of the troops can be attributed to the actual activities of the Triumvirs themselves. I think it fair to say that, for a number of years, they sought no other objective save their own preservation and, where opportunity offered, the destruction of each other.[180] People such as that have need of soldiers and so it is difficult to fault men, called to serve by unworthy masters, if, being needy, they seek to profit thereby, and they must surely be praised if they still show an awareness of other issues.

The famous scene at Misenum where Sextus Pompey would not cut the hawsers has naturally caught the imagination of generations.[181] So, we often find him depicted as someone who, in his struggles with this unpleasant trio, did not make the most of his opportunities.[182] This is difficult to sustain. A detailed discussion is plainly impossible here but the sources do seem to indicate a striving for goals different from the Triumvirs but just as limited.[183] To begin with he wished to be restored to his honours and dignities and then, later, sought a share in their power.[184] We could add that his power base was, perhaps, more solid than that of his opponents. Sicily seems to have been consistently loyal.[185] This is paralleled by the discipline of his fleet though drawn from diverse sources. Only after Misenum does disharmony arise.[186]

As we saw, indiscipline and attempts to dictate policy largely came to an end in 36, and this was mainly due to changes in government, if one may so term it. Something approximating to a stability now prevailed, with the world divided between two masters. Octavian, of course, laid the greatest emphasis on the restoration of good government but we can see this was only possible because all his energies need no longer be diverted to destroying others. The dependence on his troops which, as Appian noted, this brought about was now lessened. Octavian himself may have miscalculated here. Faced with a mutiny, he felt he had no further use for his troops and, in despising them, made matters worse.[187] But only for a time, and for what was to come Octavian was able to command the loyalty of those he commanded.

Due weight should be given to the respect Octavian had earned by finally conducting a successful campaign in Illyrium[188] but above all it was the relatively undisputed position he now enjoyed which facilitated his mode of procedure against Antony.

The material demands of the troops had still to be met. Antony showered Italy with gold but Octavian, ever vigilant, saw to it that his men received a donative even though the exactions he had had recourse to in order to raise the cash made him highly unpopular in Italy.[189] Then, at campaign's end, donatives and land were duly distributed.[190] But, these constants aside, what immediately strikes us is that, in contrast to a few years before, it was Octavian who was now in control. He it is who dictates policy and not his soldiers.

Octavian and Antony began a pamphlet and propaganda war in 33.[191] Personal abuse centring on the sexual tastes and drinking habits of both men was freely traded.[192] It was accompanied by mutual accusations of bad faith. Antony attacked Octavian for removing Sextus Pompey from office and appropriating his legions. Octavian counterattacked with characteristic shamelessness, attacking Antony for executing Sextus.[193] He declared he himself would have spared him. Octavian also charged Antony with illegal possession of Egypt and branded his association with Cleopatra a disgrace. Antony countered by claiming Octavian was hanging on to land in Italy which should have been assigned to his own soldiers.[194]

There is not a great deal of difficulty in gauging the effect of these exchanges. We saw that a number of senators were unconvinced and decamped from Octavian to Antony. There were, too, Antonian troops in Italy who had to be handled with care.[195] But the majority of the legionaries in the west elected to follow Octavian.

Reading the exchanges between him and Antony one is struck by the immediacy of the issues which divide the two. The figure of Caesar, once so prominent in men's thoughts, has almost vanished.[196] It is not just that Antony and Octavian do not wrangle over which of them is Caesar's true heir, but the troops, once so vigorous on the subject of their late chief, seem to be largely indifferent to his memory. We may speculate on why this should be so. What the soldiers had sought had been accomplished. They wanted Caesar's murderers called to account and that had been done. Further, by now, there can have been few left in the ranks who had served under Caesar himself. His name now had a symbolic significance. It no longer called forth personal affection. But above all we should remember the temperament of what we are dealing with. The Roman assemblies had always shown themselves to be volatile and changeable. As the Gracchi and others found out, enthusiasm for a policy or a cause could almost instantly vanish. I see no reason to suppose that the citizen ranker was any less intense or more steadfast in his loyalties than his civilian counterpart.

And, if the troops were unconcerned with Caesar then, as has been well observed, it is unlikely they were shocked by stories of Antony's debaucheries.[197] One cannot forbear adding that many of them probably regarded them with admiration and envy. There was, too, a certain residual affection for the man, but it was not strong enough to make them reject Octavian's slanders or accept a promise from Antony to restore the republic. For the soldiers now, Octavian was no faction leader, no protagonist in a civil war. He was the legitimate defender of *tota Italia* who was battling a foreign foe.

(d) Conclusion

There runs a line from Sulla in 88 to Octavian at Actium in 31. It may not always run straight but it runs clear. Sulla politicised the army, inviting it to help resolve a contemporary issue. Or we could put it another way: he taught his men that the enemy did not always lie without. Sometimes he could be found within. Soon he found an imitator in Cinna. But from now on political quarrels were to be terminated not by police action as in 88 but by full civil wars.

Viewing matters in a broad perspective we can say that two things remain constant between Sulla and Octavian: the soldiers' desire for profit and their willingness to intervene in politics. But at the same time there is a change of emphasis which must in some way, I believe, be connected with the fact that Caesar and the Triumvirs were not as secure in their authority as Sulla had been. Caesar had to make some concessions, the Triumvirs a good deal more. The troops are no longer content to receive what the commander may give by way of reward but are bold and forward in demanding it, knowing that those who have need of them cannot refuse. And to be politicised now does not merely mean responding when a man of authority puts an issue before them, but rather taking the initiative.

Sulla had shown the way, but in the next generation it was not always given to others to act as masterfully as he.

4

LAND AND LAND HUNGER

In our sources we hear, from the time of Marius, of grants of land to the soldier. These grants were intermittent, but in modern discussions they have great prominence and are held to be of much importance. In this section we shall try to weigh up this importance. We may accomplish this most elegantly and simply by examining separately the role of the nobility in whose power it lay to give land and of the soldier who received it.

(a) The nobility

The Duke of Wellington is said to have described troops under his command as 'the scum of the earth'. We are assured this was a purely sociological judgement and that he was fully aware of their fighting qualities.[1] Whatever the truth of that, the anecdote prompts us to begin our investigation by asking what the Roman noble thought of the legionary, since it seems reasonable to suppose that that would inform his behaviour towards him.

Most of our information comes from the loquacious Cicero. He had, for instance, a fairly low opinion of the soldier's political insight.[2] Of this it may be said that Cicero invariably tended to look down on those whose intellectual attainments did not match his own.[3] There is abundant evidence to show that while the troops may have lacked Cicero's sophistication they could grasp clearly enough the issues of the day.[4] Three other passages (*ad Fam.*11.7.2, *Phil.*8.9, 10.22) attracted Nicolet (1980, p. 133) because they seemed to cast light on this question of attitude. In the letter Cicero speaks of the soldiers as countrymen but brave and loyal. When we come to the speeches, however, they turn out to be little better than beasts. Without saying how he arrived at such a conclusion, Nicolet states that this second verdict represents Cicero's true feelings. Actually this is untenable because Nicolet has not placed the sources in context. In the letter, if Cicero speaks well of the soldiers it is because they are on his side. When it comes to the speeches it is but natural he should speak ill, for these are Antony's men. Only when we recognise that these are partisan judgements uttered in time of war can we make a reasoned evaluation. The designation as *rustici* is uncontroversial since, as has often been emphasised in modern scholarship, the legions are primarily of rural origin.[5]

We find these *rustici*, accompanied by *fortes*, described in the same slightly patronising way again in *pro Archia* 24. There we are told that when Pompey in a military assembly enfranchised a writer, his men, rude though they were, were still touched by the occasion. And when these men ceased to know their place aristocratic disdain was ready with a suitable label. Soldiers who meddled in politics were *senatores caligati*, men, in every sense of the phrase, too big for their boots.[6]

The vaguely paternalistic attitude we have been delineating did not, however, necessarily result in a consistent concern for the material welfare of the soldier. Tiberius Gracchus' complaint, that those who defended Italy from her foes had nowhere to lay their heads, is justly famous.[7] Almost as well known is his brother's prohibition on money being docked from the soldier's *stipendium* to pay for his equipment, and his bar on under seventeens enlisting.[8] Caius' laws may be, as has been suggested, a response to the contemporary economic situation[9] but it is just as likely, in my view, that he was reacting against that habitual indifference society displays towards those whom it is pleased to call its defenders. The tribune C. Licinius Macer offers some support to this notion. Some fifty years later, in 73, he was still complaining about conditions in the army.[10] So we can say that while the soldier was treated with a certain respect, active measures for his wellbeing were sporadic.

We move now to divine the implications this attitude had for the most important token of appreciation the senate had to bestow on the legionary, the grant of land.[11]

The great settlements of previous generations show clearly the senate then actually had no hesitation in granting lands, however remiss it may have been in other ways. Since we are not party to private conversations between individual senators or privileged to read records of senatorial debates we can only make conjectures as to why these settlements ceased.[12] Yet I would contend that we know enough to be able to say that the senate never completely lost the will to grant but was constrained by the circumstances in which it now found itself.

To start with, we know of some occasions when the senators were involved in land settlement. Towards the end of the second century some colonies were founded and at the end of the Sertorian War a grant was voted to Pompey's veterans but never carried out, because of lack of funds.[13] We also have on record a certain contemporary of Cicero, Servius Sulpicius Rufus, who declared his belief that public land ought to be distributed to the veteran.[14] Some think that what amounts to a lengthy rebuttal of this view is to be found in Cicero *de Officiis* 2.73–85.[15] Closer scrutiny will show the need for modification of this view.

Cicero is setting his face against *aequatio bonorum* or that process of levelling by which one class in the state is deprived of its property in order to benefit another.[16] Cicero seems to be thinking in particular of the confiscations and settlements of Sulla and Caesar.[17] Gabba (1976, p. 31) saw this, but not, I believe, its full significance. What disturbs Cicero is not so much redistribution itself but redistribution without adequate compensation, as happened in these cases. Like any good lawyer

Cicero is not above massaging the facts to make his case and so he falsely claims the Gracchi proceeded in the same way.[18] However reluctantly, Cicero, at times, is prepared to accept land being taken provided it is paid for. As might be expected, he does not want to burden the taxpayer. We can see this from his reluctance to impose *tributum* and his anxiety that public funds should not be squandered.[19]

This willingness to accept land settlement in which, without raiding the public purse, the original owners are paid off can be clearly seen in the praise he gives Aratus of Sicyon in *de Officiis* 2.81–3. This man went abroad to garner foreign money in order to finance a scheme to pay off those whose lands were being restored to their original owners newly returned from exile.[20] The distinction between this and mere seizure is obvious and real.[21] Nor is it purely academic approval of a long-dead statesman, as may be seen from Cicero's response to the land bill of the tribune Flavius (60) who was a creature of Pompey's. He supported the measure, albeit a trifle uneasily, after it had been purged of elements inimical to private property.[22] Indeed, he is on record as saying that he accepted, as a matter of course, that commanders should bring in such bills.[23]

Gabba argued that the ruling elite of Rome did not fully comprehend the changes which had come about in the Roman army at this time, and that, in consequence, their response to them was inadequate.[24] Elsewhere in this book I have expressed the belief that the changes may not have been of the order Gabba supposes, but here I suggest the Roman nobility knew perfectly well what they were dealing with. So long as Rome had constitutional government those who made up that government had nothing to fear from the soldier.[25] In the next section we shall be examining the matter in more detail but here we may say this much. There was no revolutionary movement among the soldiers: demand was voiced – and that but intermittently – by their commanders and when that demand was refused there was no violent reaction. Agitation simply died away.

I would maintain, therefore, that something other than ignorance and fear accounts for the failure of the senators to translate their benevolence into land schemes for the veterans. The reason, I believe, is the fact that such schemes were rarely, if ever, mooted in an atmosphere of calm where rational and dispassionate consideration might be given to the issue. Instead proposals for plots for the veteran became entangled with contemporary politics which proved fatal to their success.[26]

In 103 the tribune Saturninus passed a law giving one hundred *iugera* of land in Africa to Marius' veterans who had served there. We know the proposal was controversial because when a rival tribune, Baebius, tried to interpose his veto he was chased out of the forum.[27] In 100 Saturninus produced another bill, proposing colonies to benefit the troops Marius then had under his command.[28] Again there was trouble and the bill was carried by force. To do this Saturninus was able to call up those veterans who had already dispersed to their homes.[29]

Gabba believed the schemes of 103 had no real political significance. The senate did not object, and even allowed its own members to join the commissions to oversee the settlement. What was envisaged was accepted as being simply a continuation of the policies which C. Gracchus had initiated in Africa. Certain objections may be made to this. In the present state of our knowledge it is always open to us to claim Baebius may have after all been a senatorial agent. On the other side the two known commissioners have fairly certainly been identified as being of the Marian persuasion. But most of all, the political stance of Marius and Saturninus was well known and it was unlikely therefore the senators would gaze benignly on anything emerging from that quarter.[30] About 100 I think it is safe to say there is no debate. Saturninus had become completely obnoxious to his opponents and no compromise was possible.[31]

So, for all the difficulties and deficiencies of our sources, what emerges is tolerably clear. The senate may not actually have wished to oppose Saturninus in 103 but, if it did, it looks as if it was not strong enough. Hence Saturninus' schemes for Africa became a reality.[32] By 100 things were very different. Again his proposals passed into law, but with his violent death were never carried out.[33] His enemies had plainly seen to that, just as they saw to it that the assembly condemned the land bill of Sextus Titius in 99 which had similar aims to that of Saturninus.[34]

We now turn to Pompey and his various schemes to get land for his men.[35] Evidence for the first of these is scant, and scholarly debate in consequence plentiful.[36] The most important source is Dio 38.5.1–2. This represents Pompey as making a speech in 59 in which he says that, on a previous occasion, land had been granted to his veterans by the senate but, since money was short,[37] no settlement was made. The inescapable conclusion is that Pompey is talking of a measure introduced at the end of the Sertorian War for it would seem there is no other time which would fit.[38] It is true that an incident of 67, narrated by Plut.*Luc*.34, has led some to argue that, contrary to what Dio says, a settlement was actually carried out.[39] But the ultimate source is dubious and tainted. According to the story, P. Clodius, attempting to foment a mutiny in Lucullus' army, told the men that, while they continued to campaign, Pompey's men were already comfortably settled on their farms. But the character of the speaker is well known and his necessity to say something like this now obvious, so that we should, at the very least, hesitate to deploy this evidence against Dio's explicit statement.[40]

As I mentioned above, much about this episode is dark. One thing does emerge though. We cannot be doctrinaire and insist the senate consistently now opposed the grant of land, for here we find it once more playing its traditional role. Whatever differences it had with Pompey at the time, they were not enough to prevent it voting land for his troops.[41] But after this episode there was to be a change.

In 63 Rullus and some other tribunes brought forward a bill for land purchase and distribution. Everybody knew Pompey's veterans were intended to benefit but the bill was defeated.[42] In 60 Pompey made yet another effort to get land for his troops with a proposal which, as Rullus' had, made provision also for the urban plebs, but it was defeated in the senate.[43] This meant that Pompey had to enrol the aid of Caesar in his consulship of 59. Caesar's bill made all Italian land, except Campania, available for settlement. Current tenure was to be recognised and only land voluntarily offered for sale was to be purchased. This would be done at the market price and the money necessary would come from Pompey's booty. Once more the urban plebs as well as the veterans would benefit. Given contemporary attitudes to the so-called first Triumvirate, nobody need be surprised to learn there was resistance from the rulers of Rome, but Caesar ruthlessly pushed the bill through.[44]

Thus far we have been speaking of veteran settlements where the Roman aristocracy could, at the very least, attempt to influence the course of events. But now we must recognise there were also settlements carried out by generals in total disregard of any interest save their own and in which the senate was powerless to intervene. The first of these was that of Sulla.

The singular character of Sulla's settlement is not, perhaps, always recognised.[45] To start with he performed a species of *aequatio bonorum*. No compensation was paid for the land he took for his soldiers' plots. He simply confiscated what he needed from his late opponents whom he declared *hostes*. Nor was he content just to find farms for his men.[46] These settlements had a triple role to fulfil. To start with they were intended to punish those who had fought against Sulla in the Civil War. In some cases the intent was more benign. These men were to revive towns damaged in the Social and Civil Wars. Finally they would act as defence against attacks on Sulla's arrangements.[47] It will be recalled too that one of the consequences of the Sullan plantation was the scrambling of the peoples of Italy.[48]

When Caesar came to plant in 47 he recoiled from this as he did from other features of the Sullan approach. He explicitly stated he would not confiscate land and sow discord by putting old and new inhabitants together in a colony. It would come from the *ager publicus*, Caesar's own estates and purchase. In sum, the agrarian programme would be along traditional lines.[49] There is some reason, however, to believe that Caesar was not able consistently to live up to his good intentions and was eventually forced to compulsory purchase or outright confiscation.[50]

The Triumvirs, I hold, were the true heirs of the Sullan approach to settlement. I am not referring to minor matters such as the commission set up in mid-44 by Antony and his consular colleague to divide public lands between veterans and the poor which anyway had a short life.[51] Rather, I refer to what is often styled the Bononia agreement.[52] By this the Triumvirs earmarked eighteen cities and their lands for confiscation and distribution among the veterans. I do not mean to suggest either that they had consulted Sulla's *Memoirs*, but simply that, faced with the same problem of catering for large numbers, they applied the same solution as a matter of course: wholesale confiscation. Nor could they be accused of having Sulla's motivation. Wealth was the only criterion to be applied for admission to the hit list. There were, of course, complaints and remonstrations. The character and behaviour of the troops gave great offence and there were demands that other lands be confiscated in order to level the burden. Octavian did make some small concessions but in the end carried through his scheme ruthlessly and swiftly.[53] He had made himself hated by the people of Italy but had ensured the loyalty of his troops. Like Sulla, he had, in every sense of the word, divided Italy.[54]

The especial character of the settlements we have just been discussing was observed by Velleius Paterculus. In contradiction to what went before, anything founded after Eporedeia in 100 was a *colonia militaris*.[55] Plainly he saw there a difference.[56] But when we look for detail Velleius is not very helpful. For the colonies founded between the sack of Rome in 390 and the settling of Eporedeia he is prepared to give names and details of founders. But of the military colonies he merely says their *causae*, *auctores* and *nomina* are well known, and leaves it at that.[57] Presumably Velleius' putative audience knew what he was talking of but for us there must be a degree of speculation. The *causae* may refer to the desire to find land for the veteran but that is hardly unique to these colonies.[58] I would suggest Velleius has in mind some of the ulterior motives we sketched above. *Auctores* might simply be the patrons of the individual colonies[59] but I suspect Velleius is just thinking of the prime movers such as Sulla and Octavian. *Nomina* probably means the custom growing up of putting the names of such men in the colonies' titles.[60]

Thus far then, we can see that when the senate had the power to grant land to veterans it chose not always to exercise it. A time, however, came in which that power was taken away and exercised by powerful individuals. Fully to understand this change we must leave, for the moment, the Roman aristocracy and turn to the common soldier.

(b) Soldiers

Most Roman soldiers must have expected to turn to farming in one way or another when their fighting days were done. After all agriculture was the principal occupation of the ancient world, with such industry as existed rarely rising above the level of the workshop and the capacity of any city to support pubs run by ex-servicemen limited. We have a body of Roman literature dealing with agriculture which is plainly grounded in the belief that it is, on the whole, something good. I am not prepared to say how many legionaries read the elder Cato, for instance, but I see no difficulty in believing they shared his basic outlook and that many will have been aware of the social status which could come from owning land. We can establish this point easily by recording once more the fraud Clodius attempted to perpetrate on the soldiers of Lucullus. It may have been a lie that Pompey's men now had their farms but it must have been a plausible lie. He was dangling before his audience something they would find attractive.[61]

But if land was attractive it was not always easy to obtain. For much of the time, purchase was the usual method and booty the source of the necessary funds.[62] The conventional picture of the general doling out lands to his followers needs considerable modification. Such disbursements were sporadic.[63] Indeed, one could not be sure at the start of a campaign that there would be a distribution at its end. Marius, for instance, when he enrolled the *capite censi* in 107 made no promises.[64] Caesar, too, may have refrained from committing himself.[65]

And sporadic though it was, the soldier, for a long time, was dependent on the general's interest. We know the troops wanted land but the demand does not come from them. For much of the period they do not call for farms, for it is their commanders who do this. It is they who represent the interests of their men and speak for them. The general doled out booty.[66] He it was who would also seek the land.[67]

From this state of affairs there flows one consequence of great moment to which we have, in fact, already briefly alluded.[68] The rulers of Rome perceived no threat here. When a general failed in his demands those who followed him acquiesced in the situation. Nothing illustrates this better than Pompey in 60. When his request was refused his men simply departed to their homes. If we reflect upon it we can see that those who supported Marius and his henchman Saturninus prior to 100 differed not a whit from other veterans. Like them, they too eventually dispersed to their homes.[69]

The change in attitude is almost certainly to be dated to the Second Civil War. In 47 Caesar's troops mutinied, demanding the redemption of certain vague promises made after Pharsalus and their discharge, which was now overdue. According to Dio there was an element of bluff here as the soldiers were not so much interested in leaving the colours as in extracting what they could from Caesar, who would yet have need of them in forthcoming campaigns. Indeed, the same author says a similar ploy had been tried earlier at Placentia when alleged grievances were paraded, also for the purpose of extortion. Whatever the truth of this, it may be noted that, on this occasion, there was demand not for land but rather for a donative, and those who complained were taken aback to be given their discharge and told a land settlement programme would begin.[70] So for us the episode is ambiguous. The soldiers have very definitely found their voice but we do not hear them call directly for land. With the sequel that ambiguity is removed.

Immediately after Caesar's murder those of his veterans who were still in Rome awaiting settlement began to make nuisances of themselves. This is actually one of those occasions in our period when we hear of the idle demobbed soldier playing his classic role as trouble-maker and not surprisingly there were those who were able to reap a benefit. Antony now put together a bodyguard of former centurions.[71] Of more immediate concern to us here is the fear the veterans had that the lands earmarked for them would now be taken away and their determination this should not be allowed to happen. The Liberators had no choice but to agree. They promised to observe Caesar's *acta* and a little later, at the specific request of the colonists themselves, an act of confirmation was passed. The other obvious solution – continuing to send out settlers – was also applied.[72]

In mid-June of 44 Antony and his consular colleague established a commission of seven to divide public lands between veterans and the poor. Some distribution of land was actually carried out before the commission was abrogated in January 43 on the grounds that it had been established illegally. The veteran settlements were then, however, confirmed once more.[73]

After Antony's defeat at Mutina by Octavian and the consuls, the senate bestirred itself to make one of its now rare manifestations of benevolence towards the soldiers. Caesar's troops and those who had deserted from Antony were voted immunity from further service and the immediate gift of land. A commission was established to resume any of the property Antony had granted, which would then be applied to the veterans. As this latter detail held obvious dangers it comes as no surprise to learn that matters moved slowly. Indeed even in this crucial time Cicero insisted that no lands should be taken without their owners receiving due compensation. But, in any case, events, as is well known, soon made the whole exercise meaningless.[74]

The soldiers' aggressive care for their own interests manifested itself again when, in 41, Octavian set about implementing the Bononia settlement. The troops were not content with what they had been given but encroached on the lands of their neighbours, and no amount of bribery or pleading by Octavian would make them desist. Indeed they eventually turned on him and mutinied when they thought he was making concessions to the dispossessed so that in the end he had to make distribution to deserving and undeserving alike.[75] Even in 36, as he struggled to re-establish normalcy, Octavian encountered another call for land. His troops refused to undertake a foreign campaign until they had had their reward for what they had already done. It was made plain this meant land, and Octavian had no choice but to comply.[76]

This desire to settle on the land, whether on one's original farm or on one granted by the general, may have been a constant but its fulfilment was often postponed. The soldier, once he has acquired a taste for that way of life, has always shown a tendency to re-enlist and the legionary is no exception to that rule.[77] The most striking example in the late republic is, I would argue, the Fimbrians. These men first went east with the consul Flaccus in 87. They murdered their chief at the instigation of Fimbria and then went over to Sulla in 85. He left them in the east, where they took service under Lucullus in 74 before, time expired, they successfully demanded their discharge of him in 67. The natural assumption would be that by now they had had enough but that would be a mistake, for when Pompey arrived to replace Lucullus, they immediately enlisted with him.[78] Many of Sulla's soldiers seem to have been lured away when the opportunities prevented by warfare in the 70s became obvious. Some forty odd years later the Triumvirs were able to call upon *evocati* to fill the ranks of their army.[79] In this context it is worth repeating yet again that when Sulla arrived in Italy in 83 his troops could simply have gone home. Instead they elected to join him in another campaign.[80]

I would suggest that three motives chiefly account for this phenomenon.[81] The first is economic and has often been met in this work. Booty was a great lure, and though we may beg leave to doubt that many were as indigent as the much cited Spurius Ligustinus of a previous age, we can be sure that many would welcome the opportunity for betterment soldiering would bring. The soldier's life is, of course, a hazardous one but few will deny a certain glamour attaches to it and there will always be those whom it will attract.[82] Finally, it can be readily appreciated that the army provided a refuge from the drudgery of a peasant existence even if we did not have an illustrative incident recorded for us by Appian.[83] When some of Octavian's troops disliked his policies in 44 they simply walked away, but then, having time for thought, they weighed up the profits of soldiering in comparison to the toils of farming, decided the former was preferable to the latter, and promptly went back to their chief.

It is probable these men were drawing on their own experiences and not report, but there is some evidence pointing to soldiers who knew nothing of farming. When Caesar began settling we are specifically told he started with those who had some experience of farming,[84] which clearly implies there were some in his numbers who had not. How widespread this was we cannot say but some possible inkling of the upshot may be gained from the Sullan settlement. Then men of rural origin had, as a result of their experiences in the east, lost the will and the capacity to become farmers once more. Unable to shake off lordly habits acquired abroad they eventually came to ruin.[85]

Any analysis of demobilisation and subsequent settlement would be incomplete if we did not say something about those who are often dubbed 'the demob happy'. De Neeve (1984, p. 219) thought two divisions could be made of Caesar's army. One wanted land, the other money, and these would naturally sell on their portions as quickly as possible. De Neeve also believed the same was true of the soldiers of other generals. In my opinion this rigidly schematic view is mistaken. What we are witnessing is a phenomenon well attested both in Roman history and elsewhere.[86] There is no reason to suppose the veteran did not want land, but when he was kept waiting his other desire for ready cash became the greater and he yielded to it. Some of Sulla's troops certainly sold up their plots in this way and reports of footpads and the like in contemporary Rome are probably connected with this.[87] The situation in Caesar's Rome parallels this. There we find men who have sold everything and are now ready to lend a hand for pay to anybody who wants to make trouble.[88] While there is some reason to suppose that, over and above any donative he might get, the veteran sometimes received cash also to get him started in his new life, we do not have to believe there existed at any time a body of soldiers who, from the very start, sought just cash and not land. Those who sold up in this fashion did so out of mere fecklessness.[89]

The tendency of the veteran to wander off from his farm was not confined to the initial stages of a plantation and the concern it caused the planter is reflected in legislation designed to stop it.[90] Thus, Sulla, seemingly taking his cue from Tiberius Gracchus, decreed the land must be held in perpetuity.[91] For his part, Caesar forbade sale until twenty years were up.[92] Reaction of the ranker may be gauged from the widespread evasion of the law in the Sullan settlement and the bid of the Liberators for popularity by promising to abolish Caesar's bar.[93]

So we can say that what we have been looking at here is the veteran's desire for land and the obstacles that lay in the way of the fulfilment of that desire. Some of these obstacles come from the soldier himself.[94] The allure of the military life with its glamour and profit caused many to desert their holdings and re-enlist. Some, of course, squandered their competence without ever seeing their farms, and some who did not turned out anyway to be unsuitable for their new way of life. But, for most of the period, the greatest barrier faced by the soldier was his inability in the first instance to make his case effectively. In the assembly as a citizen he could only answer 'yes' or 'no' to a question and initiate nothing;[95] as a soldier he was totally dependent on his general asking on his behalf. And if the general should be unwilling or fail, then there was nothing to be done. It is only with the coming of the Second Civil War that the soldier begins to assert himself and, in terms which eventually will tolerate no refusal, demands land for himself.

(c) Conclusion

If we look at the issue of land in the last century of the republic we have to begin by recognising that two phenomena of Roman history met with in previous ages are met with now too. The soldier desires land at the end of his fighting days and his betters are not totally hostile to the notion he should have it. That said, qualifications must immediately be entered. The senate's sporadic indulgence in its traditional policy of dispensing land is to be directly connected with the form demand took. For much of the century the legionary could not ask for himself and relied on his commanders. These were usually in dispute with the senate which, for political reasons, in consequence refused what they asked. No danger was perceived or indeed existed, for the refusal met with no violent reaction. The fathers, I believe, cannot be castigated for not seeing what eventually happened: the soldiers learnt to speak for themselves and powerful commanders could impose their will and take what they wanted without having to ask.

Which, of course, brings us to those commanders and the reasons they wished to settle their men.

I do not think it rash to suggest that many acted thus because they were soldiers and respecters of tradition. Great commanders such as Marius and Pompey had a care for those they led and wished to reward them in the approved manner.[96] Further the settlers themselves would form a pool of manpower to be called upon for future campaigns. Not all possessed the clientage Pompey enjoyed in Picenum but the glamour of a great commander's name would bring veterans flocking to the colours once more.[97]

It hardly needs saying that we must avoid anachronism and attributing any deeply laid designs to those who held such an intent. To put it simply: when Pompey's veterans were settled in 59 I doubt very much if he foresaw the circumstances under which, some ten years later, he proposed to stamp his foot and summon the men of Italy.[98] Sulla's settlement, as I suggested, had broader aims than any of his predecessors. His troops could be called out when needed but beyond that they were clearly intended to repress and regenerate. Caesar then reacted against Sulla and proceeded with his plantation on more traditional lines.[99]

But, whatever the differences in their approach, Sulla and Caesar had one thing in common: both possessed absolute power and both used it.[100] However, at the

same time, they embody and illustrate a development which can only be understood completely when we introduce Octavian into the picture. When Sulla set
his designs afoot he did so without reference to anyone, least of all his soldiers. We
hear of no demand from them for farms to which he had to respond. With Caesar
there is a change. He may have been maturing his plans but there is no denying
he was provoked into putting them into action in order to quell a mutiny.[101]
Caesar's authority was restored but once the troops found their voice they did not
lose it. Upon his death they made it known, in no uncertain terms, that they
would continue to hold the lands assigned to them. In the case of Octavian we
both find authority weak and the power of the soldier strong. In effect, both in 41
and 36, he had no option but to give them what they wanted.[102]

Thus, in these three figures we see a process of degeneration. Sulla had complete mastery of his men. Caesar's, however, faltered and he had to listen to their
demands. Politicisation of the army was now reaching the stage where the legionary was not just content to respond to the programmes set before him by his
betters but was prepared to formulate his own.[103] By the time of Octavian the
Triumvir the process was complete and we have the classic textbook paradox of
the Triumvirs.[104] These men were absolute rulers who did not need to heed such
government as then existed. But they were absolute rulers only because they had
great armies, and those armies could not be compelled and remained loyal only
because they received donatives[105] and land.

On the day Caesar faced the mutineers in 47 we see that commanders discover
a new motivation here. Up until this the soldiers had, as it were, been content
with what their chief might dole out by way of land. But from now on they themselves would tell the commander what they wanted and the circumstances of the
time were such that he had better listen. In effect, all other considerations become
irrelevant. The desire of the ranker had become paramount.

Contemplating this state of affairs we can see how, in discussing the part land
played in the relations between generals and their men, we must avoid facile for-
mulations or flabby generalisations. We cannot simply, as a matter of course,
speak of the republic collapsing because commanders leading armies of landless
men who expected to be rewarded with farms made an assault on it. When we
come to speak of all-powerful men, with great ambitions, who were yet, in a very
real sense, prisoners of those they led we have to be conscious at all times that this
state of affairs prevailed only for a brief, if decisive, period of time.

We also need to bear in mind that in the desire or demand for land made by the
troops no special interest group or sectional lobby is discernible. As I argued earlier in this book, it is but common sense to believe that many of the men in these
armies held some property just as some did not.[106] Thus we cannot just say that
the demand comes from the destitute or near destitute. Those who already had
land looked for more or better. The sheer scale of the Sullan settlement must mean
such men of property were among those he planted.[107] Nor should we forget that
when *evocati* were called out from Caesar's colonies some, at the end of the new
campaign, were settled on new farms.[108]

I have stated my belief that the exceptional features of the Sullan settlement are to be connected with the powerful position he held vis-à-vis his troops. Unlike other commanders – including Caesar – he was in no way beholden to them. Hence, as I have argued, he was able to go beyond mere settlement and envisage a wider role for those he planted.[109] In a way it might not be too farfetched to speak in this instance of a kind of conquest of Italy. On the other hand, I did also suggest that, in spite of the differences in their position and circumstances, Sulla and the Triumvirs had one thing in common. In order to accommodate large numbers they both ruthlessly uprooted the inhabitants of Italy. They scrambled her peoples.[110] Caesar, of course, recognised what Sulla had done and was acutely aware of it, trying to combine his dictatorial role with a traditional approach to colonisation, deliberately and openly in the process rejecting Sullan methods. In the end he may not have been completely successful but in general Italy seems to have remained calm during his operations.[111]

This was not the case when Sulla got to work. Caesar charged him with confiscation and putting old and new inhabitants into the same settlement where they were at enmity with each other.[112] We have specific instances to substantiate this accusation. The most striking example perhaps is Faesulae in Etruria. There, in 78, the older inhabitants turned on the new and did grave damage.[113] Even in Sulla's lifetime there was trouble at Puteoli in Campania. Shortly before his death he had to intervene personally to compose a quarrel between old and new inhabitants there.[114] Trouble at Pompeii had been of long duration when Cicero alluded to it in a speech delivered in the late 60s. New and old inhabitants had quarrelled over voting rights and for some reason not clear to us today over an *ambulatio* (portico).[115] And this is the time, too, when ruined settlers appear to join the Italians they had dispossessed in Catiline's private army.[116] There is a natural temptation to go further and suppose that when the Second Civil War came Italians remembered what Sulla had done and sided with Caesar. After all many people do have long memories of ills, real or imagined. In this instance the temptation should be resisted for there is no evidence to support such a notion.[117]

If we turn to the settlement of 41 we find not only that Italy was in uproar but, in contrast to Sulla, that Octavian, who was conducting the plantations, was not in complete control of the men he was leading. The cities which were to be dispossessed protested, asking that others be made to join in and share the burden, or that, in time-honoured manner, compensation be paid. There was of course no money for this and flocking to Rome to agitate did no good either. The behaviour of the soldiers became outrageous as they encroached upon neighbouring properties and by neither exhortation nor bribe was Octavian able to check them. In fact he had to borrow from temples in order to meet their demands for money. The immediate beneficiaries of all this were of course Octavian's enemies. Sextus Pompey received some of the dispossessed and soon there came what is known as the Perusine War when the injured found a perhaps not altogether disinterested champion in Lucius Antonius. But, in the end, it was after all Octavian himself who reaped the greatest benefit when, some years later, calling out *tota Italia*, he was able to summons the men he had settled.[118]

To conclude, it would be pointless to deny that the quest for land was not a factor in the motivation of the revolutionary army. What I have tried to do is show, however, that we must avoid broad generalisation. The question, as we have seen, has many facets and diverse ramifications.[119]

5

OBEDIENCE AND DISOBEDIENCE

Under this heading we shall be considering the related offences of mutiny, desertion and fraternisation. Without wishing to labour the point or to engage in pedantic discussion, we can nevertheless set forth what will be understood by these terms in the following sections.[1]

All three of these phenomena were, in essence, a rejection of the authority of the commander.[2] Mutinies obviously can vary in seriousness but, at the most extreme, can result in the death of the commander.[3] Desertion *en masse* can plainly occur as the culmination of a mutiny but equally it may happen without any such preliminary as the troops simply walk away. Fraternisation with the enemy we would regard as akin to desertion and, as we shall see, the Romans took a similar view.

However, any study of these military crimes must begin with a discussion of what they violated, namely the *sacramentum* or military oath. Only when we have divined its nature will we be able to appreciate fully what was involved in breaches of military discipline.

(a) The oath

When Roman soldiers took service under a general they swore an oath to him which had to be renewed if a new commander should take charge. Our earliest notices make it clear the oath was designed to ensure good order and discipline. The soldier swore to follow the consul, obey his officers and execute their orders. He would not desert or do anything contrary to law.[4]

Attempts by scholars to suggest that, in the republican period, the oath had a wider scope and involved swearing allegiance to the state have foundered on a number of considerations.[5] To start with, as Harmand for instance points out,[6] sources which speak of the *respublica* are of late date.[7] It could of course be – given the state of those sources – that we have here reflected genuine republican usage, but the evidence of Vegetius who tells us soldiers swore by the Trinity counsels caution.[8] The late imperial origin of this particular feature reminds us we cannot absolutely rule out the possibility that *respublica* too could also be a late accretion to the oath.[9]

Part of the problem, I suggest, lies with us. We are totally familiar with the concept of swearing allegiance to a head of state who in his or her person embodies that state. To pledge loyalty to a monarch in a constitutional monarchy or a president in a republic is to pledge loyalty to that state. Because of this, I would argue, we tend to forget or not fully grasp the implications of the fact that the Roman republic had no formally designated head of state. I believe that from this it follows that when the legionary of the republic swore an oath to his commander, no oath of allegiance to the state was in question. For the Roman the state was no impersonal entity. He already belonged to the *civitas* (body of citizens) where every man was a soldier and was a member of the *respublica* (commonwealth).[10] At the risk of appearing frivolous we may say that the Roman could not swear allegiance to himself.

It is, I suspect, a failure to appreciate these points which has led Campbell to make two suggestion which do not seem to have any force.[11] He thinks the great dynasts of the dying republic may have inserted a reference to the state into the oath. There is however no evidence they did so[12] and no reason why they should if we remember what was said at the outset: this was an oath concerned with discipline. Campbell also argues that *respublica* was a feeble concept but this assertion rests on an insecure foundation, Suetonius *Div.Jul.*77, where Caesar says the republic is a name without substance.[13] But this has only a topical application, being uttered by a man who had in fact just destroyed it.[14] In any case this view seems to presuppose what I have argued to be false, namely that the oath was in some way bound up with loyalty to the state.

This point may be reinforced if we consider how the Romans behaved when they wished to secure the loyalty of foreigners. One instance immediately comes to mind. In 32, as Octavian and Antony faced up for the final showdown, both sides extracted an oath from their allies. It was designed to ensure not good discipline but loyalty.[15] These were not Romans and the intent was clearly to ensure that they would behave like Romans might.

Even more instructive are certain features of Italian integration with Rome. In 91, as he tried to obtain the franchise for the Italians, Livius Drusus is said to have devised an oath for them to take. One of the clauses stipulated that if the Italians were admitted to the citizenship they would regard Rome as their country.[16] We need hardly point to the sweeping and comprehensive nature of this oath in comparison with the narrow reference of the *sacramentum*. Unlike those born as Romans, those who wish to become such must swear fealty to the state.[17] By 84 the Italians had been admitted to the citizenship but had not been distributed among the thirty-five tribes. Sulla, in that year, made a bid for their support which so alarmed his opponent Carbo that he proposed hostages be demanded from them.[18] The natural conclusion to draw is that these Italians were not yet regarded as Romans, and the sequel establishes this. When Sulla came into Italy in the next year he continued with his wooing of the inhabitants and eventually signed a treaty with some of them by which all of their rights were guaranteed.[19] This is surely a pact made between two sovereign states.[20]

Thus we can see that the Romans required of others what they did not require of their own citizens – some overt gesture signifying loyalty where obedience to the Roman state was in question. The *sacramentum* was purely concerned with discipline and if we look at the recorded instances in our period we can see that its essential nature did not alter.[21]

The bulk of the recorded instances actually centre round changes of commander, which is not surprising in view of the sometimes rapid turnover in the troubled period we have to consider.[22]

We may start with Marius. His way of obtaining the Mithridatic command in 88 was dubious, consisting as it did of intimidating the assembly and running the opposition out of town. But once he had got it he proved to be a model of correctness, sending agents to administer the oath to Sulla's army which he now proposed to command. Unfortunately for him and even more for them, Sulla's troops would have none of it and they were stoned to death.[23] Pompey Strabo's men showed what they thought of their replacement commander Pompeius Rufus. They killed him shortly after the *sacramentum* was administered. About a year later political violence forced Cinna to flee the city, and like Sulla he made for the country and found what he wanted there. He persuaded the army of Appius Claudius Pulcher to desert to him and, as the new commander, administered an oath to it.[24]

We can find further examples of this kind of thing during the Second Civil War and the Triumviral period. When Caesar, during his rapid advance through Italy in 49, took some of the men from the army of Domitius Ahenobarbus, one of his opponents, into his own he administered a new oath to them. A little later the question of validity surfaced when Curio took some of these men in his army to Africa. His opponents proclaimed they were still bound by their oath to Domitius. Curio however assured them that it was the oath to Caesar which now bound them. With his capture Domitius had ceased to be a commander and his men were accordingly released from their oath.[25] One presumes there was less debate about the duty and loyalty Cornelius Dolabella's men owed him. He committed suicide in 43 when Cassius captured Laodiceia which he had been defending and joined his forces with his own.[26]

Sometimes though, it was necessary for the same commander to get the same body of troops to repeat their oath. This usually occurred when the original oath was held to have been breached. Fraternisation with the enemy, refusal to fight and outright desertion would necessitate such a repetition. This happened when Fimbria was cornered by Sulla in Asia in 85. His men began to slip away from him and he tried, with little success, to keep the others' loyalty by administering the oath once more.[27] Petreius, as he faced Caesar in Spain at the start of the Second Civil War, was more successful. When he extracted an oath it put a stop to the fraternising which was occurring between his men and Caesar's.[28]

Altogether different are the oaths administered by a general to the same body of men when one campaign follows immediately on another. This is what Caesar did, it would seem, when, with the Gallic War over, he crossed the Rubicon to start the Second Civil War. Enlistment for a new campaign required a new oath.[29]

Even clearer is the case of Sulla. As he returned to Italy in 83 with the Mithridatic War finished, he feared that his men would exercise their rights and disperse to their homes. Instead they swore a new oath as they enlisted for the Civil War which was about to begin.[30]

All of those cases, I believe, show us the *sacramentum* being applied in the traditional manner even in the most troubled times.[31] There are two cases, however, which display singular features. At the end of 43, as Antony was recruiting at Tibur preparatory to making war on Decimus Brutus, the whole senate and most of the equestrian order came to pay their respects. He made them take the *sacramentum* along with his troops.[32] It would not, I think, be fanciful to suggest that this rather odd scene was connected with Antony's insecurity at the time.[33] He was led to extend the *sacramentum* to civilians. Also in 43, just before his soldiers demanded the consulship for him, Octavian made them swear not to fight anybody who had been a soldier of Caesar's. The majority of these were in the armies of Lepidus and Antony.[34] The obvious inference to draw from this is that Octavian's grip on his men was weak and, not trusting to the binding power of the *sacramentum*, he had to have recourse to a further tie.

Our discussion will touch again on these two aberrant instances but for the moment I wish to say something further about the more conventional ones we have been considering. This is occasioned by an observation of Campbell's.[35] The oath of Cinna in 87,[36] that of Sulla in 83 and those involving Caesar and Domitius and Petreius in 49 acquire 'a much wider and potentially sinister relevance'.[37] The commander could 'order his troops against the government of the State'.[38]

The only place I have been able to find a commander accused of using the *sacramentum* in this fashion does not inspire much confidence. Just after Caesar's murder, Brutus, according to Appian (*BC*.2.140), made a speech in which he claimed Caesar had taken advantage of the military oath to lead his unwilling soldiers against the state. The speaker, the context and the detail of reluctant troops will warn us against taking this at face value. Personally I should say it is worth about as much as another accusation Brutus made against Caesar at the same time. He claimed Caesar had planted Italy in the same way as Sulla had. Whatever suspicion there may be that Caesar did not always live up to his initial declaration of moderation, there can be no doubt that he never proceeded as Sulla did.[39]

What I think we need to bear constantly in mind is that we are dealing with a state of civil war. In such a situation both sides would claim the right and neither would admit that they had set themselves up in opposition to lawful authority.[40] To take but one example here,[41] when Sulla marched on Rome his opponents enquired why he was attacking his country. He replied he was come to deliver her from tyrants.[42]

Once we have grasped this we will, I believe, have no difficulty in accepting that the essential nature of the *sacramentum* was not now altered. In the time when the state was whole a magistrate ultimately derived his authority from that state, and when he proposed to take the field he naturally administered the military oath to those he was about to command. But in these times authority often came from another quarter. The commander had achieved legitimacy because he had convinced his men in *contio* or elsewhere of the rightness of his cause.[43] And once authority was established then it was natural an oath would hereafter follow.

Thus, I see no reason to give the *sacramentum* a role or a significance greater than that it had always had. It continued to be the means by which the general disciplined his men but it was without any revolutionary significance in itself. That, as we have just seen, was to be found elsewhere. The one change which possibly occurred is that suggested by Campbell.[44] He thought that the constant changes of allegiance in the Triumviral period must have weakened its force and brought it into disrepute.[45]

But there is another oath which could bind the soldier, or so von Premerstein and his followers thought.[46] He believed we could distinguish between the military oath and others of a more general type which could be imposed on civilians and soldiers who would then be clients of those to whom they had sworn.

One's first reaction is to argue the latter detail is doubtful. In the civilian sphere clientage might indeed sometimes be involved.[47] But we have already seen that the notion that the great commanders of the late republic led armies of men who were their clients must be given up.[48] Then, an examination of our evidence for the oaths themselves offers scant encouragement for the view that they actually involved the soldier.

Some were unequivocally private. One of these was the oath to Caesar extracted from some of his political allies during his absence in Gaul. The intent was obviously to shore up his own personal position.[49] Von Premerstein (1937, p. 30) thought this resembled another oath we shall be considering shortly, that Sulla forced from Cinna in 88, but I believe a more valid comparison may be made with Livius Drusus (trib.pleb.91). As he pressed the case for Italian enfranchisement he is said to have devised an oath which was essentially one of loyalty to himself. Admitted to the citizenship, the Italians would regard Drusus as their greatest benefactor.[50] Drusus and Caesar had the same broad aim, but where Caesar dealt in individuals, Drusus dealt in nations.

Separate and essentially different are those oaths taken to preserve somebody's *acta*. When Saturninus brought forward his land bill in 100 it was decreed that once it became law the senators and probably also the magistrates should within five days swear to obey it. As scholars point out, our sources tend to concentrate on this as a device prepared for the ruin of Marius' enemy, Metellus Numidicus.[51] When he refused to take it he was obliged to withdraw into exile. It seems to have been agreed, however, that no oath could validate an invalid law and that, in consequence, Metellus' refusal was an empty gesture.[52]

Our next such oath involves the *acta* of Sulla. Despite being taken in a very public place it must be regarded as private in nature.[53] When Sulla captured Rome in 88 he brought in some reforms but feared that one, or both, of the incoming consuls, Octavian and Cinna, would try to dismantle them. So, he forced them to take an oath on the Capitol to do them no harm.[54] Aside from other considerations,[55] the way this oath was administered points to its private nature as we claimed above. In contrast to the later oath on Caesar's *acta* which was enshrined in a *lex*,[56] Sulla, as presiding officer, extracted it by refusing to grant *renuntiatio* until the candidates complied.[57] This makes plausible the suggestion that we have here something thought up on the spur of the moment when Sulla realised the coming danger. The oath was a solemn one but no doubt Cinna could excuse his subsequent foreswearing by claiming duress or simply pointing to the dubious nature of Sulla's occupation of Rome in the first place.

The manner in which it was established and administered fairly obviously points to the oath to maintain Caesar's *acta* being public. Established by decree of the senate, it was required of every magistrate as he entered upon his office.[58] After his death those who were laying claim to the title of his heirs naturally reaffirmed their commitment to this pledge. Thus, in 44, while progressing around Campania gathering troops, Antony made those he had enlisted swear to observe the *acta*. Again, after they had proscribed their opponents, the Triumvirs committed themselves to their maintenance.[59] Even those who murdered Caesar could not escape this obligation. Barely had the deed been done when they were compelled to swear they would not upset their victim's arrangements.[60]

As they scrambled to do him honour, the Romans declared Caesar's life to be inviolate and sealed it with an oath.[61] History tells us not everybody took this too seriously but it also furnishes us with analogous instances of when they did.[62] In 91 as Livius Drusus was pursuing his legislative programme he was suddenly taken ill. The Italians, who knew just how much depended on him, offered vows for his safety throughout Italy and, given the crucial situation, I am prepared to believe they were sincere.[63] Much later, in the summer of 50, as relations between the senate and Caesar became ever worse, Pompey fell dangerously ill. As in the case of Drusus, people realised how much depended upon him too, and so up and down Italy prayers and vows were made for his recovery. When that came about there was universal rejoicing.[64] One final set of oaths which have been recorded for us involve groups of men who bonded themselves together to achieve a common purpose whether legitimate or nefarious.

The first we wish to consider certainly falls into the latter category, forming as it does a lurid episode in one of the most infamous events in Roman history. Catiline, as he set his conspiracy afoot, brought his followers together to swear an oath of complicity and sealed it by passing around to taste a bowl of human blood mixed with wine.[65] Another guilty party, but less colourful, were the soldiers who mutinied in Syria in 46. They murdered their commander Sextus Caesar and put one Caecilius Bassus in his place. Then, realising they could expect to pay for this, they swore to remain together for mutual protection.[66] Then, in 42, when Octavian and Lucius Antonius were about to clash, officers from both armies intervened and managed to broker an agreement. Unfortunately this was not implemented and when the officers tried again they swore under oath to coerce their respective commanders but ultimately with no more success.[67]

There is, I would suggest, nothing rash about claiming that the famous oath made by *tota Italia* to Octavian in 32 stands broadly in the tradition of oaths such as these.[68] Indeed it is obvious he directly drew his inspiration from it. When you swear after this fashion it must be assumed you will not violate Octavian's person,[69] you will accept his *acta* and you will share in the enterprise he leads as *dux*.[70]

However, our comprehensive survey clearly reveals something else. Oaths of this type only affect the soldier *qua* soldier intermittently and incidentally. The only direct reference to such an oath being applied to serving soldiers is to those involving Antony and Octavian we have referred to above.[71] There is no evidence to support Campbell's suggestion[72] that the soldier, already tied by a *sacramentum*, would join in a general oath of allegiance if he happened to be present, and he himself says the notion 'may seem odd'[73]. The continued use of the *sacramentum* as a means of ensuring discipline which we have demonstrated is surely yet another argument against the widespread existence of this suggested practice of double oath-taking.

The incidental involvement of the soldier arises directly from the nature and purpose of Octavian's oath.[74] This is not a military oath and the soldier who might take it is not swearing in his capacity as a soldier. Like all the others making this pledge, he is swearing as one Roman to another Roman.[75]

We can now see clearly what is the significance of the *sacramentum*. He who violates it becomes *sacer*.[76] We now proceed with our study, examining those occasions when it was broken, divining why this happened and attempting to set forth the consequences.

(b) Mutiny and desertion (91–81)

Despite Gruen's suggestion to the contrary,[77] mutinies in this period can be seen to display certain broad general characteristics. We will, of course, find occasional anomalies and exceptions but overall we will be witnessing a phenomenon of the time which is susceptible to definition.

At what many, I suspect, would regard as the most elementary level, we discover the most favoured way of disposing of commanders of whom troops disapproved was stoning, a method which is, of course, found elsewhere in Roman history.[78] In one instance, that of Cinna, stabbing followed the stone throwing, while in another, Cato (cos.89), he escaped because only clods of earth were to hand.[79] By far the most exotic fate was surely that of Pompeius Rufus (cos.88). He was offering sacrifice when his troops turned on him and made him the sacrificial victim.[80]

Interesting as all this may be, it is, of course not as important as discovering what were the grievances which led to mutiny in the first place. Our sources give differing reasons in the case of Albinus, legate to Sulla in 89,[81] and it must be said all of them carry a degree of plausibility. In one account he was suspected of some kind of treachery and, in view of what was happening in Campania at the time, it is easy to see why the troops might have acted on their suspicions without giving him a chance to clear himself.[82]

Another source says he displayed *superbia*.[83] I would suggest something more than the congenital haughtiness of the Roman noble is in question here. Cinna, a few years later, is said to have perished because of his cruelty[84] but detailed accounts reveal that, in effect, this meant he was murdered while making a heavy-handed attempt to restore discipline and force his army to go where it did not want to.[85] Thus, Albinus' *superbia* may point to a haughty and unseasonable attempt to enforce his authority like Cinna over the mutinous. Whatever the truth of this, resentment at military discipline was in these times the most common cause for mutiny. Besides being allegedly stingy, Valerius Flaccus (cos.86) was inexperienced in war, a poor disciplinarian who was, like Cinna, 'injudicious in punishment'. Both met with trouble when engaged on the same enterprise, an expedition to Greece to confront Sulla. Both commanders sent on an advance party which was soon cut off by storms. The main body of troops then became restless. For Cinna this was the end and his advance guard was recalled. Flaccus was luckier. He had an able lieutenant, Fimbria, who was able to quell the mutiny.[86] Two other cases complete the tally. What drew the clods down on Cato was an attempt to impose discipline. We know he survived, but Papirius Carbo was not so fortunate. At the end of the Civil War he died when he tried to restore discipline in the army he commanded before Volaterrae.[87]

Even the most gifted commanders faced this problem and I would maintain it is a measure of their ability that they came away unscathed when, as we saw, lesser men did not. An indication of the greatness of commanders such as Sulla and Pompey is their capacity to divine the mood of their men and act accordingly. On such occasions they were wise enough not to seek confrontation. Instead they let the mutiny run its course and, in some instances, capitalised on the feeling of remorse which followed when it was over.[88] Sulla did this. His reaction to Albinus' murder was to tell his soldiers he would expect them to redeem themselves by showing even greater eagerness in the face of the enemy. Plutarch spluttered in indignation at this, but Frontinus, who was himself a soldier, was impressed.[89] Twice in the same war Marius was faced with the problem of troops who would not fight and simply judged it was advisable to make the best of things. Once, when the Romans and the Italians were equally reluctant to engage, he merely said one side was as bad as the other. Another occasion witnessed mass fraternisation so Marius consented to have a meeting himself with the Italian commander Poppaedius Silo.[90]

The army with which Pompey was despatched to finish off the Cinnans in Sicily and Africa after the Colline Gate was remarkably unruly. In Sicily itself he had to force the men to seal up their scabbards because of their lawless behaviour. When they got to Africa they took time out to dig for non-existent treasure and all Pompey could do was pretend to find this funny. But, like Sulla, he reaped a benefit for, once the mood had passed, the soldiers clamoured to be allowed to make up for their foolishness.[91] A few months later he was to be less accommodating. Disgruntled at the distribution of booty, his troops threatened to disrupt Pompey's triumph but he declared he would rather not triumph than give way and so quelled the mutiny. It has been suggested that Pompey was thus inconsistent in his attitude to mutiny, but flexible may be a more apposite term. What he had, of necessity, to condone in Africa he did not need to tolerate in Rome.[92]

Inconsistencies, too, have been detected in the career of Pompey's father, Pompey Strabo, but this particular thesis will not stand up to scrutiny. It will be recalled that Pompeius Rufus had been murdered by his own army. He had been in command only a few days, having replaced Pompey Strabo. Once he had died Pompey resumed the command and there is, to put it no more strongly, a grave suspicion he had engineered the mutiny.[93] I find it difficult to believe, however, that Strabo, as some maintain, either discovered the hidden potential of his army before Sulla or at any rate was his imitator.[94] The inspiration he and his men sought had been all around them in the mutinies with which the Social War had been punctuated. Sulla's march and the unseating of Marius had been nothing but the most spectacular of these.

For some the murderous devotion we have just mentioned sits ill with stories that by the end of his career Strabo had become an object of hatred to these sup-posedly loyal troops.[95] But we must remember the circumstances of the day, particularly the ravages of the plague.[96] If we do, we can see that Heftner's sugges-tion was correct (1995, p. 76), that soldiers had become disillusioned with his endless manoeuvring which may have seemed something like dithering. Mutiny eventually came, most likely when Strabo lay ill and there was a delay in appoint-ing his successor Cassius, all of which will, at a vital moment, have left the army without much-needed direction. The young Pompey seems to have aborted it by a personal display of bravery, but this procured only a brief stay for the army fell to pieces when Strabo died.[97]

Mutinous troops were not the only hazard for the general. These were times in which the commander was well advised to keep an eye on his staff. Pompey, as son of the commander in 87, was the target of an assassination attempt by his *contu-bernalis* which he managed to foil.[98] Yet, a few years later, he was, according to one account, implicated in the murder of Cinna.[99] Cato, as we have had occasion to mention, may have escaped the clods but he succumbed to the dagger of the younger Marius when he offended family honour by boasting he had done better than the elder Marius on the field of battle.[100] We saw how Fimbria rescued Flaccus from a mutiny. What looks like a personal quarrel led him soon after to engineer one of his own. Taking advantage of Flaccus' unpopularity he posed as the sol-dier's friend, complained of Flaccus' treatment of him and eventually forced him to flee to Nicomedeia, where he was killed.[101] Another notable assassin was Albinovanus, who established his traitor's credentials in the Civil War by mur-dering his fellow officers at a banquet before fleeing to Sulla.[102]

We now turn to mass desertions and switching of sides. The first of these in our period comes in 90. The Italian commander Papius Mutilus took Nola and the garrison accepted his offer to join him. Their officers, however, refused and he had them starved to death.[103] When Sulla finally caught up with Fimbria the latter's troops deserted to him, as did those of the consul Scipio when he entered into parley in the Civil War. A little later Scipio lost a second army to Pompey in what appears to have been a similar encounter.[104] Some further desertions which Appian records for the second year of the war were obviously inspired by the declining

Cinnan fortunes but were no doubt made in the knowledge the Sullans would welcome the fugitives.[105]

Mutinies had, of course, occurred before in the Roman army. What distinguished this period from those which had gone before was the number we find concentrated in a relatively short period.[106] When we come, however, to investigate what it is about the troops of this time which so predisposed them to seek the remedy for their grievances in violence then we find few statements in our sources which would be of help. In describing the death of Carbo at Volaterrae, Valerius Maximus (9.7.3) says he was killed trying to restore discipline which had slackened as a result of the Civil War, which last statement, I submit, can admit of a number of interpretations. In the specific instance of Cato, Dio fr.100 is more informative. The consul's soldiers came from the city and were past the normal age for service. Hence they could ill tolerate discipline. Scipio's army too came from the city and this could explain why his grip on it was not as tight as it might have been. But urban origin cannot always be invoked as an explanation for unrest. Norbanus also drew his troops from the city but he saw to it they were not lured away by Sulla.[107] So far as the parley or the mass desertion is concerned we fare rather better. Self-interest may have played its part here. The troops of Fimbria and Scipio will have wanted to be on the winning side[108] and when Hortensius found himself cut off in Greece in 86 he had no other option but to join Sulla.[109]

Syme (1939, pp. 159–60) was inclined to be dismissive of claims by the Triumvirs that they had tried to avoid shedding Roman blood, but I can see no reason to doubt reports that soldiers in this period refused to fight those they regarded as belonging to the same race. The rebels in the Social War, of course, were not Romans but many had fought alongside them and, as Italians, were regarded as being akin to them.[110] Hence the encounters with Marius and Sextus Pompey. With the coming of civil war for the first time it is understandable Roman should not want to fight Roman, and so we should believe Appian when he says that was why the Fimbrians joined Sulla.[111] The reluctance of Cinna's men to face Sulla may have been grounded in the fear of what would happen to them if they did, but that may not be all. At the time there was in Italy a general reluctance to go to war and Cinna's troops may simply have reflected the distaste many felt for conflict with fellow Romans, a distaste plainly shared by Scipio's troops once fighting started. They, it will be recalled, had, like the Fimbrians, fraternised with the enemy and allowed themselves to be seduced by them. Sulla himself seems to have shared these sentiments since he first tried to avoid war by negotiations and then strove to lessen its impact. The behaviour of his troops was at first exemplary, he tried to lure enemy armies to his side and became reconciled to a number of his opponents.[112]

So far as both mutiny and desertion are concerned there is one other reason why we find so much of it in these years. Quite simply these soldiers knew they could get away with it. We hear virtually nothing about mutineers being called to account. The only instance I have come upon is that of the man who tried to organise the mutiny against Cato. He escaped military discipline and was instead sent to Rome, where he was rescued by a tribune.[113] More than immediate danger prevented the likes of Sulla and Pompey from proceeding against the mutinous. Even when the mood changed they dared not have recourse to punishment, however light.[114] And for a very good reason: they could not risk alienating those who served under them. Both the Social and Civil Wars were characterised by the desperate attempts of both sides to overcome shortages and maximise the number of men at their disposal.[115] Soldiers were precious. They knew their own worth and so did those who led them. They must not be needlessly provoked.

One feature deserves especial note. In the Social War mutiny was the predominant mode of protest chosen. In the Civil War we hear more of desertion. This does not come about by chance. The Italians may have been related to the Romans but essentially the Social War was fought against an external foe and Roman soldiers did not normally desert in great numbers to foreign enemies.[116] When we come to the Civil War there is an important change. Now those who are not happy with their lot – often simply because they are fighting their fellow countrymen – can cross over to where Romans are waiting to receive them.

From an analysis of cause we pass naturally to a consideration of significance. To what extent can we say that the mutinies and mass desertions we have been studying are symptomatic of some kind of revolutionary spirit in the Roman army of this time? Any such probing must begin by recognising that in even the most disciplined and well-ordered armies there can occur moments of indiscipline and temporary wavering which only by a most rigid and pedantic application of a definition can be called mutiny.[117] Sulla, as I suggested, inherited Cato's unruly and murderous troops and turned them into the highly disciplined force with which he won two wars. These same men hesitated at Chaeronea and wavered at Orchomenus but I do not think we need describe this as mutiny.[118] And where an incident can be classified as mutiny we have to differentiate between the gravity of the offence in itself and its wider consequences. Plainly, taking time out to look for non-existent gold is a far less serious matter than stoning one's commander to death, but what concerns us is the long-term effects both might have. Common and all as mutinies were in the Social War, they appear to have been of short duration and not to have affected the prosecution of a war which the Romans, in effect, brought to an end in two years.

It is elsewhere we must look for a pernicious consequence of these mutinies. We find it, I believe, in the fact that troops now discovered they could rid themselves of an unpopular commander with impunity. So far as Pompey Strabo and Sulla were concerned this had a considerable effect on the course of events. Both men exploited the sentiment in their efforts to ensure their own survival. There, however, the resemblance ends. Restored to his army, Pompey could do no more than intrigue, and his attempts to play one side off against the another led to the victory of Cinna. Sulla, for his part, elected to play the reformer – a somewhat premature decision in 88, but he was to be allowed to do so again.[119]

When we come to the Civil War with its attendant desertions and changes of side, we may perhaps think that the numbers involved made some difference.

Certainly they would have been welcome as we can see from the frantic lobbying of Italian communities in the winter of 83.[120] Something of the psychological damage inflicted can be seen in Carbo's massacre of Celto-Iberians when their colleagues, infected by the general mood, had repeatedly deserted.[121]

The connection we have drawn between impunity for acts of insubordination and the generals' need for men in these wars could hold dangers for the modern scholar in that he or she might wish to assimilate this situation to that described by Appian *BC*.5.17 where the Triumvirs are said to have been the prisoners of their men. We should not make such an assimilation. When Appian describes Triumvirs as prisoners he is thinking of how the soldiers of that period did actually dictate policy to those who were supposedly set over them.[122] No general of the period 91–81 found himself in this position, and with good reason. Unlike the Triumvirs, those who took the field now were not, as Appian says the Triumvirs were, invested with a dubious authority but were the properly constituted magistrates of the Roman republic. Nor did they resemble the Triumvirs in seeking a personal *dominatio*. The Social and Civil Wars were fought over real issues and the victors in the latter established no lasting lordship. We can best appreciate the difference in generations if we contemplate two paradigmatic figures. Both Octavian and Pompey Strabo sought to use their armies to advance themselves. Octavian looked for and found great *dominatio*; Strabo, for all his intrigues, could not imagine anything more than a second consulship coming his way.[123]

(c) Mutiny and desertion: Caesarian period (49–44)

The first instance of desertion we hear of is in early 49 when Thermus the Pompeian praetor was abandoned by his troops at Iguvium. They, however, did not go over to Caesar but, evidently judging the campaign they had enlisted for over, returned to their homes.[124] At Auximium there was a virtual replay of the scene when Attius Varius' men deserted him, with some returning home and others enlisting with Caesar.[125] As Caesar's advance continued, the garrison commander at Asculum, Lentulus Spinther, had to flee after being deserted by his men, some of whom were later impressed by Caesar.[126] Caesar next had to face Cn. Domitius Ahenobarbus, who had recruited among the Marsi and Paeligni and stiffened their resolve by promises of a land distribution from his own estates. But he, too, eventually went the way of the others. Besieged in Corfinium he also was deserted by his troops.[127]

We have now to turn attention to the provinces, where we encounter, on the whole, fraternisation and parley. In Spain Caesar, contrary to the bloodthirsty desires of those he commanded, hoped to bring matters to a peaceful conclusion by cutting the food supplies of Afranius and Petreius. As the armies faced each other the soldiers on both sides began to mingle and mix. The Pompeians offered to desert but demanded guarantees for the safety of Afranius and Petreius. Petreius, however, was able to recall his men to their allegiance and renew the *sacramentum* they had broken. He succeeded in inducing some of them to murder some of

Caesar's men. But in the end the Pompeians had to surrender anyway. Caesar promised those who had a domicile in Spain immediate discharge. The rest would receive it at the river Varus and this was duly done.[128]

In Africa a somewhat similar incident took place.[129] There C. Scribonius Curio was operating in the Caesarian interest. A small group of Marsi who were in his army slipped across to his opponent Attius Varus and told him Curio's whole army was disaffected.[130] Varus was persuaded to face down Curio's army. In his army was that Quintilius Varus who had been captured at Corfinium by Caesar and released unharmed.[131] This man now sought to seduce those of Curio's men who had also been at Corfinium by trying to claim they were still bound by their oath to Domitius and reinforced his case with the promise of a bounty. For a little while there was consternation in Curio's camp but eventually he was able to persuade his men to obey their oath to Caesar and when battle was finally joined he emerged the victor.[132] In 49, the Governer of Syria, Metellus Scipio (cos.52), despite losses near Mount Amanus, had styled himself *imperator* and embarked on a career of extortion among the neighbouring communities. These good works were carried out even though a Parthian invasion was feared, and his troops began to mutter they would march against a foreign foe but not a citizen and consul. Their commendable scruples were soon quieted, however, when they were led to billets in Pergamum and allowed to plunder the nearby towns.[133]

In this war Caesar was twice faced with mutiny. The first of these took place in 49 at Placentia as he made his way back from Spain. The troops claimed they had not received a donative promised when they chased Pompey out of Brundisium and they said the war was being deliberately prolonged so that their discharge was now overdue. One source, Dio, claims they were not really seeking a remedy for these grievances but rather seeing how far they could push Caesar in his hour of need in order to extract the maximum by way of concessions from him. Caesar faced down the mutineers, claiming it was the enemy, not he, that was prolonging the war by running away and refusing to fight. They had done well in Gaul but now, in violation of their oath, they wished to quit before the war was done. He proposed decimation and cashiering but, needing every man for what lay ahead, he allowed himself to be persuaded to settle for the execution of the ringleaders.[134]

Early in 48 another instance of fraternisation led to parley. As the two sides faced each other at the river Apsus in Illyricum Caesar took advantage of this to send P. Vatinius to talk peace. The Pompeians promised that Aulus Terentius Varro would come to speak with him, but in the event Titus Labienus appeared. He had nothing of worth to say and a sudden shower of missiles put an end to the talks. Any lingering doubts about the way things were going were removed when Labienus exclaimed he wanted Caesar's head.[135]

The second mutiny Caesar had to face occurred in 47 and was more serious than the first.[136] Troops stationed in Campania mutinied because vague promises made after Pharsalus had not been kept[137] and because they had been retained under arms beyond their alloted time. A promise of another donative was spurned and the agent sent to announce it, the future historian Sallust, had to run for his life from the angry audience. The troops now marched on Rome, killing two more envoys on the way. Caesar himself then faced down his men and asked them what they wanted. They said their discharge and did not mention the donative. Here again, as in the previous mutiny, some of our sources claim money was the real objective. Caesar was about to set out on another campaign and as he would have need of them they proposed to profit thereby. He, however, nonplussed them by saying he granted them the requested discharge. The promised monies would follow when he triumphed with his other troops. Shamed, the men began to quieten down, hoping Caesar would relent, because of his needs, but he simply called them *Quirites*. They asked to be taken back and eventually he relented except in the case of the tenth legion. He then announced a land settlement programme and finally agreed to forgive the tenth.[138]

In the next year we find a mutiny in Syria. The sources are a trifle confused but the essential point is that Q. Caecilius Bassus killed his commander Sextus Caesar, who had been appointed by Caesar in 47. According to some accounts Sextus was an incapable commander who resented Bassus and brought him before an assembly. There the troops turned on the commander and stoned him to death. Then they bonded together and swore an oath so as to avoid retribution.[139]

That same year Caesar tried yet again to seduce an opponent's troops. Facing his inveterate foe Scipio (cos.52) in Africa, he tried to subvert the loyalty of the latter's men by distributing pamphlets among them promising pardon and the same rewards as were given to his own soldiers. Scipio countered with his own pamphlets, but his campaign was not a great success since he called for the liberation of the people and the senate but said nothing about any monies which might be disbursed.[140]

In this Second Civil War there were obviously many Romans who had no qualms whatsoever about killing fellow Romans.[141] The bloodthirsty Labienus well illustrates the type so far as Pompeians are concerned.[142] Not that Caesar's troops were blameless in this regard. At Thapsus in 46 they showed what they were capable of when they massacred the defeated despite Caesar's effort to stop them.[143] But, on the whole, their attitude can fairly be described as benign. For instance we saw how they fraternised at Ilerda although to start with they wanted to fight, and we know there were other parleys and moments of fraternisation just as there had been in Sulla's war.

The reasons for this state of affairs are two, and they are the same as they had been some forty years before. Romans now, as then, could shrink from slaying Romans.[144] It could be argued that when Appian and Dio say that, just before Pharsalus, both sides were acutely aware they were about to fight against their fellow countrymen to whom they were bound in many cases by personal ties, they were indulging in a *topos* or playing the flabby *litterateur*.[145] But such a view is revolting to common sense and is, in any case, amply refuted by the exemplary case of Caesar.

This neatly takes us to our second point: the character of the commander who set the war afoot. Sulla made great efforts to avoid the war and then to conclude it swiftly by encouraging desertion, even if he has received little credit for it.[146] Caesar, who acted likewise, has, and deservedly. His *clementia*, which was to cost him his life, is so well known as to need no attestation and so we may believe him when he speaks of wishing to settle matters without shedding blood. He did not wish to lose any of his men and he was trying to avoid bringing suffering on his fellow citizens.[147]

From this we pass to a consideration of the two mutinies Caesar faced in this period. The grievances were money and delayed discharge from service, as we know.[148] The problem of arrears of pay for the army had been an intermittent one in the late republic.[149] As recently as 56 it had led to mutiny. Then the soldiers of Lucius Calpurnius Piso (cos.58), enraged at not being paid, set fire to his head-quarters in the, fortunately for him, mistaken belief that he was inside.[150]

However, the most interesting and fruitful comparison is not with Piso but with Lucullus. In the case of both Caesar and Lucullus the grievance was dis-charge. But the monetary issue was present too. At the time of the mutiny against him, Lucullus had acquired, probably unfairly, a reputation of being stingy with booty and this sharpened the temper of his men.[151] Caesar, for his part, had not been lavish with money and this by now was beginning to be resented.[152] For both men this was a problem of their own making. Lucullus had stopped his men plun-dering Greek cities and Caesar had spared both provincials and defeated Pompeians. The outcome of the agitation was, however, very different. In the demand of the Fimbrians for release there was no element of extortion. And from Lucullus there came no offer of further material reward, only an abject begging which resulted in their consenting to undertake garrison duty.[153] However, with Caesar, as we know, the mutineers were able to gain an advantage for he had something to give. And it is here that the importance of those mutinies lies. Their duration was short so they did not affect the prosecution of the war, but in them we find Caesar buying allegiance at a price. For the first time soldiers are not content just to receive what their commander might deign to give. They speak for themselves, they make specific demands and their commander must listen.[154] The inchoate mutinies of a previous generation were no more.

(d) Mutiny and desertion: Triumviral period (44–31)

Just as in the earlier periods we have been looking at, so now here again we encounter mutiny, desertion and switches of sides. The evidence may be set forth as follows.[155]

In the confusion immediately following the death of Caesar, Antony claimed to fear for his own safety and, with the blessing of the senate, enrolled a bodyguard of centurions and other experienced men known to him personally. Later in the year he arrested some of them because allegedly they had been suborned to kill him by Octavian.[156] Both he and Octavian had to face mutiny. As relations between the two deteriorated Octavian's men objected to being led against Antony and not against Caesar's murderers. Many simply walked away and he could do nothing to stop them. When they changed their minds and returned, he had no option but to receive them and acquiesce in the lie that they had just gone home to collect their weapons.[157] Antony's problems proved to be as great, if not greater. In October he headed for Brundisium in order to collect the Macedonian legions for use against Decimus Brutus, only to find the troops turning on him because he, too, was not pursuing the tyrannicides with sufficient zeal. A donative designed to soothe was dismissed as beggarly and the subsequent application of a modified form of decimation only shortened tempers further and gave Octavian the opportunity to display, for the first time, a deadly facility he was to show again and again: the ability to seduce other commanders' troops. Now he sent subversives, in the disguise of traders, into Antony's camp to distribute seditious pamphlets, and on the road to Rome he had the satisfaction of adding to his ranks the deserting fourth and Martian legions.[158]

Octavian's success naturally encouraged imitators. Early in 43 Asinius Pollio, governor of Further Spain, and Munatius Plancus, stationed in Gaul, found themselves (or more accurately their men) very much in demand as Antony and Lepidus offered them various inducements.[159] When Antony had Decimus Brutus bottled up in Mutina he too got to work and sent his agents into the town. They were, however, detected and the enterprise failed.[160] After Antony's defeat at Mutina, Octavian, who sought reconciliation, was careful to give any of Antony's men who came his way a choice of remaining with him or returning to their commander, and he allowed Ventidius, who was nearby with legions gathered to aid Antony, to proceed on his way.[161] But even as Octavian was about these activities the senate was trying to undermine him by means of envoys, to whom his troops however paid no heed.[162] This therefore failed and an essentially illegal action helps to explain a seemingly bizarre story from the previous year. According to this, matters had gone so far that Cicero had berated Antony for suppressing the mutiny at Brundisium.[163]

Just after Antony's reverse at Mutina, Lepidus and his army suffered a fate almost identical to that of Scipio Asiagenus a generation before.[164] He and Antony opened communications and their troops mingled and mixed, with the result that Lepidus' men went over to Antony and he himself was obliged to follow.[165] With the final defeat of Decimus Brutus four of his legions joined Antony. Some others went to Octavian, and about this time Asinius Pollio finally succumbed to Antony's charms and came to his side.[166] Then, when Octavian advanced on Rome itself to obtain the consulship, three of the defending legions deserted to him together with their commanders, save for one who committed suicide. A rumour that the fourth and Martian legions were about to desert Octavian gave momentary hope to his enemies but soon proved to be false.[167]

So much for Italy. As might be expected, the Liberators too had been busy in the east. In the previous year in Thessaly, Marcus Brutus had scooped up some of the remnants of Pompey's army.[168] Then in Macedonia he managed to subvert the loyalty of the troops of Antony's brother, Gaius. Being of a very high mind, he kept Gaius himself in honourable captivity, only to find he had introduced the proverbial cuckoo into the nest, for Antony proceeded to make several attempts to foment mutiny. Brutus' patience, however, did not snap until early 42 when news of the proscriptions induced him to make away with his troublesome guest.[169]

Meantime Cassius had entered his province of Syria and there he encountered the mutineer Bassus, whom we have already met with in the previous section.[170] By now the retribution he feared had materialised and he was being besieged by Staius Murcus and Marcius Crispus. Cassius on his arrival raised the siege and joined the armies of both besieged and besiegers to his own.[171] Sieges continued to yield Cassius manpower. Cornelius Dolabella had put together an army in Asia with which he invaded Syria. He soon found he was no match for Cassius and was penned up in Laodiceia. With the fall of the town he committed suicide and Cassius impressed his men.[172]

Interest in the next year, 42, naturally centred on Philippi and on a mutiny which was feared but never actually happened. We hear that both Brutus and Cassius feared that Caesarians in their ranks[173] would prove disloyal but these anxieties turned out to be baseless. It was not until the end of the second battle that Brutus' officers urged accommodation with the enemy and the rank and file consented to be divided among Octavian's and Antony's armies. Traffic on that day was not all in the one direction. In a sea battle, said to have been fought on the day of Philippi, defeated Triumviral sailors went over to the victor Murcus.[174]

Whatever euphoria Octavian may have felt was soon dissipated, one suspects, upon his return to Italy in 41, when he had to face mutinies. There was one at Placentia and the mutineers extorted money from the townsfolk.[175] But there was another far more serious, at least from Octavian's point of view. At this time he was busy settling veterans on the land.[176] Some of the soldiers, however, found out he was making some concessions to the dispossessed and they reacted with anger. They killed a centurion who tried to impose order and for a time turned on Octavian himself. He eventually quelled the mutiny by giving land to the deserving and undeserving alike. Shamefaced, the troops asked to be punished for what they had done but Octavian wisely said their own bad consciences would be punishment enough.[177]

Rather more cheering, to start with anyway, must have been the news received at the start of the Perusine War that two of Lucius Antonius' legions had mutinied. Octavian, ever open to the possibilities offered by this kind of situation, hurried to take advantage of it. Lucius, however, was too quick for him, buying back the strays with a donative. A little later Antony's quaestor M. Barratius Philippus arrived in Italy. Having some kind of quarrel with his commander he spread false report that Antony disapproved of Lucius' actions. As a result some of the latter's troops decamped to Octavian.[178]

However Octavian did not always have to scheme and intrigue to increase his army. In the next year Fufius Calenus died and Octavian inherited his troops.[179] Then, with the end of the Perusine War, there was witnessed what looks like a piece of play-acting. When Lucius' troops surrendered, Octavian gave it about that he intended to punish them, but then, yielding to the pleas of his own men, forgave them and enlisted them in his ranks.[180] Then, as the victorious Caesarians pursued the rest of the defeated, two legions belonging to Munatius Plancus were persuaded to come over to Agrippa.[181] Far away in Syria, Q. Labienus, son of Caesar's old officer, invaded the province at the head of a force of Parthians. He had originally been sent to Parthia to look for help by Brutus and Cassius. However he was long detained there and only now obtained an army. Some moderns brand Labienus a traitor but it should be borne in mind that even Pompey had thought of looking for help in the same quarter. At any rate, when the garrison of Syria went over to him they need not be branded as traitors either. Once Brutus' men, they now served Antony and would have found it easy to return to their old allegiance as personified by Labienus.[182] To complete the year's tally of insubordination we have the reports of the mixing and mingling before the peace of Brundisium. Soldiers of both sides met to argue and accuse, with Octavian's troops declaring they wished to reconcile Antony and Octavian.[183]

Up until now we have not heard much of the kinds of tensions on a general's staff which characterised the period 91–81 and led to several assassinations.[184] With the coming of 40, that changed. It was a very good year for disposing of unsatisfactory underlings. Antony put his agent Manius to death because he had urged Fulvia to the Perusine War. He also did something which clearly shows why he was destined to be a loser in these struggles. The consul designate of 39, Q. Salvidienus Rufus, offered to desert Octavian. Antony's response was to tell Octavian, and Rufus was executed. In keeping with the spirit of the age, Sextus Pompey made away with Staius Murcus whom he was beginning to find an irritant.[185] Another lieutenant of Sextus, the Greek Menas, showed more skill and finesse and in the years 38 to 36 scurried to and fro between Sextus and Octavian. He eventually settled with Octavian but unsurprisingly the latter kept a close watch on him.[186]

However, greater rewards than the allegiance of Menas were to come Octavian's way in 36. To start with he destroyed the power of Sextus Pompey in a sea campaign.[187] Then he took over Lepidus' army and dismissed its general into private life. This last was carried out by Octavian in the manner we have by now become familiar with.

After Sextus' defeat Octavian and Lepidus quarrelled. The troops were weary of war and Pompeians in Lepidus' army feared their terms of surrender would not be secure until Octavian approved them. He immediately set about subverting their loyalty. He then appeared before Lepidus' camp and the troops within started to drift over to his side, with the cavalry coming last of all. Lepidus now had no option but to throw himself on Octavian's mercy. But, as often happens, triumph is followed by disaster, actual or potential. Octavian's troops now mutinied.[188] Discharge was the issue, along with the demand for payment of rewards equal to those given to the soldiers who fought at Philippi.[189] Octavian seems to have thought he was now in a strong position because his first response was to threaten. Traditional severe punishments would be administered. The troops treated this with contempt and Octavian was obliged to change tack. Since the domestic wars were now over[190] he proposed to lead them against a foreign foe, the Illyrians. The answer was not encouraging. His men did not intend to go anywhere until they had been rewarded for what they had already done. Octavian then began to distribute crowns and other honours, but a military tribune, Ofillius sharply reminded him these were no substitute for land and money.[191] The crowd shouted approval and Octavian quitted the rostrum in anger. He was, though, sufficiently master of the situation so as to ensure that, by the next day, Ofillius had disappeared, never to be seen again. He had, however, made his point and land was now distributed to those who served at Mutina and Philippi while a donative was given to those who remained with the colours.[192]

With this incident the tally of Triumviral desertions and mutinies is complete.[193] With the victory over Sextus, Octavian regarded the period of civil strife as at an end.[194] The war in Illyricum which now followed was, as Octavian had declared, a foreign war,[195] as was that subsequently against Antony and Cleopatra. And in these wars there was no place for mutiny or desertion.

In this period desertion or switching of sides becomes virtually commonplace and it requires no profound investigation to account for the phenomenon. This was the age of the desperate. Ruthless men sought to shore up their position and undermine that of their opponents.[196] At a time when people recruited extensively among slaves we need not be surprised to discover that they did not scruple to gather to themselves the disaffected from other armies or join the soldiers of a defeated opponent to their own.[197] Often, of course, commanders were not content to wait until fortune gave them an increase but took a hand in the business for themselves. A generation or so before, Sulla's subversion of the loyalty of his enemies' troops had earned him the title of 'fox' from a reluctant admirer. Now, as we have just said, the practice has become commonplace and our sources are littered with instances of metaphorical mining and burrowing. If we were to nominate the chief victim we would have to say it was Lepidus, who twice had an army snatched away from him thanks to the machinations of others. Conversely the palm for mastery of these arts must be awarded to Octavian, who emerges as an inveterate seducer of other men's troops and whose crowning achievement in this department was the second and final luring away of Lepidus' men in 36.

In spite of the abundant opportunities to decamp, soldiers continued from time to time to voice their grievances by mutiny and, having discovered their voice under Caesar, they did not now lose it. Two themes are discernible. When Antony and Octavian seemed to be about to clash they were quickly told their concern should be the destruction of the Tyrannicides. Then, when Octavian was proving to be unsatisfactory in the matter of donatives and land, he soon faced unrest, just as his adopted father had.

Speaking generally, the sources give the impression that the soldiers of this time were of good quality and worth wooing.[198] We have just seen their tendency to switch allegiance but once they had elected to follow a commander they considered themselves bound by the *sacramentum* and submitted to discipline.[199]

If we want to estimate how far this tendency towards indiscipline, however manifested, affected the course of events we have first of all to remember its temporal limitations. In effect we are really looking at a period of eight years from the assassination of Caesar in 44 to 36 when Octavian began to restore order.[200] After the latter year opportunities for switching sides became distinctly limited. Octavian, it is true, was to have trouble with legions and their demands even after Actium.[201] But there was by then nowhere for the rebellious to go, and even in 36 Octavian seems, for all of his difficulties, to have realised he was now beginning to act from a position of some strength. Order was being restored and there was no place for indiscipline.[202] The change that was coming in the world was illustrated and encapsulated in the differing fates of two soldiers. The first incident dates to 41. One day, at the theatre, a common soldier sat in the places reserved for the *equites*. Octavian had him removed, only to be set on, as he left the theatre, by a mob of soldiers who thought their comrade had been killed. Only his sudden reappearance saved Octavian.[203] The other story, from 36, and its different sequel we are familiar with. Then when a barrackroom lawyer raised his head Octavian felt sufficiently secure to have him removed forever.[204]

Next, however, we have to ask how far, in these eight years, what we may dub fluidity of loyalty helped determine the course of events. Self-evidently, tampering with the loyalty of an opponent's troops and bringing them over to your own side must, from your point of view, be a good thing.[205] But, at the same time, increase in numbers, however desirable in itself, is not decisive in winning battles and wars. That may be attributed to luck and skill.[206] In fact, I can find here no record of somebody overwhelming the opposition by sheer force of numbers. But we do hear on occasion of the psychological boost that came with this kind of recruiting. For instance when, in 43, it became known at Rome that Cassius had managed to garner twelve legions in the east, the senate rejoiced.[207]

I believe that it was in two particular areas that the mutinous attitude of the soldiers was decisive in determining the course of history. Whatever other motives drove Octavian and Antony into partnership and impelled them to continue in it, the attitude of their soldiers was decisive here. To start with, the soldiers would not allow them to pursue private quarrels while the Tyrannicides went unpunished. Then, after Philippi, they would not support Octavian in his attempt to fight Antony, whom they regarded as the victor. The other instance is Lepidus. It was the desertion of his troops which finished him off as a political force and thus brought closer the final encounter between Octavian and Antony.

(d) Conclusion

The *sacramentum* or oath taken by the soldier on enlistment was a pledge to obey the commands of the lawfully constituted magistrate of the republic under whom he was to serve.[208] To violate this by mutiny, desertion or the like was a serious matter. We can see this from the fact that the violator became *sacer* and thus liable for the most extreme punishments. We have also seen how many did wantonly and without regard break their oath. But we need also to be aware the *sacramentum* was not an act of fealty to the Roman state itself but rather, as we have said, to one of its representatives. In times of civil war, though, a commander's legitimacy was often doubtful and his standing a matter of dispute. Hence the soldiers sometimes decided – and were often encouraged to do so by a rival general – that lawful authority lay elsewhere and so they went there.[209]

Acts of disobedience of the sort we have to consider are to be found, in the main, in the periods of civil strife.[210] Thus we find them in the period of the Social and the First Civil Wars and then again in the Second Civil War and the Triumviral period.[211]

Mutiny is to be found in all periods but tends to predominate in the earlier.[212] Its nature, however, changes with time. In the Social War especially, we witness, I think, a widespread but inchoate anger which arises from diverse causes.[213] By the time Caesar had to face down his men, things were different. These soldiers were articulate and they knew what they wanted: money and land.[214] And that was how it was, too, for the Triumvirs. For all the praise that is sometimes heaped on Caesar for his handling of the mutiny, there is no escaping the fact he had to give in to the demands made upon him, and so in turn did the Triumvirs. The soldiers got what they wanted.

Certainly in all periods mutineers went largely unpunished, but this simple statement could, if we are not careful, mask the great change which had occurred. The motive for forbearance was the same in all cases. With the desperate need for manpower nobody could afford to alienate his soldiers. Where there came a difference was in the position of those who forbore. In the Social War, and arguably in the First Civil,[215] commanders could claim to act as they did in the legitimate interests of the state. By the time we come to Caesar his legitimacy is doubtful and that of the Triumvirs is questionable indeed.[216] Hence they were vulnerable in a way the earlier commanders had not been and became a prey for demanding troops.[217]

Nevertheless we have to recognise the comparative rarity of mutiny after the Social War and we can explain it if we are prepared to be daring and speak of 'mutiny without alternative'. When the Romans engaged a foreign foe they were not given to deserting in great numbers. Hence in the Social War they had no other means of expressing discontent or seeking a remedy for grievance and so we have 'mutiny without alternative'. But, as we know, in times of civil war, they could desert to the other side and be made welcome.[218]

Syme's dictum that 'Sulla could not abolish his own example' has virtually achieved the status of a mantra.[219] In this department deservedly. He appears to have been the first to practise the art of seduction of other men's troops. The novelty of his procedure may be gauged from Carbo's famous chagrined remark about the lion and the fox.[220] Naturally he found imitators first in Caesar and then the Triumvirs, under whom, as we saw above, changes of allegiance proceeded at a dizzying pace. In the case of both Sulla and Caesar it is possible to argue that over and above the desire to increase their own numbers, or at least neutralise the forces of the enemy, they also sought to limit the duration of the war. It is very difficult to claim that last for the reptilian Octavian who, with his ceaseless seductions, can be seen as Sulla's bastard heir.

Only occasionally do we catch a glimpse of the psychological effect which came with switches of allegiance. A lot of the time such changes and mutinies had no decisive effect on the course of events, but there were occasions in the Triumviral period when they had. It was in those days, too, that they may have done something to prolong the war in that they were one of the main ways the protagonists had of filling their ranks.

6

THE REVOLUTIONARY ARMY FROM SULLA TO AUGUSTUS

Now that we have examined the differing facets of the question piecemeal and in detail, we are in a position to offer a broad and comprehensive picture of the role of the Roman army in the Roman revolution.[1]

I hold that in order to understand properly the role played by the army in the revolution we have first of all to give full recognition to the fact that that role was played out over roughly two generations. We speak of a period which stretched from the time of Marius and Sulla[2] to that of Octavian who became Augustus. This I submit should at least lead us to wonder if, over such a stretch of time, there is not the possibility for development and change and that the static view of the revolutionary army as something fully formed and unchanging from its inception may not fit the case. We are fortunate in being able to pinpoint the exact moment revolutionary potential was revealed but we can also see clearly that further innovations were to follow. We can put the point in a kind of shorthand by reference to those who commanded these armies. Sulla was not Caesar.[3] And Octavian was not Caesar.[4] In other words, a statement that is valid for one age and its representative revolutionary figure may not be valid for another.

If we keep this before our minds as we approach our sources we shall discover that in one crucial passage (*Sulla* 12) Plutarch demonstrates that he, at least, could not make such a distinction. He depicts the army of Sulla as having the same characteristics as those of the Triumvirs and its leader in terms appropriate to them but not to himself. In view of our uncertainty as to how Plutarch arrived at this conclusion it seems unfair to accuse him of deliberately adopting a static approach, although we cannot acquit him of giving us a kind of ahistorical back projection.[5] Actually, divining the source of Plutarch's error is probably of less moment than recognising that he has been uncritically followed by a number of modern scholars, with a consequent misunderstanding of the particular period.

As we start our investigations proper we find that some current notions about what Marius did are misconceived. Because of the emphasis modern historians put upon his reforms of 107 we have, for ease of discussion, begun our consideration of the beginning of the revolutionary army at that point where it is conventionally supposed to have had its start, but researches reveal Marius did few, if any, of the things he is sometimes supposed to have done. He did not make of the Roman army an army of mercenaries; he did not preside over legions who were concerned only with material reward to the exclusion of all other considerations; he did not introduce into the ranks a body of men intent on pursuing their own special objectives. Above all he did not create a revolutionary army.

There appears to be general scholarly consensus that the number of *capite censi* that Marius admitted in 107 was quite small and that commanders who came after him did not follow his example. They had no need, for their requirements were met by enrolling those who had a property qualification. It was not until the Social War with its great demands for manpower that commanders turned once more to the landless, a source that was to be tapped again and again in the great conflicts which followed. Yet now and later these men remain elusive, for all of the alleged importance many attribute to them. We have no exact numbers for them nor do we know how they stood in proportion to the men of property in the legions. All we can say for certain is that there may have been more of them in the Triumviral armies than earlier. Nor do we find them, as we have remarked, forming a distinct group with interests and areas of their own to prosecute. Plainly those who have and those who have not as soldiers share a common outlook. Irrespective of competence, all have been absorbed into the same ethos.

The subscription of all legionaries to the same ideals and the failure of the Marian reform to create a revolutionary temper can be seen first of all in the economic motivation for the action of the troops in 88. They followed Sulla because they feared, rightly or wrongly, that if Marius took command he would lead other troops to the east and they would lose the Mithridatic booty. Quite simply this is a constant. The Roman soldier ever, regardless of what he owned, hoped to profit by war, and the needy, and perhaps less needy, now continued to think precisely as their ancestors had. There is nothing new here.

On the political level there is of course something new but it has nothing to do with Marius. The latter did not create some kind of new army which Sulla was the first to exploit. To put it in Herodotean terms, Sulla did not put on a Marian shoe because there was no shoe there in the first place. Indeed we must take from him the accolade (if that is the right word) he is sometimes accorded of showing remarkable insight in seeing possibilities in the Marian army which its creator failed to spot. What Sulla did shows no particular insight at all.

The issue of historical inevitability can best be left to the philosopher. However the working historian can recognise from time to time in history a given set of circumstances awaiting a moment for a trigger or catalyst to produce a result almost entirely predictable. What happened in 88 was one of those occasions.[6] The increasing violence of Roman political life meant that men sought to protect themselves by counter-violence. Self-evidently the army would, on the surface, seem to provide the best protection of all, and it is safe to say that sooner or later somebody would try and find out if it really did. Had Sulla not turned to the legions, then I maintain somebody else in trouble would have. As it was, the purest chance and accident of his position meant that it fell to him to discover and exploit for the first time the revolutionary potential of the Roman army. To put it bluntly: he, not Marius, created the revolutionary army.

Seeking precision, we can describe what Sulla did on that day in 88 in various ways. We could accuse him of corrupting the *contio*, for he introduced into the military gathering issues and concerns which had no business there but properly belonged in its civil counterpart in the city. I would hazard a guess and say that Sulla himself, who declared he wished to rid Rome of tyrants,[7] would probably have said he had read his men a fundamental political lesson: Rome's enemies were not always to be found beyond her gates; sometimes they were to be discovered cavorting in the Forum. However I believe the most apt formulation, because it brings out the consequences of the act and the indisputably ruinous precedent it set, is that which says Sulla politicised the Roman army. The men he addressed, irrespective of origin or status, had sunk their individuality in a common military identity. They were not now being asked to slough off that identity, but were however invited to remember they were also citizens. They were called to participate directly in politics, have a view on the issues of the day and help to settle them by force of arms.

Once or twice in the course of this work I have been at pains to emphasise that the grasp the ranker had of these issues was often uncertain and his response simplistic, being at times little more than subscription to a slogan. This, however, does not upset our thesis in any way. The Romans are not the only people to have had limited political perceptions and act upon them. We can easily acknowledge too that slogans are often very potent indeed.[8] In incidents such as the negotiations between Sulla and Scipio Asiagenus we catch a glimpse of what seem to have been sophisticated exchanges, but we do not need to assume that every legionary had a copy of *de Republica* in his knapsack in order to envisage him functioning as a political animal. Pondering the behaviour of the citizen in assembly helps further to put matters in perspective. There his reaction was often simplistic and he could be changeable. The fate of Caius Gracchus is instructive for us when we contemplate former Caesarians, despite the initial misgivings of Brutus and Cassius, quite happily serving in the army of the Liberators. Like the modern elector from one election to another, the Roman, be he citizen or soldier, could change his mind. We may deplore his motivation. We cannot deny that it was his right.

Sulla then was not at the head of an army of mercenaries nor was he able as a patron to call out men who were his clients. But there were two circumstances, one personal and one characteristic of the times in which he lived, which may have made it just that little bit easier for his troops to follow him. On the personal level his charisma had, a little while before, been enhanced when he was awarded a grass crown for saving his men from great danger.[9] Speaking in a more general fashion we recognise that this was a time when mutiny was common and in the prevailing atmosphere a number of armies got rid of their commanders. Thus Sulla's men will have had few qualms when they resisted the pretensions of Marius.

Desertion, of course, is sometimes the consequence of, sometimes a substitute for, mutiny. In the Social War mutiny was the favoured mode of expressing discontent, for the Roman soldier did not normally desert *en masse* to a foreign foe. With the coming of the First Civil War there was now a change. Not only did desertion become more common but it was positively encouraged, especially by Sulla. People were being invited to come over to the right side.

We of course can see that there were two great periods of mutiny and desertion in the last century of the republic and they coincided with the two periods of turmoil and violence which, though separated by a generation, were responsible for the state's destruction: the period of the Social and First Civil Wars and the period of the Second Civil War and the Triumvirate. That this should be so is hardly remarkable. A comparison of the two periods however will prove enlightening.

To begin with, in that second period desertion tends to lose that slightly pejorative colouring imparted to it by our sources, especially Plutarch, in the earlier. Then enticement of the enemy, particularly by Sulla,[10] is often represented as something underhand accomplished by outright bribery. Whether this echoes contemporary opinion or is rather the writer's own moralising I cannot pretend to say. But what is certain is that Caesar, in the next generation, fell under no such opprobrium when he imitated Sulla, whom even the most hostile sources acknowledge to be a master in the art of seducing other people's armies. Both men had the same objectives: to increase the size of their armies and shorten the length of the war.[11] Increase became the principal objective and the practice itself became ever more widespread with Octavian, Sulla's most distinguished imitator in this department at least. This is directly attributable to the current state of the Roman world. Desperate to fill their ranks in order to destroy their common enemies and then each other, the Triumvirs did not scruple to use every means possible to add to their numbers.

Returning to mutiny, we soon discover that its nature has undergone even greater change than desertion. In our first period of domestic strife it can be said to be the expression of blind rage. The troops of the day simply lashed out at their commanders. When we come to the second we find that the mutineers have set and definite aims and are not afraid to articulate them.[12] We encounter this for the first time in the two mutinies Caesar had to face down. The theme and the issues are clear: conditions of service, and reward when that service is done.

In the earlier of the two periods of strife the role of the soldier is essentially to react, not imitate. Thus, twice Sulla's troops signal approval of a programme of political action which is entirely of his devising and without demur they accept such booty and land as he gives them. This acquiescence is, of course, classic behaviour for Roman troops and we must emphasise it continues after the First Civil War is done. Pompey's troops make no fuss when at campaign's end land is voted but then not given.

Everybody knows that once Sulla had by his march on Rome created the revolutionary army, he almost immediately found imitators. Just a few months later, Cinna's actions match his in every particular: worsted in street violence which took its rise from a political quarrel, he fled to the army. There he laid a political pro-gramme before the troops and assured them they should have their accustomed soldierly recompense. War and the good things of victory then followed.[13] Speaking in broad general terms those who came after Cinna acted in essentially the same manner. There may be variations in the details of their stories but at base these men set a political agenda before their men with the assurance, explicit or not, that they would enjoy the booty which was always the soldier's expectation. However in the next generation Sulla's imitators differ from the master in three respects. The first of these accounts for the changed nature of mutiny we remarked upon earlier.

Knowing as we do what Caesar achieved, it is easy to forget that initially his position was insecure. His troops were aware of this and for the first time took the initiative, demanding what before they would have been content to receive and Caesar, it may be emphasised, had to give.[14] Of course, these were simply episodes in his career and he was able eventually to stamp his authority on events. Yet they boded ill, for it was far otherwise with his self-proclaimed and unworthy heirs, the Triumvirs.

Although they attempted to give their rule the cloak of legality these men were even less secure than Caesar had been. Although they claimed to be acting in the interests of the state and to be advancing its interests, it is difficult to escape the conclusion they were warlords pure and simple who had flourished in and contrib-uted to the weakness of that state. There is every reason to suppose that their power rested on foundations much less stable than that of Sextus Pompey, whom they lost no opportunity of denigrating as an outsider and a renegade.

From this weakening of the authority of the leader there follows the need to recruit as widely as possible in order to shore up that authority or merely, at times, to survive. And such recruiting did not just mean abandoning the levy. It also involved the subversion of other people's troops. Of course, those taken into the ranks by such irregular methods still expected to be rewarded. No more than in the case of the armies of Sulla and Caesar do we find, however, some special class of landless men pressing their own particular suit. Rather we are witnessing some-thing which is ageless but perverted. It is ageless in that, in an undifferentiated fashion, the legionary, irrespective of origin, looks forward to booty. But it is per-verted because reward comes not from conquering a foreign enemy but from oppressing the subjects of Rome. And the demand for reward has become insist-ent. The legionary knows his own worth and, it may be said, the worth of those in authority over him, so in consequence he is not afraid to demand. His attitude is sometimes characterised as mercenary and it may very well be such a charge is not totally without foundation. Yet, on the other hand, I for one find it difficult wholly to condemn needy men if they sought an advantage for themselves in a sit-uation created by the merciless and unscrupulous. In a further effort to put the matter into perspective we can finally recall that this kind of behaviour was not unknown in the assembly. There the citizen instituted no comprehensive revolu-tionary programme, but he could on occasion extract limited material benefit from his betters.

Out of this logically follows the Triumviral record of extortion. Sulla's Civil War was over quickly and was, in part at least, bankrolled by the booty of a foreign campaign in Asia.[15] Caesar, in the earlier days, also tried to avoid being a burden to Italy and the provinces but when we come to the Triumvirs we find prolonged warfare being paid for by every means possible. Nothing illustrates the distinction I am trying to draw between the generations better than the various settlements of Italy. When Sulla set his afoot he was beholden to no one; he was not answering a call for land from any quarter. In consequence, aside from doing what was right for his men, he was able to accomplish twin aims. He chastised his enemies and at the same time set about restoring the prosperity of Italy. As we look back on his work we can see that he accomplished what was virtually Rome's second conquest of Italy. Caesar was different. In contrast to Sulla he made his settlement in response to a definite call from his mutinous troops. Over and above this he had no discernible aims to pursue. Recognising the ill feeling created by Sulla's scrambling of the population of Italy, he did all in his power to purchase the land he required. For Octavian, however, such a course was not possible. His troops made it clear they wished to be settled and he had no choice but to give them exactly what they wanted. In order to do this he embarked on a scheme of expropriation which equalled that of Sulla perhaps, but which had no discernible purpose save his own self-preservation.

But we cannot just speak of the economic factor; we must also reckon with the political which parallels it, because it is a manifestation of the same attitude. In the age of the Triumvirs, soldiers had still to be enthused. We can think of the Liberators with their call to Freedom or of Octavian who rallied the legions to destroy a foreign queen. But, as in the material, there is here in this department, too, a like development. Soldiers who clamour for loot also make their political opinions known spontaneously. When Octavian and Antony appear to be somewhat hesitant in pursuing Caesar's murderers they are soon reminded by their men of where their duty lies. Again Octavian's troops may offer to obtain an office for him but they also arrange a political match for him.

At the present time there is much debate about just what role the assemblies really played in the working of the Roman constitution and how great was the actual power of the people. There is therefore a certain frisson involved in contemplating what is happening here. Just as the Roman republic was coming to an end the Roman citizen, for the first and only time, realised his latent potential. Being under arms and having weak masters he was able to initiate and dictate policy. This of course did not last. When Octavian restored the republic (or at least created his own version of it) there could be no place for such things. The common soldier, along with the common citizen, was thrust back into his position of subordination.

The imitation of Sulla by the leading men of the period of Caesar and the Triumvirate provides a clear element of continuity with that earlier generation. But here again we detect a vital difference. People still deployed the revolutionary army as a weapon but for different ends from those that Sulla had.[16] He fought

98

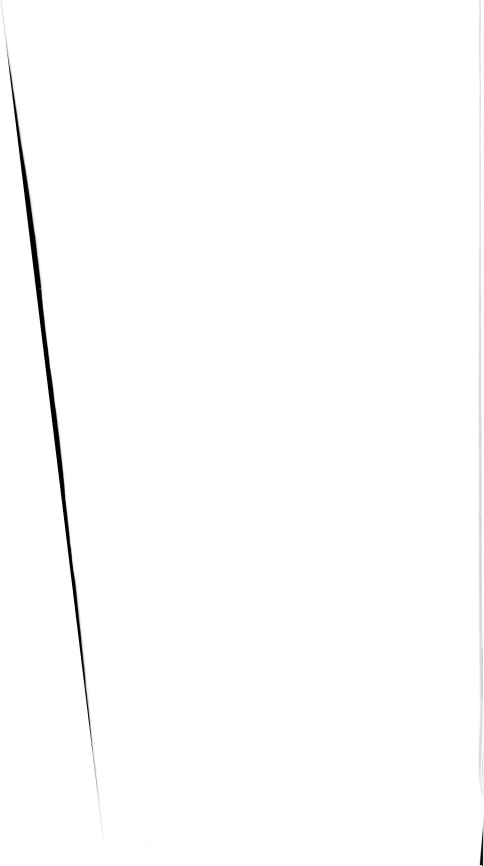

to re-establish senatorial government and used his victory to bring in laws to strengthen the republic. Caesar's ultimate aims are a matter of dispute, with monarchical ambitions being attributed to him then and now, but few doubt that he destroyed senatorial power. The impotence of Cicero and his friends abundantly illustrates this. The Liberators briefly offered the possibility of the preservation of the republic. The Triumvirs for a time showed little interest in anything except revenge and self-preservation. Eventually one of them, Octavian, began to grope his way towards a solution of the state's contemporary problems.[17] Like Sulla, he too sought the goals of order, stability and renewal, but the ord_ he established, for all its deliberate superficial resemblance to the ways of old, r far different from that of his predecessor.

In the 1790s when the French revolutionary armies swept across Europe were inspired by novel and exciting doctrines which they were anxious to abroad. The armies of the last century of the Roman republic were no less tionary but their concerns were far different. They were invited to int_ domestic affairs. Apprised of the state of contemporary politics they int_ armed citizens. Two periods of such intervention brought diverse resul_ intervention, however momentarily, brought the possibility of salv_ republic. The second brought its destruction.

Appendix 1

THE CONSPIRACY OF CATILINE

Between the failed coup of Lepidus (cos.78) and the rather more successful one of Caesar in 49 only one instance of insurgency is recorded, the conspiracy of Catiline.[1]

In one respect the inspiration for this plot is Sullan. That is to say that while the conspirators, as we shall see in a moment, sought different things from Sulla, they nevertheless looked to him as a model for what might be accomplished by direct violent action. Catiline had had first-hand experience of this as a participant in the First Civil War, and should he ever forget it he had P. Cornelius Lentulus to remind him of the prophecy which said three Cornelii were destined to rule Rome.[2]

But as we have just said, Catiline and his fellows did not seek what Sulla sought. When Sulla made his move he had already made a success of his life. Victorious over the Samnites, he was now consul and about to conduct an eastern war. Already formulating notions for the reform of the state, he had much to lose and he acted to preserve it. In contrast the Catilinarians were to all intents and purposes failures. Catiline himself is paradigmatic. He came from an old patrician family but yet had made three unsuccessful bids for the consulship. These were men who had not advanced as far in their careers as they expected. In some cases they had been knocked back, and many felt that other unworthy men occupied offices of state which were rightly theirs.[3] In some cases tempers may have been further sharpened by debt.[4]

The solution to their woes which Catiline promised those who would follow him could be said to have a certain elegant simplicity but to be lacking in the complexity and sophistication of Sulla's legislation. Catiline declared his associates would have *libertas*, riches, honour and glory. These would be gained by wiping out those now in power, taking their places and abolishing debt.[5]

But a group of disgruntled aristocrats does not make a revolution on its own. Wider support must be drawn upon, and for this the Catilinarians turned to Italy.[6] The recruiting sergeant, if we may so phrase it, turned up in virtually every region of the peninsula.[7] The main area however was Etruria. These Italians dispossessed by Sulla made common cause with his settlers who had come to ruin.[8]

Sulla, Cinna and Lepidus had of course recruited in Italy but in one vital aspect Catiline differed from them.[9] They already stood at the head of the armies which they were now supplementing. Catiline was raising his own illegitimate force. In so doing he was directly exploiting the habitual misery of the countryside. He stands in the line of those who sought to stir the peasantry from their wonted passivity. If he has a predecessor it is Flaminius the tribune of 232; if he has a successor it must be Milo in 48.[10] The availability of veterans from the Sullan wars is not especially significant.[11] There had always been ex-soldiers living in rural areas. What is significant is that this is one of the occasions they found a leader. The Roman peasant will not initiate: he will await someone like Catiline to give him direction.[12]

Thus, in whatever other ways we regard Catiline,[13] we cannot make of him the leader of a revolutionary Roman army. Rather he tried to capitalise on the grievances of the Roman peasant.

Appendix 2

SELECT CHRONOLOGY

107	Marius admits *capite censi* to the army.
103	Saturninus' first land law.
100	Saturninus' second land law.
91	Social War begins.
89	First Mithridatic War begins.
88	Sulla's march on Rome.
87	Cinna and Marius take Rome. End of Social War.
85	End of First Mithridatic War.
83	Rome's First Civil War begins.
82	First Civil War ends.
81	Constitution and land settlement of Sulla.
78	Revolt of consul Lepidus.
77	Lepidus' revolt suppressed.
72	Death of Sertorius.
70(?)	Lands voted to Pompey's soldiers but not granted.
63	Rullus' land bill. Conspiracy of Catiline.
60	Pompey's request for land for eastern veterans rejected by senate.
59	Caesar as consul obtains land for Pompey's veterans.
59–49	Caesar campaigns in Gaul.
49	Second Civil War begins. Caesar campaigns in Spain.
48	Pharsalus. Caesar at Alexandria.
47	Caesar in Asia Minor. His land settlement begins. He campaigns in Africa.
46	Caesar's African campaign continues.
45	Caesar campaigns again in Spain.
44	Assassination of Caesar.
43	Siege of Mutina. Establishment of Triumvirate.
42	Philippi. Octavian begins settlement of Italy.
41	Perusine War.
40	Peace of Brundisium.
39	Peace of Misenum.

36 Octavian eliminates Sextus Pompey and fellow Triumvir Lepidus.

31 Actium.

Note: for more details consult MRR.

NOTES

1 Introduction

1   App.*BC*.1.98–104. For Appian, Sulla's dictatorship is also a tyranny. Cf. also *BC*.1.3.

2   See n.6.

3   Appian himself points out that, in contrast to Caesar, Sulla restored *demokratia*. Caesar, of course, he believed aimed at kingship – see App.*BC*.2.107–11.

4   Compare Tac.*Ann*.1.1.

5   Hence the title of Syme (1939) where it is narrated and analysed.

6   The power wielded by the people has, of late, been scrutinised, a scrutiny initiated by Millar (1998). But ultimately we cannot evade the fact that their assemblies never realised whatever potential they might have had, in either the legislative or the electoral sphere, and never mounted a serious sustained challenge to the ruling oligarchy. I believe that here we should follow Gabba (2003) p. 187 rather than Millar. He says, 'we must distinguish between the political use of a formality deemed indispensable, and effective participation, even under guidance, in a political decision'.

7   For the emperor as the source of all power see Tac.*Ann*.1.2–3 with Syme (1939) pp. 369–86. Syme (1939) p. 7 speaks of an oligarchy behind this façade, a notion Brunt (1988) p. 4 dismisses as 'banal'. But there is no contradiction here. There was still an oligarchy of birth and wealth but it was no longer freestanding. Its position depended on the goodwill of the emperor. Brunt's further contention that our system with its small ruling class, answerable to an electorate, is an oligarchy only in the literal sense of 'rule of the few' is disingenuous. As a member of an Oxford College, Brunt must have known we are speaking here of an 'oligarchy of position' which refreshes itself and recruits by the exercise of patronage and not by appeal to birth.

8   Not, of course, as great as the subsequent fall of the empire.

9   For discussions see Brunt (1988) pp. 68–81; Smith (1955) pp. 47–72; Greenidge (1904) pp. 1–99.

10 See 2(b).

11 It may be noted that these struggles were not invariably violent. Marius achieved his first consulship peacefully after taking advantage of a *popularis* movement. See Sall.*Jug*.84.

12 Wiseman (2002) pp. 285–310 attempts to explain the history of the late republic as a struggle of *optimates* and *populares*. The attempt founders on the intermittent nature of the struggle. Cf. Meier (1966) p. 208.

13 It is well known that Gruen (1995) unconvincingly maintained this was so even in its final years.

14 Evans (2003) p. 153 n.46 suggests Marius and Sulpicius made the mistake of supposing Sulla would simply give way as Metellus Numidicus had in 107: MRR1.553.

15 See further below.

16 Interestingly he was the first reformer since Tiberius Gracchus not to meet a violent end.

17 The mistaken view that Sulla's reforms were the work of several years can be found for instance in Mackay (2004) p. 132.

18 Hence I style him the 'last republican' (2005b).

19 Sulla himself cannot have been in any doubt about what could happen. After all, he had had to deal with Cinna in 88 and Lepidus in 80.

20 Brunt (1988) p. 72 emphasises the desire for security after the Civil War.

21 In the nineteenth century this oligarchy was sometimes castigated as essentially worthless. It might be fairer to say they were probably no worse than any other group of politicians to be found at other times and in other places.

22 On Caesar's contempt for institutions see Meier (1996) pp. 358–60, 449–50.

23 See Hatscher (2000) pp. 179–80.

24 One is irresistibly reminded of the United States, where supposed injuries to *amour propre* awaken calls for redress. The difference, however, is that in the States nothing more than frivolous lawsuits result. In Rome there came the destruction of the republic.

25 Seager (2002) p. 171; Meier (1996) pp. 364–7. Contra Jehne (1987).

26 See his own admission in Suet.*Div.Jul.*77.

27 Though it should not be forgotten that their dominance was, for a time, challenged by Sextus Pompey, son of Pompey the Great. For him see Hadas (1930) and Powell and Welch (2002).

28 I have deliberately lightly annotated this section. The essential detailed information may be found in Scullard (1982) together with citation of sources and modern bibliography. More recently, Mackay (2004) and Bringman (2002) also offer dependable narratives and further bibliography. Boatwright, Gargola and Talbert (2004) cannot be recommended, being wordy in exposition, eccentric in citation of ancient sources and thin in references to modern work.

29 Background: Keaveney (2005b) pp. 69–72.

30 Trans.: R. Warner (Penguin).

31 Brunt (1988) p. 257 n.78; Meier (1966) pp. 103, 240; Nicolet (1977) p. 135; Wiehn (1926) p. 92.

32 See, for example, Beard and Crawford (1999) pp. 7–8; Potter (2004) pp. 83–4.

33 See further 2(a) on the warlord.

34 Keaveney (1983b) pp. 58–9.

35 On Sulla's position see Keaveney (2005b). The notion that the high have made themselves beholden to the low seems to underlie the similar charges made against Marius and others. Their careers, too, are on record and provide no support for it. There is another anachronism in Plut.*Sulla* 6. See further 5(b). The possibility of similar ahistorical writing in Dio is discussed in 3(b).

36 It has variously been suggested to me that Plutarch regarded Sulla as a corrupter (P. Stadter) or that, by the time he came to write, the rapacious and oppressive republican general had become a *topos* (John Madden). Plut.*Sulla* 30 suggests, however, he simply found Sulla a bit of a puzzle, as many have done. Note that others get the same treatment in Plut.*Brut.*29.

37 Trans.: J. Carter (Penguin).

38 Rudé (1964) pp. 132–5.

39 I do not share Jongmann's pessimism about writing of historical change: Jongmann (2003) pp. 120–1. Nor, self-evidently, do I believe, as he does, that we have to write static history. His descriptions of a 'world of changeless change' seem to me merely an unhelpful conceit.

40 Although the discussion largely proceeds along chronological lines within each section, this is not a narrative history. As an aid to the reader I have therefore appended a table of events in Appendix 2 at the end of the book. Except where they are obviously AD, all dates are BC.

2 The leaders and the led

1 See 3.

2 To the possible charge that some of what we are about to describe are simply *topoi* – see Paul (1984) p. 238 – we may reply that many of the figures we shall be considering were men of considerable attainment and thus it is difficult to see what else they might have done to achieve the greatness they undoubtedly possessed.

3 Plut.*Pomp*.64. Cf. Heftner (1995) p. 68.

4 Plut.*Mar*.34. Antony was another recorded exerciser and people said this was about the only good thing he did after being left in charge of Rome by Caesar in the Second Civil War (Plut.*Ant*.6).

5 Plut.*Mar*.20.

6 Plut.*Mar*.7; Sall.*Jug*.96. Antony is also said to have made himself popular in the mess (Plut.*Ant*.47).

7 Plut.*Caes*.17; Suet.*Div.Jul*.57.

8 Suet.*Div.Jul*.66.

9 We are talking here of day to day discipline – see Harmand (1967) pp. 418–19. Large-scale mutiny and the indiscipline of the Triumviral armies are matters for separate consideration See 5.

10 Suet.*Div.Jul*.65–7 with Butler and Cary (1927) p. 128. Wellington had something of the same attitude – see Longford (1992) p. 237.

11 Plut.*Sulla* 6 with Holden (1886) p. 76 and Keaveney (2005b) p. 74.

12 Wiehn (1926) pp. 93–5 emphasises the importance of the commander's personality.

13 Keaveney (1992) pp. 124–6.

14 Plut.*Mar*.21.

15 Keaveney (1992) pp. 108–9.

16 Plut.*Sulla* 19, 29 with Valgiglio (1960) pp. 90–1; Keaveney (2005b) pp. 78–80, 122.

17 Plut.*Sert*.19 with Konrad (1994) pp. 168–9 and Goldsworthy (1996) p. 162 who draws attention to Caes.*BG*1.52 where a legate orchestrated a necessary manoeuvre. Conversely we read in Plut.*Mar*.26 how Marius lost contact with his left wing at Vercellae, a report which should perhaps be treated with some scepticism as it is by Valgiglio (1956) p. 120 and Carney (1970) p. 39. See now however Evans (2003) p. 34.

18 Caes.*BG*3.14, 6.43, 7.17. Cf. Plut.*Caes*.16 and Goldsworthy (1996) p. 163.

19 App.*Mith*.49. Cf. Harmand (1967) p. 464.

20 *BC*.3.69, *BG*.2.25.

21 Plut.*Caes*.52; Suet.*Div.Jul*.62 with Butler and Cary (1927) p. 126.

22 App.*BC*.2.81.

23 Plut.*Crass*.26.

24 For the general who leads from the rear see Goldsworthy (1996) pp. 150–4.

25 Even though, as Goldsworthy (1996) p. 159 points out, the uniforms of both sides in a civil war will have been pretty much the same.

26 *Sulla* 2.

27 Plut.*Ant*.4. Trans.: I. Scott-Kilvert (Penguin).

28 Caesar: Suet.*Div.Jul*.45; Pompey: Plut.*Pomp*.2; Lucullus: Keaveney (1992) p.6. Honourable scars earned in battle might, one supposes, be distinguishing features for display but Roman attitudes here were somewhat complex and tended actually towards the reserved. See the useful discussion of Evans (1999).

29 Plut.*Luc*.28. Trans.: B. Perrin (Loeb). *De Vir.Illust*.74 praises his dress sense.

30 Plut.*Crass*.23.

31 App.*BC*.2.90.

32 See Gelzer (1968) pp. 246–52.

33 Plut.*Pomp*.35.

34 Plut.*Pomp*.19.

35 Keaveney (2005b) pp. 14–16.
36 Plut.*Pomp*.7. Here is recorded the first of three single combats engaged in by Pompey. For the others see *Pomp*.19, 35 already referred to above.
37 Suet.*Div.Jul*.61 with Butler and Cary (1927) pp. 125–6.
38 Plut.*Sulla* 29.
39 Brunt (1988) p. 261, for instance, is cursory. Harmand (1967) pp. 462–4 is more informative but still brief.
40 On personal faith see the discussion of individual commanders below.
41 Goldsworthy (1996) p. 250 perhaps underestimates the importance of religious ritual for the soldier.
42 The absence of a mention of a 'rôle culturel' for Caesar in the *de Bello Gallico* does not mean he did not perform it. See Harmand (1967) pp. 464–5 and the remarks below.
43 For a description of a general from an earlier period doing this see Val.Max.7.2.5.
44 See Keaveney (1982b) for a full discussion.
45 Plut.*Sulla* 9, 17, 27.
46 Plut.*Crass*.19 with Angeli Bertinelli (1993) pp. 405–6. Lucullus had considerably happier dealings with this river. See nn.50, 56.
47 *Bell.Af*.75. The term *lustratio* in *BG*.8.52 may mean no more than 'reviewed'. See Harmand (1967) p. 464 n.189.
48 Plut.*Brut*.39.
49 I make no judgement on whether some were *post eventum* or contemporary whose full significance was only realised after the disaster.
50 Plut.*Crass*.19, 23 with Angeli Bertinelli (1993) pp. 405, 409–10; Val.Max.1.6.11 with Mueller (2002) p. 156.
51 Plut.*Luc*.24 with Piccirilli (1990) pp. 316–17 and Keaveney (1992) p. 105.
52 Plut.*Sulla* 27 with Keaveney (2005b) pp. 106–8.
53 Suet.*Div.Jul*.59. See Front.*Strat*.1.12.2.
54 Front.*Strat*.1.12.4.
55 Keaveney (2005b) pp. 108–9.
56 Beard et al. (1998) pp. 84–7; Mueller (2002) pp. 103–5.
57 Plut.*Mar*.17 where other relevant signs and portents are also listed; Front.*Strat*.1.11.12; Val.Max.1.2.3a, cf. Mueller (2002) p. 70.
58 Keaveney (2005b) pp. 33–5 and further Keaveney (1983a) pp. 45–9.
59 For an exception see n.44.
60 Keaveney (1983a) pp. 55–69 especially pp. 60–5 for Sulla. Pompey: Beard et al. (1998) pp. 144–5.
61 *Pro.Leg.Man*.47–8. The most reasonable suggestion is that Pompey took his from Sulla, cf. Wistrand (1987) pp. 39–41.
62 But significantly not Sulla.
63 The aid of wind and weather which Cicero mentions is not a frigid conceit but a genuine manifestation of *felicitas* which could alter the forces of nature. Compare, from Sulla's career, the rainstorm which followed the surrender of the Acropolis garrison because of thirst (Plut.*Sulla*. 14); the wreathing of weapons by flowers from a nearby meadow which foretold victory (Plut.*Sulla* 27); the rain which held off until Sulla's funeral was completed (Plut.*Sulla* 38).
64 Lucullus: Keaveney (1992) pp. 82, 85, 105, 108–9. Sulla: Keaveney (1983a) pp. 58–9, (2005) pp. 71–2, 169.
65 Meier (1996) pp. 400–1 seems to take this view.
66 Lukewarm belief: Weinstock (1971) pp. 26–8; Atheism: bibliography in Harmand (1967) p. 465 n.191.
67 Weinstock (1971) pp. 112–16.
68 See briefly Mueller (2002) pp. 109–10.

69 So Plut.*Sert*.11–12, 20; Val.Max.1.2.4 and Gell.15.2.4 but not App.*BC*.1.110. Cf. also Front.*Strat*.1.11.13.

70 As do for instance Wardle (1998) p.141 and Spann (1987) p. 63.

71 See Konrad (1994) pp. 123–4, 171.

72 App.*BC*.2.116, 152–3; Suet.*Div.Jul*.59.

73 Plut.*Caes*.52; Suet.*Div.Jul*.59; Dio 42.58.1.

74 Plutarch thought it might. Weinstock (1971) p. 98 offers no reason for his belief that the story is entirely fictional. It may not be inappropriate to recall here that Plutarch (*Mar*.17) said some people thought Marius' devotion to Martha was feigned. He himself was suspicious of charlatans (*Mar*.42).

75 Lintott (1968) p. 40 n.2 is not adequate here.

76 Plut.*Ant*.22, *Quaest.Rom*.83. Plutarch pointedly contrasts Antony's chivalrous behaviour towards Brutus' body.

77 Keaveney (2005b) p. 129.

78 Dio 43.24. 3, 48.48.5.

79 Suet.*Div.Aug*.15; Dio 48.14.3–4.

80 Syme (1939) p. 212 for instance.

81 Made by Weinstock (1971) pp. 398–9.

82 It should not be forgotten that even Crassus had had his successes.

83 *Bell.Af*.31.

84 3(a).

85 3(b).

86 3(b).

87 3(c).

88 See (d) below.

89 A consideration of the broader 'charisma' will be found in (d) below.

90 Brunt (1988) pp. 253–5, 276–8. Cf. Gabba (1976) pp. 24–6; Gruen (1995) pp. 367–8. The behaviour of city troops in the Social War, 5(b), points to unreliability.

91 There is a lengthy exposition of this view in Greenidge (1904) pp. 59–86. It is stated more briefly in, for instance, Smith (1955) pp. 61–2; Beard and Crawford (1985) pp. 5–6; De Blois (1987) pp. 8–9; Rosenstein (2004) pp. 3–6.

92 (2004) pp. 26–56.

93 (2004) p. 155.

94 It is agreed the peasant was never totally wiped out. See Rich (1983) pp. 297–8 and Brunt (1988) pp. 246–7, 273 for instance. Jongmann's attempt (2003) pp. 111–13 to overthrow our literary evidence seems misconceived to me.

95 (2004) pp. 55, 91.

96 We can all agree soldiers returned with booty but Rosenstein (2004) tends to veer between minimising its impact (pp. 76, 163) and recognising its importance (pp. 81, 101). I should say that, given the low standard of living (see below), even a small amount of booty will have made a great difference to a man's fortunes.

97 (2004) p. 80.

98 Terrenato (1988) p. 104. It is worth remembering however that not everybody will have been in a position to accumulate such a surplus. In pre-famine Ireland most peasants could boast only of a pig and a manure heap: Woodham Smith (1962) p. 18.

99 Storage problems: Scheidel (2004) p. 7; Rosenstein (2004) p. 16 and more graphically Woodham Smith (1962) pp. 30–1. Roman famines: Virlouvet (1985) pp. 11–19, cf. Brunt (1987) pp. 703–6. France: Cobban (1963) p. 15; Rudé (1964) pp. 46–7.

100 (2004) pp. 60–1.

101 As he, in effect, admits in (2004) p. 223 nn.195 and 196.

102 Salmon (1970) pp. 55–81 followed by Rosenstein (2004) p. 59. See further below.

103 Brunt (1988) pp. 512–13.

104 (2004) p. 59.

105 Nicolet (1980) p. 117; Rich (1983) p. 326. See further 4(b).

106 The intermittent nature of colonial programmes may be seen from the catalogue in Salmon (1970) pp. 110–11. For their initiation by the Roman elite see Salmon (1970) p. 19 or Gargola (1995) pp. 52–3. For the first century see 4(a).

107 Incidentally manpower would not, as Rosenstein (2004) p. 153 seems to suppose, be lost by sending people to Latin colonies. These would still have to fight for Rome.

108 And this is sometimes underestimated. See 3(a).

109 (2004) pp. 144–5.

110 Rosenstein (2004) p. 271 n.19.

111 (1970) pp. 112–13.

112 Brunt (1987) pp. 193–4; Rathbone (1993) p. 147; Rosenstein (2004) pp. 57, 234 n.68.

113 Although there is debate on the matter – see Gabba (1967) p. 14 – it seems to me there is no reason to deny the existence of the tax mentioned by App.*BC*.1.7 or to evade the inference from the same passage that it was not collected in any systematic fashion.

114 Foxhall (1990) pp. 106–7; Rosenstein (2004) p. 78.

115 (2004) pp. 69–70. Brunt (1987) p. 137 shows a keener awareness of the issue, as does Jongmann (2003) p. 113.

116 Woodham Smith (1962) pp. 30–1. The eventual consequences are well known.

117 Livy 42.34. Cf. Harris (1971) p. 48; Harmand (1967) pp. 12 n.8, 231 n.2; Rathbone (1993) p. 145.

118 Such a plot would be viable with a potato crop – Woodham Smith (1962) pp. 24–31 – but not otherwise.

119 Against Brunt's doubts – (1987) p. 395 – about his eligibility for the levy see n.168. For a parallel case of economic hardship see Woodham Smith (1962) p. 23.

120 Livy 42.34.2: *in quo* surely refers solely to one *iugerum* while *donatus ab imperatoribus* (34.11) must refer to material rewards, for which see Goldsworthy (1996) p. 276. It beggars belief that in his long career Ligustinus was unable to garner some loot which, even on Rosenstein's minimalist view (see n.96), would have made a difference. An increase in acres need not be accompanied by the erection of a bigger house since at the time there was a certain vogue for the smaller dwelling – see Rosenstein (2004) p. 279 n.107.

121 Lough (1960) pp. 14–63; Rudé (1964) pp. 98–100.

122 For these see Rudé (1964) pp. 46–7 and Cobban (1963) p. 105.

123 Italian rural violence is catalogued in Brunt (1987) pp. 551–7. Many of the instances he records are later than this period however.

124 And rash if we thought only in terms of a failure to consume sufficient calories. On calories see Brunt (1987) pp. 137–8; Rosenstein (2004) pp. 69–70.

125 Despite his extravagant claims this emerges with great clarity from Millar (1998).

126 The Triumviral period is the exception. See 5(d).

127 MRR1.225. Rosenstein (2004) p. 154 takes this as evidence that, even after a comprehensive colonial programme, there still remained a surplus population to be drawn off, but equally the evidence is such as to permit us to say deracination was already well advanced, see de Sanctis (1967) pp. 323–4. In any case, in the desire of the elite to exploit the *ager publicus* we clearly have a clash of interest with the people. See n.106. For a later attempt to exploit rural discontent see Appendix 1.

128 In contrast with some other societies which witnessed rapid demographic change. De Blois (1987) p. 8 draws attention to such a rapid change in Holland between 1650 and 1750.

129 Rosenstein (2004) p. 223 n. 147.

130 App.*BC*.1.8, 10, 18 with Greenidge (1904) pp. 75–6.

131 ORF3 no. 152. Cf. Rosenstein (2004) p. 276 n.76. Brunt (1987) p. 395 is purely speculative.

132 Gabba (1976) pp. 5–12 has been questioned by Rich (1983) pp. 309–16; Lo Cascio (1990); Rathbone (1993).

133 Caius Gracchus seems to have decided to continue to implement his brother's schemes and make that implementation more effective. See Greenidge (1904) p. 209.

134 Plut.*Tib.Gracch*.8. Laelius' bill could have been introduced in either his tribunate, his praetorship (145) or his consulship (140). The date of the tribunate would fall between 160 and 147. On all of this see Taylor (1962) p. 24, who suggests 151 as the date of the tribunate. Astin (1967) pp. 307–11 contributes little save the suggestion the bill was proposed in the consulship and the distinctly odd notion that Laelius was not trying to deal with a crisis.

135 Cic.*de Offic*.2.73; MRR1.560. For the resemblance to Tiberius see n.73 below. Such misrepresentation of Philippus as Cicero may have made does not affect our argument. See 4(a) n.17.

136 Plut.*Tib.Gracch*.9.

137 See the start of this section.

138 See (2001) and especially p. 60 and see further nn. 85 and 86.

139 As may also be said of Scheidel (2004). The dilemma is neatly encapsulated either in Morley's inability to decide if the population of Augustan Italy was in the region of 5–6 million or 12–14 million or in the problems encountered in calculating the slave population: De Ligt (2004) p. 745.

140 So, for example, Rich (1983) pp. 296–7 and Morley (2001) p. 60.

141 Frere (1987) pp. 16–26.

142 Morley (2001) p. 60 seems to accept this.

143 (2004) pp. 17–18.

144 De Ligt (2004) p. 729 n.11.

145 In addition to the evidence cited above, see that collected by Astin (1967) pp. 171–2. For some further remarks on the value of this tradition see n.148. Contrast Rosenstein's approach with the naïve one of Jongmann (2003) p. 105.

146 (2004) pp. 156–7.

147 See Young (1929) pp. 276–7 with Maxwell's note p. 392.

148 Cobban (1963) pp. 22–6, 46, 56–62, 96–7, 103–6. The relentless opposition of vested interests to any attempt at reform may serve to answer Morley's question – (2001) p. 60 – why would the Roman nobility be so ready to oppose Gracchus if he had got it right? As with the French, they could not bear the sacrifices his schemes would entail. See further below.

149 As would Laelius.

150 Figures and discussion in Astin (1967) pp. 335–8 and Brunt (1987) pp. 70–83.

151 (2004) p. 157.

152 (1987) pp. 71, 79. See (1987) pp. 33–5 for factors which might lead to a defective census.

153 Cic.*Pro Arch*.9, *Pro Cluentio* 14; Dio 37.44.1.

154 So repeatedly Rosenstein (2004) pp. 59, 82, 157. See also Evans (1988) pp. 128–9, who unfortunately seems to take Brunt's hypothesis (n.152) as proven fact.

155 Herod.4.84, 7.27–9, 38–40, 60. On communications in the empire see Keaveney (2003b) pp. 30–2. On the levy Dandamaev and Lukonin (1989) p. 233.

156 The evidence, collected by Brunt (1987) pp. 391–2, is anecdotal but nevertheless suggestive.

157 Evans (1988) pp. 124–6.

158 De Ligt (2004) p. 744 does not seem to have allowed for this.

159 Harris (1971) pp. 41–53; Rich (1983) pp. 316–18; Rosenstein (2004) p. 60, 157; De Ligt (2004) pp. 742–3.

160 It is, perhaps, worth adding that what we have just said about Tiberius also holds good for his predecessor Laelius.

161 A century separates Greenidge (1904) p. 111 and Rosenstein (2004) p. 156 but they both make the same point.

162 Note that Philippus claimed only two thousand people owned property in the state (Cic. *de Offic*.2.73).

163 (2004) p. 156.

164 (2004) p. 165.

165 Thus, incidentally, the people in question would evade the normal fate of the vagabond: descent into brigandage – Cobban (1963) pp. 48–9 or premature death through want – Woodham Smith (1962) p.27.

166 Plut.*C.Gracch*.5. Rich (1983) p. 319 argues that commanders who indulged in this practice risked appeal to the tribune (n.68) but this supposes those who enlisted would want to appeal.

167 *Proletarii* could be called up legally. See Rich (1983) pp. 290–2, who has not seen the possible implication of Tiberius' speech.

168 Made by Rathbone (1993) pp. 145–6. Doubts about its connection with a supposed reduction of the minimum census for the *assidui*, cf. Rosenstein (2004) p. 156 and n.132 above, do not, in my opinion, affect the general thrust of the argument.

169 Keaveney (2003b) p. 77.

170 Livy 34.45.2, 39.23.3.

171 Livy 39.29.8–9: Apulia. For the other incidents see Greenidge (1904) pp. 86–8.

172 Diod.Sic.34/35.2.1–24, 25–48 with Keaveney (1998) pp. 73–82.

173 Plut.*Tib.Gracch*.8. Dating: MRR1.485. Possible route: Nagle (1976). Badian's doubts – (1958) pp. 172–3 – about the authenticity of the report seem to me to rest on doubtful *Quellenforschungen*.

174 Morley (2001) p. 60 thought Tiberius might himself have been extrapolating from areas where the slaves had become predominant to the whole of Italy in order to make a better case. I hope I have been able to make clear in my text why it is equally possible he could have made a deduction based on the situation as it was then known. See further n.175.

175 App.*BC*.19. Morley (2001) pp. 57–8 discusses the possibility that a slave-run villa might be more productive than a free. If it were, then his speech suggests Tiberius would not have been impressed. Morley (2001) p. 60, pursuing the notion of extrapolation on Tiberius' part, thought Tiberius might also have played on fears the slaves might revolt. It has escaped his notice that by now they already have.

176 Although we might remark that subsequent history entitles us to say Tiberius was prescient when he warned of this threat, and this is especially so if we were to subscribe to the view that great plantations were not yet that common in his day. He drew the correct conclusions from Sicily.

177 Sall.*Jug*.86 with Evans (1994) pp. 75–6 and Gabba (1976) pp. 1–19 whose view of a progressive lowering of the qualification before Marius is however disputed. See previous section. Sallust says specifically he probably acted thus *inopia bonorum*. For the more sinister motivation he suggests could lie behind such recruiting see below n.221.

178 Gell.16.10.14; Ps.Quint.*Decl*.3.5. See the discussion of Gabba (1976) pp. 13–14.

179 As Rich (1983) p. 328 and Carney (1970) p. 32 n.163 saw, although the latter may perhaps rely too much on Marius' land settlement for proof; for that see 4(a) and below. Evans (1994) p. 120 appears more sceptical of the notion.

180 As Rich (1983) p. 326 points out, this is the implication of Sall.*Jug*.85: *capite censos plerosque*.

181 Sall.*Jug*.86. See further below.

182 Brunt (1987) p. 430; Evans (1994) pp. 75–6; Rich (1983) p. 324.

183 MRR1.558

184 [Front.] *Strat*.4.2.2.

185 Evans (1994) p. 118 seems close to this position. Badian (1958) p. 198 n.3 appears to ignore the distinction.

186 (1958) p. 198 n.2. He also wonders if the whole passage is not just anti-Marian propaganda.

187 See 5(c) for instance.

188 Saturninus' African settlements might reasonably be expected to house some of the veterans of this army. Unfortunately there is scholarly disagreement about their extent. See Badian (1958) pp. 198–9; Brunt (1987) pp. 577–88, (1988) p. 278; MRR3.21. This, of course, means we have no real idea how many troops were settled here. For instance Brunt (1987) p. 570, who argues for a minimalist view, naturally assumes the majority were brought home but I cannot see why he thinks [Front.] Strat.4.2.2 supports this contention, nor does he explain why Marius bothered to bring them back if he was going to reject them.

189 (1994) p. 118. Less happy perhaps is his suggestion that [Front.] Strat. 4.2.2 can be taken to mean Marius appealed for recruits. Evans also speaks of the hope of reward these men had. We should remember, however, that Marius made no promises. See 4(a).

190 A point Evans (1994) p. 75 seems to have overlooked.

191 In the case of Pompey, for instance, 4(b).

192 Evans (1994) p. 120. Again we may invoke Pompey (n.191) or Caesar's *evocati*: 4(b).

193 For Marius' African booty see Plut.*Mar*.12. Evans (1994) p. 81 n.89 thinks the amount may be inflated. In any case he neglects to consider donatives and distributions for which see Harris (1971) p. 102 and Schneider (1977) p. 106.

194 For the background see Keaveney (2005a) pp. 76–80. A radically different view will be found in Carney (1970) p. 42 n.200.

195 Liv.ep.69.

196 Evans (1994) p. 122 overlooks Plut.*Mar*.38 which attests the presence of soldiers in the assembly who must, as Gabba (1967) p. 105 argues, be numbered among the rustics in App.*BC*.1.29–32.

197 For the booty from these wars see Plut.*Mar*.21, 27. The spirit of Spurius Ligustinus (see (b)) may be invoked here. Again here (see n.190) Evans (1994) pp. 122–3 argues – wrongly in my view – that only a part of Marius' army would have been offered land.

198 Badian (1958) p. 211 n.2; Evans (1994) p. 121.

199 Gabba (1976) pp. 14, 18. Contra Badian (1958) p. 197.

200 Smith (1958) pp. 44–5; Gabba (1976) p. 15.

201 (1983) pp. 327–9. Cf. Keaveney (2005a) pp. 144–5, (2005b) pp. 115–16.

202 The most sophisticated and subtle expression of this notion I have seen is Gabba (1976) pp. 26–37.

203 3 and 4.

204 (1984) p. 70. It may be instructive to compare this with the crude caricature of the helots as 'relatively ignorant simple people' in Talbert (1989) p. 30.

205 For example, De Blois (1987) p. 12.

206 For Sulla in the Social War see Keaveney (2005b) pp. 41–4 or (2005a) pp. 139–40, 152–7.

207 Keaveney (2005b) p. 48.

208 Sec.1(b).

209 *Huic accedebat quod L. Sulla exercitum quem in Asia ductaverat, quo sibi fidum faceret, contra morem maiorum luxuriose nimisque liberaliter habuerat. Loca amoena, voluptaria facile in otio ferocis militum animos molliverant. Ibi primum insuevit exercitus populi Romani amare, potare; signa, tabulas pictas, vasa caelata mirari; ea privatim et publice rapere, delubra spoliare, sacra profanaque omnia polluere. Igitur ei milites, postquam victoriam adepti sunt, nihil reliqui victis fecere.* Trans.: J. C. Rolfe (Loeb).

210 McGushin (1977) ad loc. puts it more delicately, saying history has been distorted to make a moral point. Some seem to take it seriously. See, for example, De Blois (1987) p. 44 and Meier (1966) p. 240.

211 The *victoriam* referred to here is obviously that of the Mithridatic War.
212 As Meier (1966) p. 240 emphasised. Cf. 1(b). There is no basis to the assertion of Brunt (1988) p. 31 n.60 that App.*BC*.5.17 is applicable to earlier armies. See further n.227. The claim (Dio 41.8.6) that Caesar's army was largely composed of barbarians probably reflects contemporary propaganda and is as false as Sallust's verdict on Sulla's army. The only justification for it is the existence of a legion of non-Romans called Aleudae – see Harmand (1967) p. 33 n.58; Gelzer (1968) p. 196 and Shackleton Bailey on Cic.*ad Att*.7.13.3.
213 (1983) p. 328. For him the period of quiet is 70–50. Cf. Brunt (1987) p. 725.
214 For a discussion of the recruitment on both sides see Brunt (1987) pp. 466–8, 473–80; on Caesar see Chrissanthos (2001) pp. 66–8. For more on slaves in armies see below and (d).
215 Cf. Brunt (1987) p. 474 and my remarks further below.
216 Dio 42.55.1. For a fuller discussion of this mutiny see 5(c).
217 It is not inevitable because, of course, one could get that experience working for somebody else.
218 (1983) p. 329.
219 Trans.: J. Carter (Penguin).
220 Brunt (1987) p. 409; Rich (1983) p. 328 n.207.
221 Cf. Paul (1984) pp. 172–3.
222 On this see Gabba (1976) pp. 13–14, 29–30.
223 *BJ* 86. See Gabba (1976) p. 180 n.113 – accepted e.g. by Paul (1984) p. 217.
224 Many later sources speak of the steadiness of armies drawn from men of property. See, for example, Plut.*Mar*.9; Val.Max.2.3.1; Gell.16.10. Cf. Gabba (1976) pp. 17–18.
225 *BC*.4.137.
226 Holmes (1928) p. 72.
227 To suggest (cf. n.212) that Appian might be thinking of armies from other periods as well is to demean what Gabba (1970) p. 40 calls an 'acuta analisi'. Brunt (1988) p. 480–512 attempts to calculate the number of men under arms in the period.
228 See (d).
229 Nepos *Eum*.8.
230 See 5(d).
231 See the detailed treatment in 3(c).
232 Special importance attaches to the notion of quiescence in this study. See both 3 and 4.
233 Nicolet (1980) pp. 105–9 points out how the city, in a sense, extends into the field; Brand (1968) pp. 63–82, 99–107. Cf. also Goldsworthy (1996) pp. 251–2, 279–82.
234 See 5.
235 All treated fully in Harmand (1967) pp. 349–82.
236 Gruen (1995) pp. 112–13; Goldsworthy (1996) p. 14; Smith (1958) pp. 60–1.
237 Familiarity: *Bell.Af*.45 (admittedly enunciated by a centurion). Camaraderie: Tac.*Agric*.25.
238 Harmand (1967) p. 367. See further below on Lucullus.
239 See 5.
240 Keaveney (2005b) p. 52; Gelzer (1969) pp. 195–6.
241 See, for example, Gabba (1976) pp. 27, 35 whose explanation of the growth of professionalism is implicitly refuted in what follows here.
242 Gelzer (1969) pp. 187–8; Hatscher (2000) pp. 199–200.
243 It should be noted that the standing of the officers in 88 is largely conjectural but I think it a reasonable conjecture. These men shared their sentiment with the senate: Keaveney (2005b) pp. 53–4.
244 Keaveney (1992) pp. 15–17.
245 Dio 41.4.2–4; Plut.*Caes*.34.
246 Cic.*ad Att*.7.12.5, 13.1, *ADFam*.16.12.4. That Cicero, under the circumstances, should not mention the less elevated personal motivation is understandable. Labienus' subsequent career I think justifies his verdict now.

247 At any rate I am persuaded by Brunt (1988) pp. 497–8 that there is no reason to accept Syme's theory (1979) pp. 62–75, that Labienus was a long-standing Pompeian who now returned to his true allegiance. See also his remarks on Matius in (1988) p. 40. This would seem to be a good point to say something about another avenue open to the officer who was faced with the dilemma of choosing sides, a solution we think of as typically Roman: suicide. Instances of this seem to cluster largely in the period 43–41. In 43 when Octavian took Rome Caecilius Cornutus the city prefect committed suicide. At the fall of Laodiceia to Cassius both Dolabella and Marius Octaviaus made away with themselves while M. Juventius Latrensis did likewise when Lepidus' army deserted to Antony. After Philippi not only did Brutus and Cassius kill themselves but they were joined in death by others. In Africa in 41 a certain C. Fuficius, who had once been a centurion, plainly adopting the manners of his betters, also fell on his sword: App.*BC*.3.92, 4.62, 131, 135, 5.26; Dio 47.30.571; Vell.Pat.2.63.2, 71.2; MRR2.373.

248 Compare, for instance, Badian (1958) pp. 1–11 and Gelzer (1969) pp. 62–101 on the one hand with, on the other, Brunt (1988) pp. 382–442. We are not, of course, concerned with foreign peoples or princes who may have had a client relationship or ties of *hospitium* with the great at Rome; on these see briefly Brunt (1988) pp. 386, 392–3.

249 Among those who would say to a great extent we find Syme (1939) p. 15; Smith (1955) pp. 127–8; Gabba (1976) pp. 26–8 who may be contrasted with the more sceptical Brunt (1988) pp. 435–8 and Rouland (1979) pp. 352–401. That patronage played a part in the army's career structure is undoubted: Goldsworthy (1996) pp. 31–2, cf. *Bell.Af.*54 but, as I hope will emerge from our discussion, that is an entirely separate and unrelated issue to what we are about to consider.

250 A representative sample is provided by the following: Syme (1939) p. 15; Harmand (1967) pp. 445–7; Carney (1970) pp. 33–4; Beard and Crawford (1985) pp. 7–8. Von Premerstein (1937) pp. 22–5 has been very influential.

251 See 3. Due weight may also be given to some of the less formal ties which bound the commander and his troops. On these see further below.

252 Something that would anyway be difficult to invoke, I believe, in the case of Sulla in 83 (Plut.*Sulla.* 27) for instance. If he had the client army Harmand (1967) p. 445 supposes he had, then it would be hard to account for the doubts he had about their attitude.

253 Vell.Pat.2.16.1–3 with Gabba (1976) p. 186 n.53 though he perhaps overestimated the importance of the episode. There is no reason to suppose, as Beard and Crawford (1985) p. 8 do, that the contemporary army of Pompey Strabo was private. On private armies see also Wiehn (1926) pp. 76–7.

254 App.*BC*.1.67; Plut.*Mar*.41; Gran.Lic. p. 35 Cr. with Bennett (1923) pp. 11–13; Carney (1970) p. 62; Rawson (1978) pp. 133–4 with 3(a) and further below. Gabba (1967) p. 187 suggests that in order to reach the number of a thousand whom Plutarch and Licinianus say followed him from Africa we have to assume some of them were veterans of his settled there. Conceivably these could be clients but they might be a trifle old by now.

255 Seager (2002) pp. 20–1, 26. Brunt (1988) p. 260 n.87 suggests the *oiketai* of Diod.Sic. (see 38/39.10) may actually be clients of other leading men, which interpretation I think diminishes the force of the remark. In any case the reference to an army snatched suggests recruitment and the fate of Scipio's army at the hands of Pompey (Plut.*Pomp*.7).

256 The conjecture of Badian (1958) p. 277 that Pompey drew on his clients for the army he led against Lepidus (cos.78) is, as Brunt (1988) p. 436 points out, just that: conjecture. Lepidus himself may have had hopes of clients in Cisalpine Gaul: Badian (1958) p. 276 and Seager (2002) p. 31. For his directly attested following see below.

257 Cic.*Quint.fr*.2.3.4 with Seager (2002) p. 115. The danger of invoking *clientela* to explain an incident is I think exemplified by Harmand (1967) p. 446 who assumes Pompey's difficulties in 61 arose from disarray among his clients.

258 Pompey and Picenum: Cic.*ad Att.*7.16.2, 8.11a, 12a–c. Caesar's advance: Gelzer (1968) pp. 195–8. Brunt (1988) pp. 436–8 seems to take this as evidence for the weakness of the client–patron relationship, ignoring the practical difficulties Pompey's clients now faced. So far I am aware patrons did not require clients to commit suicide.

259 Plut.*Crass.*6; App.*BC.*1.80; Liv.ep.84 with Badian (1958) pp. 266–7; Ward (1977) p. 60. Wiehn (1926) p. 83 thought of *hospitium*.

260 I think Diod.Sic.38/39.12 supports the idea that Marius traded on his name. For the clientage see the discussions of Badian (1958) p. 244; Brunt (1988) p. 260; Lovano (2002) p. 122. In view of what they were facing it is strange the Cinnans did not earlier turn to this reliable source of manpower, but dissensions in the Cinnan high command (cf. e.g. App.*BC.*1.85) may not have helped. Gabba (1976) pp. 105–22 and Spann (1987) pp. 160–74 are at least able to agree that Sertorius did not recruit among clients.

261 See Brunt (1987) pp. 480–5, (1988) pp. 259–60, 437–8, Syme (1939) p. 125. Brunt's minimalist approach leads him, one fears, to underestimate the value to Octavian of his clientage. If Pompey could draw on it so could he, and he could use it after a like fashion. On these recruitments of civilian clients see Rouland (1979) pp. 371–4.

262 Gabba (1976) p. 186 n.53; Beard and Crawford (1985) p. 8.

263 Cic.*Parad.Stoic.*45, *de Offic.*1.25. For other versions, a bibliography of the debate the statement has aroused and a helpful discussion see Whitehead (1986). There is no reason to follow Mouritsen (2001) p. 62 who thinks a bodyguard is in question.

264 Keppie (1984) p. 98; Gruen (1995) p. 369.

265 Spartacus: Ward (1977) pp. 68–9; Whitehead (1986) pp. 73–4. Economic background: Marshall (1972) p. 51; Keaveney (1992) p. 51.

266 Pompey's letter: Keaveney (1992) pp. 51–2. Crassus and Pompey: Plut.*Crass.*6, 7.

267 People might make the dangerous assumption you were on the other side: Plut.*Pomp.*8. See also Wiehn (1926) pp. 80–1.

268 Plut.*Mar.*41–3, *Sert.*5; App.*BC.*1.67; Lic. p.35 Cr.; Cic.*post Red.ad Sen.*38, *post Red.ad Quir.*7.19–20 with Bennett (1923) pp. 11–13; Gabba (1967) p. 188; Konrad (1994) pp. 66–7.

269 *BC.*4.137, 5.17. See (c) above also for other possible implications of Appian's statement.

270 Plut.*Pomp.*16, or at least he was until the Triumviral period when a certain fluidity is detectable in recruiting methods. See 3(c). See also Appendix 1.

271 Vell.Pat.2.68.1–3; Dio 42.23–25; Caes.*BC.*3.4, 20–2; Plut.*Mar.*41.

272 Sall.*Cat.*59.3; Caes.*BC.*1.1–13; Dio 41.11.1–3, App.*BC.*2.38. Emendation in Sallust – a possibility considered by de Neeve (1984) pp. 177–8 – is probably unnecessary. Brunt's suggestion – (1988) p. 260 n.87 (after Cuff) – that Domitius, on the basis of Diod. Sic.37.13, could be a *patronus* of the Marsi typically ignores other possibilities for which see Keaveney (2005a) pp. 117–18.

273 Foxhall (1990) esp. pp. 99, 103–4, 111; de Neeve (1984) pp. 175–92.

274 Catiline: Sall.*Cat.*28.4. Domitius: Dio 41.11.1. With him compare Visius in Cic. *Phil.*7.24.

275 Keppie (1984) pp. 140–4.

276 Marius: Keaveney (2005b) p. 88. Cinna: App.*BC.*1.65; *de Vir.Illust.*69.

277 Plut.*Mar.*41; Flor.2.9.11; Schol.Gron. p. 286 St.

278 Caes.*BC.*3.2.

279 On the basis of *Bell.Alex.*2, *Bell.Hisp.*20 Westermann (1955) p. 67 argues Caesar did not recruit slaves but he ignores Macrob.1.32 (for which see Harmand (1967) p. 258), which might suggest that he did in some circumstances. See also Rouland (1977) pp. 83–4.

280 Brunt (1987) pp. 231, 474.

281 Dio 47.27.2, 48.19.4, 27.2, 34.4; Suet.*Div.Aug.*16; Vell.Pat.2.73.3; Liv.ep.123; Cic.*ad Fam.*11.10.3.

282 See for example, Badian (1958) p. 236 n.3; Lovano (2002) p. 34, and contrast the approach of Sartori (1973).

283 Gruen (1995) pp. 428–9. On attitudes see Rouland (1977) pp. 91–7.

284 See Westermann (1955) pp. 66–7. We may compare this with the experience of thirty years before (n.44) when those in need could not get a single slave to join them.

285 Note what happened when slaves were no longer needed. After defeating Sextus Pompey, Octavian either executed or returned to their masters the slaves in his opponent's army (App.*BC*.5.131; Dio 49.12.4–5). Gabba (1970) p. 218 thinks Octavian was branding the Sicilian War as servile but his cold-blooded act may have had another purpose. He was in the process of turning himself from a gangster to an elder statesmen and bringing back order to Italy – 5(a). With such an aim there could be no place in the legions for irregular recruits.

286 A point made for instance by Brunt (1988) pp. 260–1.

287 Hatscher (2000) pp. 19–69 has a long and thorough discussion of the concept.

288 *New Shorter Oxford English Dictionary.*

289 This is the list (p. 75) presented by Hatscher (2000) pp. 74–96 in his discussion of republican charismatic leaders. From an earlier age he adds Scipio Africanus, cf. (b) above. Brunt's doubts – (1988) p. 261 – about Sulla's charisma are probably to be explained in the light of the eccentric verdict in (1988) p. 463 n.29.

290 Drexler (1935) pp. 217–27, followed by Badian (1958) p. 228 n.5; Gabba (1976) pp. 27, 185 n.52. There have been doubts though. See nn. 294, 295.

291 Drexler (1935) p. 218.

292 5(b), (c), (d).

293 Compare, for instance, the parley at Ilerda; Gelzer (1969) pp. 215–16 or what is narrated in *Bell.Hisp*.19. This latter is an example of self-preservation pure and simple. It is invoked by Drexler (1935) pp. 225–6 however as a specimen of military clientage. See above for why I would hold that view to be untenable.

294 I am not sure that Gabba (1976) p. 186 is right to see this as a purely incidental issue. See further below. Brunt (1988) p. 258 points out that the author of *Bell.Af.* was aware of wider issues.

295 I am not convinced we need to follow Gruen (1995) p. 375 when he suggests that now, four years into the war, allegiance to the state would anyway be blunted. The protagonists would still claim to represent the state.

296 Trans.: J. Carter (Penguin).

297 Kapuściński (2001) p. 254.

3 Politics and profit

1 Compare Gabba (1976) pp. 27, 35 and Brunt (1988) p. 275.

2 Note my remarks in Keaveney (2005a) p. 14 and in (d) below. Cicero veered between attributing no political insight and some limited to the soldier (*Phil*.10.2, 13.33) as the situation developed after Caesar's death. For Cicero's changeability see Syme (1939) pp. 150–9. We should remember soldiers attended assemblies: Gabba (1976) p. 28; Keaveney (2005a) p. 77; Nicolet (1980) p. 143.

3 Harris (1979) pp. 102–3. Brunt (1987) p. 724 wisely withdrew his earlier (p. 412) objection to this view. Rosenstein (2004) pp. 9, 101 tends to play down the importance of such booty. This may owe something to his general thesis and also to the notion he appears to have conceived of what constituted subsistence level for the peasant. See 2(b). Evans (1988) pp. 131–2 rather inaccurately dubs this a mercenary mentality.

4 For the events of 88 see Keaveney (1983b), (2005b) pp. 72–103. On *contiones* see Pina Polo (1995). On the vexed but important question of whether the commander could be heard at these *contiones* I find the affirmative answer of Pritchett (2002) pp. 1–80 convincing. See my review in *Les Études Classiques* 2003, pp. 212–13. Since Marius seems to have tried to administer the *sacramentum* (Plut.*Mar*.35) – see 5(a) – we may presume the troops were

misled or heard too late he did not intend to dismiss them. On the profit motive see Carney (1970) p. 55 n.253. For Marius' reforms see 2(c).

5 See 2(d). Gruen (1984) p. 61 suggests economic factors may not have been of such moment to the officer classes as they were to the rankers, but I would say the rapacity of the Roman noble is not to be underestimated.

6 Plut.*Tib.Gracch*.16–20; App.*BC*.1.31.57; Val.Max.3.8.5; Keaveney (2005a) pp. 134, 182; Greenidge (1904) pp. 110–44. See also the discussion in 2(a).

7 I do not subscribe to the notion that Pompey Strabo is to be reckoned as an imitator of Sulla. For him see 5(b).

8 Greenidge and Clay pp. 171–2 with Keaveney (2005a) pp. 175–80 and Lovano (2002) pp. 32–4.

9 App.*BC*.1.65–6; Vell.Pat.2.20.3–4; Bennett (1923) p. 10. Smith (1955) p. 106 is perhaps a trifle harsh in attributing Cinna's desire for restoration to mere selfishness.

    Appius Claudius Pulcher: MRR2.48. The suggestion in the Loeb Liv.ep.79 that his *imperium* was in some way improper seems to rest on a misunderstanding of Cic.*Dom*.83. The issue of the powers of the assembly was to surface again in a few years. See below n.25. On the army and the theatrical see Goldsworthy (1996) pp. 148–9. For the importance of insignia see Wiehn (1926) p. 86.

10 So, for instance, Badian (1958) p. 236 to the exclusion of the political dimension sketched above.

11 Liv.ep.79; Vell.Pat.2.20.4; Schol.Gron. p. 286 St. As Lovano (2002) p. 37 n.41 points out, *corripuit* is ambiguous. On this point see further below on Sulla and Fimbria.

12 See, for instance, the hesitant remarks of Bennett (1923) p. 10 and Lovano (2002) p. 37.

13 Bennett (1923) pp. 6–7; Keaveney (2005a) p. 179 n.37.

14 Lovano (2002) pp. 36–7 makes unnecessary difficulties. Compare, too, stories about recruitment of slaves: 5(a).

15 Bennett (1923) p. 10.

16 Although his ally Marius shortly afterwards did this to Ostia: Liv.ep.79.

17 For this see Polyb.10.16.5 with Walbank ad loc. Cf. Brunt (1988) pp. 411–12.

18 App.*BC*.1.67. For other aspects see 5(a).

19 For Flaccus and Fimbria see MRR2.53, 56, 59 and section 4(a) below. For the encounter between Sulla and Fimbria see App.*Mith*.59–60 and *de Vir.Illust.* 70.

20 Either a reference to the murder or to the fact that he held a commission from the Cinnans whose standing in Sulla's eyes is well illustrated in App.*BC*.1.79.

21 Having been declared a *hostis* by the Cinnans (App.*Mith*.51).

22 The cynicism of Syme (1939) pp. 159–60 seems to me excessive. See 5(b).

23 Keaveney (2005b) pp. 112–14. See also 5(b), (c).

24 *De Vir.Illust*.70; Plut.*Sulla* 28.

25 Lewis and Short. Picking up n.11 above, note that Vell.Pat.2.20.4: *corruptis primo centurionibus ac tribunis, mox etian spe largitionis militibus* could be taken to mean that first the officers were seduced and then the men by the added inducement of cash.

26 Liv.ep.82.

27 See further 1(b), 5(a).

28 Keaveney (2005b) pp. 108–9; Hatscher (2000) p. 143; Brunt (1988) p. 263. It has been suggested to me that this would make it easier for them to accept the Peace of Dardanus which they detested (Plut.*Sulla* 24).

29 Sall.*Cat*.11

30 Plut.*Sulla* 27. Doubted by Valgiglio (1960) p. 126.

31 Keaveney (2005b) pp. 112–13, 157–8.

32 Keaveney (2005b) pp. 112–13. Millar (1998) pp. 53–4 is not satisfactory in every respect.

33 But note that the issue of the powers of the assembly raised by Cinna (n.9) surfaces again here: Cic.*Phil*.12.27.

34 Keaveney (2005b) pp. 112–13.

35 Plut.*Sulla* 27; Caes.*BC*.1.39. Valgiglio (1960) pp. 126–7 thought the report of Sulla's loan exaggerated but does not know about Caesar's. Equally Meier's view – (1996) pp. 382–3 – that Caesar wished to stiffen the resolve of his men before the first serious fighting is not persuasive. His army was no stranger to war. See (c) below.

36 In the light of App.*BC*.1.76 for instance I see no need to accept Hatscher's suggestion – (2000) pp. 144–5 – that Sulla might have whipped up hatred of the Samnites in order to inspire his troops.

37 Badian (1958) p. 269; Gabba (1976) pp. 103–15; Spann (1987) pp. 39, 169–74; Konrad (1994) pp. 96–7.

38 On the background see Gruen (1995) pp. 12–17; Seager (2002) pp. 30–2; Keaveney (2005b) pp. 173–4.

39 Greenidge and Clay p. 233 with Keaveney (2005b) p. 343 n.9.

40 Plut.*Pomp*.16; App.*BC*.1.107 with Gabba (1967) pp. 292–5; Schol.Gron. p. 286 St.; Flor.2.1; Exup.6; Sall.*Hist*.1.67, 69 M/59, 64 McG. McGushin (1992) p. 129 thought the initial decision to send Lepidus to Etruria showed confusion among the fathers. More likely, as Seager (2002) p. 31 believes, it showed fear of civil war. People remembered where head-on confrontation with Cinna had led. Gruen (1995) p. 14 thinks the senate did not take Lepidus seriously but I doubt this. More likely he was benefiting by the three-way split (Keaveney (2005b) pp. 185–7) in the political world of post-Sullan Rome.

41 Gelzer (1968) pp. 145–54, 164–90; Meier (1996) pp. 364–7; Seager (2002) pp. 137–51.

42 On the crossing of the Rubicon see below n.91.

43 Caes.*BC*.1.7. For Caesar's movements and the location of this *contio* see Gelzer (1968) p. 193 n.3 which, despite Brunt (1988) p. 258, did not take place at the Rubicon. Later sources (App.*BC*.2.330; Dio 41.41) add little to Caesar's own account. Gelzer rejects the detail in Suet.*Caes*.33 that he indulged in a little histrionics after the manner of Cinna (3a) but such displays were not unusual. See Aldrete (1999) pp. 41, 67–9. The substance of the letter addressed to the senate earlier (Dio 41.1.3), refuting charges made against him and recounting services to the state, resembled pretty much what we find here, one suspects. For further repetition of Caesar's case see n.47.

44 Plut.*Caes*.34; Cic.*ad Att*.7.12.5, 13.1, *ad Fam*.16.12.4; Dio 41.4.2–4. For a discussion of this desertion in the context of a consideration of the relations which bound a soldier to his commander see 2(d) but contrast it here with Sulla's experience in 88: (a) above.

45 The essential loyalty of his troops may be gauged when we remember that the two mutinies he faced (see below and 5(c)) were concerned not with the legitimacy of his enterprises but with conditions of service. The significance of this emerges when we recall in contrast that Lucullus came to grief precisely because his men would not accept the legitimacy of what he proposed. See Keaveney (1992) pp. 124–5.

46 Caes.*BC*.1.72–2, 84–7, 3.19; App.*BC*.2.42.56; Lucan 4.174–262; Dio 41.47. For the fraternising of Caesar's officer Curio in Africa see Caes.*BC*.1.27–35. The phenomenon of fraternisation is discussed fully in 5(c) where some later instances are also noted.

47 Caes.*BC*.3.22.

48 Caes.*BC*.1.12. On Thermus' rank see MRR2.262.

49 Caes.*BC*.1.13.

50 *Milites Domitianos sacramentum apud se dicere iubet*: Caes.*BC*.1.23. For this oath see 5(a). Prior to this Caesar had held a *dilectus* of troops who had fled from the consul Lentulus in Picenum: Caes.*BC*.1.15–16.

51 Dio 41.23.1, 62.1. Cf. Keppie (1984) p. 110. Note, however, that in Spain too some elected to go home: Caes.*BC*.1.86.

52 Keppie (1984) pp. 104–5; Parker (1958) p. 58.

53 For the Caesarian armies see Brunt (1987) pp. 474–80.

54 Caes.*BC*.3.60–1.

55 *BC*.2.72–4.

56 Caes.*BC*.3.90. Appian seems to echo him by speaking of 'offering fair terms', 'win by benefits', 'dismissed unharmed' (*BC*.2.73, Loeb trans.) See further nn. 60, 65.

57 Despite what Caesar himself claims in *BC*.1.3.

58 Gelzer (1968) pp. 192–3. When Caesar eventually got to Rome and summoned the senate he found himself facing a rump: Gelzer (1968) p. 208.

59 Caes.*BC*.1.8 with Leach (1978) pp. 174–5 and Seager (2002) pp. 154–5.

60 App.*BC*.2.50–2. Once more (see n.56) Appian echoes a contemporary. Cicero speaks of Pompey's strategy as 'Themistoclean'. We also know that Pompey backed up rhetoric by edict. The senators were to come to Thessalonika where the legitimate government now was. See Gelzer (1968) pp. 211–12 and note the remarks of Seager (2002) p. 154.

61 Plut.*Cat.Min*.54. Caes.*BC*.3.13 speaks of panic in Pompey's army just as it reached Dyrrachium which was calmed after the troops, following the example of Labienus, swore loyalty. Plainly the circumstances called for a renewal of the *sacramentum*. See 5(a). Note that when Scipio sometime later made a similar appeal to Caesar's it did not meet with success because it was not backed with money.

62 See Leach (1978) pp. 186–8; Brunt (1987) pp. 473–4.

63 Seager (2002) p. 163 speaks of Pompey's 'moral advantage'.

64 Dio 41.17.3. He adds that this last detail was a sham and both sides sought only their own interests. Brunt (1988) p. 258 seems inclined to accept this observation at face value, but we should perhaps consider that he is here being ahistorical and attributing attitudes to Caesar and Pompey which are more characteristic of the Triumvirs (see next section). Certainly Plutarch is guilty of such a practice (see 1(b)) and Dio himself may indulge in it elsewhere. See n.95.

65 Dio 41.57.1–2. Compare the sources in n.56 above.

66 Seager (2002) p. 150; Gelzer (1968) pp. 209–10.

67 Caes.*BC*.3.3 He also gathered a fleet and won supplies from the same area.

68 Caes.*BC*.2.18, 21.

69 Caes.*BC*.3.32–3.

70 *Bell.Alex*.48–64.

71 The situation up until 47 is sketched by Chrissanthos (2001) p. 70.

72 Gelzer (1968) pp. 167–8; Chrissanthos (2001) p. 70 n.138.

73 Suet.*Div.Jul*.68.

74 Caes.*BC*.1.39. Note the comments in (a) n.35 above and in Keaveney (2005b) p.207 n.30.

75 Chrissanthos (2001) p. 70. For a comparison with Lucullus see 5(c).

76 Suet.*Div.Jul*.26 with Butler and Cary (1927) ad loc. Suetonius gives no date but somewhere in the region of 51–50 seems most likely. See Harmand (1967) p. 266 and Keppie (1984) p. 103.

77 App.*BC*.2.47, 92; Cic.*ad Att*.11.22; Caes.*BC*.3.5; Dio 42.52.

78 These are fully discussed in 5(c).

79 So, for instance, Harmand (1967) p. 298. Chrissanthos (2001) pp. 67–9 is more acute.

80 Caes.*BC*.1.40, 32, *BG*.8.54; Dio 40.65; Plut.*Caes*.29, *Pomp*.57; App.*BC* 2.29–30 with Gelzer (1968) p. 144, 181, MRR2.250. I am inclined to disagree with Leach's view ((1978) p. 165) that Caesar paid the departing troops to spread false report, and I am sceptical too of Meier's view ((1996) p. 340) that Appius Claudius Pulcher had simply been fooled.

81 App.*BC*.2.30; Plut.*Pomp*.57, 60. See Seager (2002) p. 146.

82 Caes.*BC*.1.8–11 with Gelzer (1968) p. 195. Cf. 2(d). It is worth pointing out that, if there were some flaws in Pompey's plan, those like Cicero (*ad Att*.8.16.1, 9.5.4) and Favonius (Plut.*Pomp*.60) who pointed them out only did so after Caesar actually began his advance.

83 See n.43 above.

84 Suet.*Div.Jul*.33. Cf. Pritchett (2002) pp. 52–8.

85 Cf. Gelzer (1968) p. 283 n.1.

86 Dio 42.49 with Gelzer (1968) pp. 258–9.

87 Dio 42.50 with Gelzer (1968) p. 262.

88 Gelzer (1968) pp. 270–1.

89 Gelzer (1968) p. 298.

90 Suet.*Div.Jul*.38; Dio 43.21.3; App.*BC*.2.102 with Gelzer (1968) pp. 284–5.

91 Sources and discussion in Gelzer (1968) p. 193 n.3. The impact of the crossing of the Rubicon may be gauged from the fact that it has attracted the attention of the fantasist both antique (Suet.*Div.Jul*.32) and modern (Wiseman (1998) pp. 60–3).

92 To anticipate: we shall encounter a difference with the Triumvirs. See next section.

93 See the next section.

94 See above.

95 42.49.4–4. This should not be interpreted in the light of a superficially similar remark of Crassus – 2(d).

96 See n.64.

97 See 2(c) and next section.

98 As Gelzer (1968) pp. 187–8 observed.

99 So, for instance, Hatscher (2000) p. 179.

100 Keaveney (2005b) pp. 50–63, 105–7.

101 See in summary Keaveney (2005b) p. 183.

102 Gelzer (1968) pp. 37–8.

103 Suet.*Div.Jul*.31–2; Plut.*Caes*.32, 60; App.*BC*.2.35.

104 *BC*.3.57. Cf. Dio 41.32.

105 See his discussions in (1968) pp. 217, 232.

106 This is not to deny that these sentiments informed the eventual legislation as Gelzer (1968) p. 239 claims, but they do not in themselves constitute any kind of coherent programme. Furthermore it is questionable if the legislation was intended, as Sulla's had been, as a permanent remedy for Rome's political ills. See next two notes.

107 Gelzer (1968) p. 332 but see also pp. 329–30; Meier (1996) pp. 456–8 and 1(a).

108 I find Meier (1996) pp. 364–7 persuasive on this point but see Jehne (1987) contra especially his summary remarks pp. 448–51.

109 Holmes (1928) pp. 1–69, Botermann (1968) pp. 1–15 and Rawson (1994) pp. 468–79 all provide narrative and comment.

110 This sentiment is carefully analysed by Botermann (1968) pp. 172–6.

111 Botermann (1968) p. 15 points out that just before Octavian departed for Rome delegates from the legions waited upon him and asked him to avenge Caesar. As she points out, there may be differences in the sources as to the composition of these embassies but we can be sure they represent a spontaneous initiative by the troops.

112 App.*BC*.3.40, 45. This mutiny is discussed further in 5(c). See also n.129.

113 App.*BC*.3.41–2. See 2(b).

114 App.*BC*.3.29–30, 39. Rawson (1994) p. 476 thinks we may have a doublet here. The accounts of Plut.*Ant*.16 and Dio 45.7.3–83 do not mention tribunes.

115 App.*BC*.3.48.

116 Cf. Botermann (1968) pp. 50–1.

117 App.*BC*.3.21. Some of this money may have found its way to the troops: Dio 45.7.2.

118 See further 5(c) for this mutiny.

119 These transactions of Octavian and Antony are tabulated by Keppie (1983) p. 42. To his list of sources add Cic.*ad Att*.16.8.1, 9, 11.6; App.*BC*.3.42. Cf. Syme (1939) pp. 107, 125, who seems to conflate two seperate donatives.

120 Cic.*Phil*.13.33. Cf. Rawson (1994) p. 489. For Cicero's attitude to the common soldier see also 2(a). When things were going his way he tended to be more benign in his judgement. See for instance *Phil*.4.4–5 on these same legions.

121 App.*BC*.3.88.

122 App.*BC*.3.86; Dio 46.41.5. Botermann (1968) p. 149 thought Appian had gone back to Octavian's propaganda. Certainty is, of course, impossible.

123 Cic.*ad Fam*.11.13.3. Cf. Holmes (1928) p. 59.

124 App.*BC*.3.88; Dio 46.43. Appian represents the centurions as citing precedents, such as the two Scipios for instance, for Octavian's consular bid. This detail suggests three possibilities: it is simply an addition by Appian himself; the centurions had been primed by Octavian; it did in fact originate with the soldiers. If the last were true then Cicero (n.120) may be mistaken about the political sophistication of the legionary.

125 Plut.*Ant*.20; Dio 46.56.3–4 with Holmes (1929) p. 72; Botermann (1968) p. 167.

126 App.*BC*.3.97. At the outset of his campaign in 44 he had behaved in a strictly traditional fashion, hardening his troops and securing booty with a campaign against Alpine tribes – Holmes (1928) p. 34. See further n.160.

127 App.*BC*.4.62.

128 Cic.*ad Fam*.10.32.4. On the seductions see 2(c).

129 App.*BC*.3.51.

130 App.*BC*.3.74; Dio 46.31.3–4; Cic.*ad Fam*.12.30.4. Cf. Holmes (1928) p. 65. Decorations were usually welcome but not invariably. See Goldsworthy (1996) pp. 276–8 and 5(d).

131 Dio 46.38.2.

132 Cic.*ad Brut*.1.1.8.5, *ad Fam*.11.14.2, 12.20.4.

133 See 4(a) and note the contemporary foundation of Lugdunum. See Holmes (1928) p. 64.

134 App.*BC*.3.88.

135 App.*BC*.3.90; Dio 46.44.2.

136 App.*BC*.3.94; Dio 46.46.5. See Weigel (1992) pp. 73, 75.

137 Botermann (1968) p. 87 poses this question. See further her discussion (pp. 102–4) of the attitude of Bassus' (cf. (b)) troops who eventually joined Cassius (App.*BC*.4.59).

138 Details and discussion in Holmes (1928) pp. 75–80 and Botermann (1968) pp. 89–96, 101–7. Note that they even approached the Parthians for help. The contradictory accounts handed down to us carry a faint echo of the shame which was felt at this. See Keaveney (2003a).

139 App.*BC*.4.133. For Brutus see Holmes (1928) p. 59.

140 This was the eventual conclusion of Botermann (1968) p. 104 with regard to the troops of Bassus (n.137).

141 Dio 47.42.3–5 is uncharacteristically succinct. Syme (1939) p. 205 emphasises that this was the end of liberty.

142 App.*BC*.4.117–20, 126.

143 App.*BC*.4.66. For Appian on tyranny and kingship see Keaveney (2005c) pp. 429–33.

144 App.*BC*.4.90–100.

145 App.*BC*.4.89, cf. 124.

146 App.*BC*.4.100. Both sides also made money available to their soldiers for sacrifice but here the Liberators were said to have been more generous (Plut.*Brut*.39). Cf. 2(a).

147 App.*BC*.4.117–18; Plut.*Brut*.43–5. Dio 47.47.2.

148 App.*BC*.4.120; Plut.*Ant*.23.

149 For this settlement see 4(a).

150 App.*BC*.5.20, 30, 54. Syme (1939) p. 208 n.1 suspects Appian may have idealised Lucius. See also Pelling (1996) p. 15.

151 App.*BC*.5.20 with 5(a).

152 Or, in another account, the Caesarian veterans settled in Ancona. They may have been mindful of the oath they swore in 43: Dio 46.42.3.

153 Dio 48.12.1–3; App.*BC*.5.23.

154 App.*BC*.5.15; Suet.*Div.Aug*.14.

155 App.*BC*.5.53, 57, 59, 64 with Holmes (1928) pp. 104–5.

156 Holmes (1928) pp. 106–8; Hadas (1930) pp. 95–7.

157 Dio 48.37.

158 For the campaigns see Holmes (1928) pp. 108–16 or Hadas (1930) pp. 100–47.

159 Weigel (1992) p. 91. See further 5(c).

160 App.*BC*.5.129–32; Dio 34.3–5, 49.15–16. Cf. Syme (1939) pp. 232–4. The purge of slaves who had made their way into the army was another sign that abnormal times were coming to an end.

161 Holmes (1928) pp. 122–30, 136–8; Syme (1939) pp. 259–75; Pelling (1996) pp.28–34, 39–40.

162 Holmes (1928) pp. 143–4. See further below.

163 Holmes (1928) pp. 140–1. The soldiers, of course, received a donative after Actium: Holmes (1928) p. 171.

164 Nep.*Eum*.8. Cf. 2(c).

165 Sall.*BJ*.86.

166 Plut.*Brut*.22, *Ant*.16.

167 App.*BC*.3.42, 48, 88.

168 Dio 45.12.1–2, 46.26.5.

169 (1955) pp. 127–8.

170 (1939) p. 125.

171 It is worth pointing out here that essentially this is what they did also in assembly. In the absence of any more sophisticated approach, the Roman people, as the opportunity presented itself, extracted whatever they could from their betters. See further below for a refinement of this argument and the previous section for Caesar.

172 A brief excursion to Gaul by Octavian in 39 seems to have yielded nothing (App. *BC*.5.75).

173 There is an interesting twist in the tale of Lepidus' capture of Messana. In order to buy the allegiance of the garrison he allowed it to join in the sacking of the town by his own troops (App.*BC*.5.122).

174 As my concern is chiefly with how the leaders got themselves into this position, together with emphasising the timeless nature of the soldiers' demands, and not with the detailed mechanics of how the monies were gathered, I offer only a selection of sources, ancient and modern, to support the picture presented in the text: Cic.*Phil*.3.3, 12.12; App.*BC*.4.5, 60; Plut.*Ant*.21; Dio 46.31, 47.18, 48.34; Vell.Pat.2.73.3; Syme (1939) p. 214; Pelling (1996) pp. 6, 10–11; Huzar (1978) pp. 89–90, 102, 124; Holmes (1928) pp. 90–1.

175 See further below on this mutability.

176 See previous section.

177 Botermann (1968) p. 49 puts it neatly, 'Sie konnten damit rechnen, von ihnen potentiellen Feldherren zu werden, und begonnen, sich als unabhängig uber den rivalisierenden Politiken stehende Macht zu fühlen, die sich an den ihr Zusagenden vergeben konnte'. See also Polverini (1964) pp. 450–2 and the further remarks on the leaders below.

178 Holmes (1928) p. 72.

179 App.*BC*.3.4 with Hadas (1930) pp. 63, 100.

180 Cf. App.*BC*.5.13.

181 Holmes (1928) pp. 107–8.

182 See, for example, Hadas (1930) p. 61. Contrast Powell (2002) pp. 103–5.

183 Cf. Powell (2002).

184 Hadas (1930) pp. 60–1, 95. Powell's comparison, (2002) p. 110, with Sertorius is apt.

185 Powell (2002) pp. 109–10; Stone (2002) pp. 135–7.

186 The fleet was manned by volunteers, mercenaries, slaves and refugees from the proscriptions. See Welch (2002) pp. 38–43, 53.

187 Dio 49.13.

188 Cf. Pelling (1996) p. 46.

189 Dio 50.7.3 with Syme (1939) pp. 282–4.

190 Holmes (1928) pp. 159–60.

191 See further Syme (1930) pp. 276–8; Huzar (1978) pp. 185–205; Pelling (1996) pp.40–4.

192 Suet.*Div.Aug.*69–70.

193 Antony's culpability is disputed. See App.*BC.*5.144.

194 Dio 50.1–2.1; Plut.*Ant.*55. A little more in the same vein, not cited here, may be found in these sources.

195 Suet.*Div.Aug.*17; Dio 50.6.3.

196 Pelling (1996) pp. 44–5 is to be preferred here to Huzar (1978) p. 204.

197 Pelling (1996) p. 44.

4 Land and land hunger

1 Longford (1992) pp. 212–13.

2 *Phil.*10.2, 13.33.

3 See Keaveney (1992) pp. 11–12.

4 See 3.

5 See Gruen (1995) pp. 368–9 for example.

6 Dio 48.12.3. See further 3(c).

7 Plut.*Tib. Gracch.*9

8 Plut.*C.Gracch.*5; Diod.Sic.34/35.25, cf. Greenidge (1904) p. 208.

9 Gabba (1976) pp. 6–7, 23. For some criticism of his views see Rich (1983).

10 Sall.*Orat.Mac.*27, cf. Keaveney (1984) pp. 357, 367. A comparison with the position of the soldier in the imperial army will bring the matter into even sharper relief. For this see Garnsey (1970) pp. 249–51.

11 As Keppie (1983) emphasises, soldiers could never expect land as a right. For a eulogy of the soldier as defender of the state see Cic.*Phil.*3.38, 4.4–5.

12 See Salmon (1970) pp. 112–13.

13 Colonies: Gabba (1976) p. 38; Pompey: see discussion below.

14 Varro LL5.40.

15 See, for instance, Gabba (1976) pp. 30–1.

16 See especially *de Offic.*2.73, 78–9. The same notion will also be found in *de Rep.*1.43.

17 For Cicero's attitude to Caesar's settlement see *ad Fam.*13.4, 5, 7, 8, 17. See further below. The inclusion of Marcus Philippus in this company (*de Offic.*2.73) leads us to suspect he too would seize without recompense or alternatively that he was being misrepresented like the Gracchi (n.18).

18 See Gabba (1976) p. 31. Cicero tells the truth in *Leg.Ag.*2.10, 31.

19 *De Offic.*2.72, 74 and *Tusc.*3.48 which contains yet another protest at *aequatio*. See also *Sest.*103 and Auct.*ad Herr.*1.12.21.

20 Contrast this with the behaviour of those mentioned in *de Offic.*2.80.

21 Although it seems to have eluded Brunt (1988) pp. 266, 274.

22 *Ad Att.*1.19.4. Note also what is said in *Leg.Ag.*2.12, 68, 70 and see Gruen (1995) p. 390.

23 Cic.*Leg.Ag.*2.54. In general on attitudes to agrarian legislation see now Fezzi (2001).

24 Gabba (1976) pp. 18–19.

25 The remarks of Smith (1955) pp. 101–2 are to the point here. For my implicit arguments against Gabba, see for instance 2(c).

26 Gabba (1976) p. 41 sees the connection between land and politics but does not in my view always draw the correct conclusions from it. Keppie (1984) p. 63 merely assumes hostility without explanation.

27 *De Vir.Illust.*73 with Evans (1994) p.117 and Schneider (1977) p. 133 who points out Baebius need not necessarily be regarded as a senatorial stooge. See n.30.

28 For background see Keaveney (2005a) pp. 76–80. A radically different view will be found in Carney (1970) p. 42 n.200.

29 Liv.ep.69; Plut.*Mar.*38 which was overlooked by Evans (1994) p. 122. The troops Plutarch mentions must, as Gabba (1967) p. 105 says, be numbered among the rustics in App. *BC.*1.29–32.

30 Gabba (1976) p. 41; Greenidge (1904) pp. 127, 148–9; Badian (1958) p. 199, (1964) p. 38; Keaveney (2005a) pp. 77–80; MRR1.573, 3.109.

31 Smith (1955) pp. 99–101; Gabba (1976) pp. 41–2.

32 The debate about its extent; cf. Badian (1958) p. 199; Brunt (1987) pp. 577–88, (1988) p. 278; MRR3.21 does not affect our argument.

33 Gabba (1976) pp. 42, 199 n.167. Keppie (1983) p. 39 thinks there was some distribution but admits there is no direct evidence to support his view.

34 Cic.*de Leg.*2.12, 31. Cf. Gabba (1976) p. 200. Note also that a little earlier Marcus Phillipus, like Laelius before him, had been prevailed upon to withdraw a radical land proposal. Cf. n.17. Possibly a further clue to senatorial attitudes in 103?

35 For reasons which will, I hope, become clear I do not proceed in chronological order and leave Sulla to one side for the moment.

36 Gabba (1976) pp. 151–3; Smith (1957); Marshall (1972); Gruen (1995) p. 37.

37 Like Marshall (1972) p. 47 I am inclined to believe this detail to be true and not an excuse for inaction. Contra Gabba (1976) p. 34.

38 Marshall (1972) pp. 44–5; Gabba (1976) p. 152.

39 Gargola (1995) p. 246 n.4.

40 Smith (1957) p. 82; Keaveney (1992) pp. 122–3.

41 Background: Seager (2002) pp. 35–7. I would not accept Marshall's suggestion, ((1972) p. 51) that Pompey needed these troops and so used the money shortage as an excuse not to implement the law. This would be unnecessary as he should always call on *evocati*. Cf. Keaveney (1982a) pp. 539, 542; Keppie (1983) p. 53.

42 Seager (2002) pp. 68–9. For another view see Ward (1977) pp. 152–62.

43 Seager (2002) pp. 81–2.

44 Gelzer (1968) pp. 72–4.

45 On the settlement see Keaveney (1982a).

46 He was certainly more than the simple imitator of Marius Brunt (1988) p. 280 supposes he was.

47 For some further observations on this see Keaveney (1982a) pp. 543–4.

48 See section 2(b).

49 App.*BC.*2.94, 120, 140; Dio 42.54.2; Suet.*Div.Jul.*38. Schneider (1977) p. 183 thought Dio harmonised with the vague benevolence of [Caes.] *BC.*3.57 and I suspect the donative in Suetonius may be the necessary things of App.*BC.*2.94. Typically (cf. Keaveney 1987) Dio and Suetonius agree that Caesar had scattered his settlers all over the countryside but assign differing motives for this. Dio says Caesar wanted to avoid their being a terror to their neighbours or a possible source of rebellion, while Suetonius attributes it to Caesar's desire not to evict. Both explanations are perfectly plausible being compatible with Caesar's declared aims. Naturally some veterans maintained a corporate identity – see Keppie (1983) p. 57 – but I am not sure we need follow de Neeve (1984) p. 131 who thinks they were intended to form garrisons.

50 Keppie (1983) pp. 55, 58; de Neeve (1984) p. 132; contra Schneider (1977) pp. 189–90.

51 MRR2.332–3, 335.

52 App.*BC.*4.3. Cf. Dio 47.14.4, ILS 886 with Keppie (1983) pp. 61–3. On the comparison see also Botermann (1968) p. 165.

53 App.*BC.*5.12–13, 27; Dio 48.6–8. See Keppie (1983) p. 60. Note that a modification proposed by Lucius Antonius was never carried out (App.*BC.*5.20) – see also next note.

54 Had the peace of Misenum concluded in the next year with Sextus Pompey been implemented, there would have been further trouble. The proscribed were to return to their estates and there was widespread fear enemies would thus live side by side. App.*BC*.5.74 recalls what had happened with the Sullan colonies. See above.

55 1.15.1. On the term see Salmon (1970) p. 128.

56 On this point Gabba (1976) p. 38 is to be preferred to Brunt (1988) p. 241 n.4.

57 1.14–15.

58 See Brunt (1988) p. 241 n.4 against Gabba (1976) p. 39.

59 Gabba (1976) p. 39.

60 Gabba (1976) pp. 194, 138, 139.

61 On land and status see de Neeve (1984) p. 220. For Clodius see Keaveney (1992) pp. 122–3.

62 Rosenstein (2004) p. 101. Schneider (1977) p. 103 is inadequate. Cf. Rich (1983) pp. 298–9 and Keaveney (1982a) pp. 537–8.

63 A point emphasised by Keppie (1984) p. 39.

64 See Evans (1994) pp. 116–17 (esp. n. 90) although he draws, I believe, the incorrect inference from the evidence.

65 So Keppie (1984) p. 40. Of some commanders, I suggest, there could be no hope. Even if his reputation for stinginess was undeserved, the circumstances under which Lucullus parted from his troops make it unlikely he contemplated giving them land. See Keaveney (1992) pp. 117–27. Pompey's constant desire (this section passim) for land for his men is patent, on the other hand.

66 Harris (1971) p. 75.

67 On this trait of passivity see also n.93.

68 Previous section.

69 For Pompey and Marius see previous section. Throughout the period there are references to the continuation of the customary dispersal after campaign. See, for example, Plut.*Sulla* 27; Caes.*BC*.1.12–13.

70 Suet.*Div.Jul*.69; Dio 41.26–35, 42.52.1–55.3; Plut.*Caes*.51; [Caes.] *Bell.Af*.19, 28, 34; Cic.*ad Att*.11.21.2, 22.2; App.*BC*.2.47, 92–4. Cf. Gelzer (1968) p. 219.

71 App.*BC*.2.120. Botermann (1968) pp. 23–4 points out this should not be seen as an attempt to establish a tyranny in the classic Greek fashion but could be taken as evidence for Antony's relations with the senate.

72 Dio 44.34.1–2, 51.4; App.*BC*.2.123, 135, 3.87; Cic.*Phil*.2.100, *ad Att*.14.21.2, 15.5.3, *ad Fam*.11.2.1–2.

73 MRR2.332–3, 335; Botermann (1968) pp. 64–5.

74 Dio 46.29.3; Cic.*ad Fam*.11.20–1, *Phil*.5.53; App.*BC*.3.82. As Shackleton Bailey on *ad Fam*.20 shows, Appian does not contradict our other sources in that the commission is concerned with the assignment of property made under *acta* now annulled. I cannot agree however that *ad Fam*.21 is to be taken to mean it was not concerned with its division to the troops. See also Botermann (1968) p. 61. Brunt (1988) p. 266 argues that an agrarian law of Pansa embodied these provisions. Strangely although he elsewhere – (1988) p. 463 n.29 – calls Sulla a historical Busiris devoid of statesmanlike qualities, he now laments because the senate did not adopt the Sullan approach to veteran settlement. In the course of this chapter I have suggested why they would not, and now, of course, it was too late because they could not.

75 App.*BC*.5.12–13, 16; Dio 48.6–93. Cf. Keppie (1983) p. 60 and further (a). The remark about deserving and undeserving in Appian could mean that men already in possession of land got more. I am more inclined to take it as meaning that people who had not done their full term of service contrived to get a plot.

76 App.*BC*.5.128–9; Dio 49.14. Cf. 3(c).

77 Keaveney (1982a) pp. 539–43.

78 Keaveney (1992) index on Fimbrians. Certain considerations may lead us to conclude these men were exceptional. Given their length of time away from Italy it is highly unlikely they now had any homes to go to and, in view of their situation, any trade save war. Any hopes of land must have resided with Pompey, not Lucullus (n.65).

79 Keaveney (1982a) p. 542; Keppie (1983) pp. 37–8, 60, 62.

80 Keaveney (2005b) pp. 106–7.

81 Leaving aside, of course, the fact that when the levy operated those liable for conscription would have to answer the summons. For some further remarks on this topic see 2(b).

82 Keaveney (1982a) p. 542.

83 *BC*.3.42. It seems to me de Neeve (1984) p. 220 may miss the point.

84 Dio 42.55.1.

85 Keaveney (1982a) pp. 540–1 against Brunt (1987) p. 310.

86 Keaveney (1982a) p. 542.

87 Keaveney (1982a) p. 539.

88 App.*BC*.2.120.

89 Keaveney (1982a) p. 536; de Neeve (1984) pp. 219–20; Brunt (1988) pp. 270, 272.

90 Obviously the calling up of *evocati*, for which see for example Keaveney (1982a) p. 542 and Keppie (1983) p. 62, would not be affected by these laws. Plainly the intention was that some, at least, would return to the lands they had been granted. See also n.108.

91 Keaveney (1982a) p. 535. Both Gabba (1976) p. 205 n.228 and de Neeve (1984) pp. 220–1 think this was purely a mechanical copying of Tiberius' ordinance. The latter points to a number of passages of Appian (*BC*.1.96, 100, 104, 2.141) which speak of a mutual dependence between Sulla and his veterans which, as de Neeve sees it, is incompatible with an act of coercion. This may mistake the relation of Sulla to his troops, cf. 3(a), and it certainly, in my view, mistakes Sulla's purpose as outlined here by Appian. He is speaking at this point not of a defence of Sulla's constitution but of the forming of a bulwark against the resurrection of Sulla's Italian enemies, something which would require tying the veteran to the land. In any event it is easy to see why the soldier would welcome a law sanctioning his possession of the land. He would have received an expression of legitimacy under the *Leges Corneliae*. See Keaveney (2005b) p. 155 and n.92.

92 App.*BC*.3.2. Strangely those who deny serious intent to Sulla in his wish for inalienability (n.92) seem to have no difficulty believing Caesar meant what he said. Interestingly Brutus – perhaps not the most reliable witness – accused Caesar of wanting to pin down Italy as Sulla had (App.*BC*.2.140).

93 Keaveney (1982a) p. 542; App.*BC*.3.2, 7. See also Botermann (1968) pp. 13–14.

94 But not all, it should be said. For the frauds perpetrated on the common soldiers by the officer class in the matter of assigning land see Keaveney (1982a) pp. 538–9.

95 As Nicolet (1980) p. 137 among others emphasises.

96 The sporadic nature of land grants would indicate not all shared this outlook or, perhaps, shunned the political controversy a proposal might bring.

97 2(d). Note also how the Triumvirs could call on Caesar's veterans: Keppie (1983) p. 53.

98 For a like anachronism attributed to Sulla see Plut.*Sulla* 6 where he is represented as preparing for a coup during the Social War.

99 See previous section.

100 Despite the sanction of a *lex* in both cases: Keaveney (2005b) p. 136; Keppie (1983) pp. 50–1.

101 App.*BC*.2.92–4.

102 2(b).

103 This has been discussed fully in 3(c).

104 Ultimately grounded on the acute remarks of App.*BC*.5.17 (cf. also 4.35).

105 On the donative see especially 3(c).

106 See 2 (c).

107 See further below on the scrambling of the population of Italy.

108 Keppie (1983) p. 64.

109 This uniqueness may be illustrated by a comparison with Pompey in the next generation. He reverted to the conventional pattern. He asked the senate for land and seems to have no wider aim in mind other than settlement itself. For Caesar see below.

110 As was recognised in the case of Sulla by Scheidel (2004) p. 20. His concern for demographics leads him to ignore the rich ancient source material which enables us to appreciate, in a very real fashion, something of what these disturbances must have been like.

111 So Keppie (1983) p. 58 who attributes to him 'a degree of tact' not shown by the Triumvirs or, as we shall now see, by Sulla before him.

112 App.*BC*.2.94.

113 Keaveney (1982a) pp. 523–5. The violence at Abella in Campania was probably the work of Spartacus, Keaveney (1982a) pp. 517–18.

114 Keaveney (1982a) pp. 520–2.

115 Cic.*pro Sulla* 60–2 with Keaveney (1982a) pp. 519–20 and Berry (1996) pp. 250–7 who perhaps too readily accepts a suggestion of Wiseman that the older inhabitants might have been excluded from the *ambulatio*.

116 Sall.*Cat*.16.4. On Catiline see Appendix 1.

117 Against the thesis of Syme (1939) pp. 86–94 see the arguments of Brunt (1988) pp. 7–8. If we can make some kind of connection between the Gracchan Age and the Social War (Keaveney (2005a) pp. 119–20) none, it would appear, can be made between the Sullan settlement and the Second Civil War.

118 App.*BC*.5.12–14; Dio 48.6–8. See Hadas (1930) pp. 82–3 and Syme (1939) pp. 207–8, 288–92.

119 It will be noted that I have laid emphasis on the fact that it was only after a certain point that soldiers could put pressure on their commanders and that those commanders had to respond. On the reasons for this see especially 3(b), (c).

5 Obedience and disobedience

1 Mutiny is not a topic which has received a great deal of attention from scholars. Brunt (1988) pp. 257, 259, 261 acknowledges the prominence the phenomenon acquired in this period but his attempt at analysis (pp. 268–9) is perfunctory. Gruen (1995) pp. 372–4 has a useful discussion of mutiny between the Social and Second Civil Wars, although his bracketing of it with wavering in the face of the enemy may not be acceptable (see n.116). The mutinies in Caesar's armies in the Civil War have been exhaustively studied by Chrissanthos (2001). The utility of the general survey by Messer (1920) is not in doubt. Scholars complain of its alleged shortcomings but still turn to it. For desertion we have only Evans (1988) pp. 126–7, which discusses desertion by individuals in the context of avoidance of the levy. We, however, will be concerned with desertion by large numbers of troops.

2 And as such liable for gruesome punishments for which see Brand (1968) p. 74, 103–7. As we shall see, however, such punishments were now rarely inflicted, a point overlooked perhaps by Campbell (1984) p. 22. See also n.75.

3 Under this head we shall also be considering assassination of the commander by his subordinate, something which we shall encounter not infrequently in what immediately follows. Mutiny or the fomenting thereof constituted *maiestas* (treason) because it diminished the dignity, grandeur and power of one to whom the Roman people had given that power (Cic.*de Inv.*2.52).

4 Polyb.6.21.2; Dion.Hal.10.18.2, 11.43 with Smith (1958) pp. 31–2; Harmand (1967) pp. 258–60; Brand (1968) pp. 91–3.

5 Parker (1958) p. 25; Campbell (1984) p. 24; Nicolet (1977) pp. 309–10.

6   (1967) p. 299.
7   Servius *ad Aen.*2.157, 8.1.
8   Vegetius 2.5 with the discussion of Campbell (1984) pp. 23–4.
9   Although he opted for a republican origin for this clause (n.5) Campbell was prepared to entertain the possibility that it was late and represented a time when many soldiers had only a nominal connection with the emperor. This has certain attractions but below I shall try to show the clause is probably earlier. See n.74.
10 See Brunt (1988) pp. 299–300; Nicolet (1980) pp. 89–92.
11 (1984) p. 20 and n.4.
12 See the evidence on the oaths below and also nn.71 and 72.
13 On the authenticity of the utterance see Gelzer (1968) p. 274.
14 The qualifications of Meier (1996) p. 440 seem excessively subtle to me. Campbell also invokes the mention of *libertas* in the centurion's call in Caes.*BC.*3.91 but this has nothing to do with the oath and implies nothing either about the actual condition of the *respublica*.
15 Dio 50.6.6.
16 Diod.Sic.37.11 with Keaveney (2005a) pp. 95 n.54, 98 n.77 with additional bibliography. Note that this is a different matter from the other clause which bound them to Drusus. This was designed to ensure personal loyalty once they have become Romans. The one we are considering deals with admission to citizenship. See further n.50.
17 Here I think it worth mentioning that when the Italians rose in revolt diverse populations were in question. As they had no common nationality it comes as no surprise to learn they formed a confederacy which was underpinned by a most solemn oath of loyalty to each other and by the exchange of hostages. See Keaveney (2005a) pp. 117, 123–4 and next note.
18 Liv.ep.84; Val.Max.6.2.10. See Keaveney (2005a) p. 185. Ghilli (2001) p. 438 n.611 is mistaken in claiming an oath was extracted.
19 Liv.ep.86 with Keaveney (2005b) pp. 115–16, (2005a) pp. xiii, 187.
20 Previously there had been enabling acts to admit the Italians. See Keaveney (2005a) pp. 170–1 . Evidently there had been a shift in perception.
21 As we shall see, there are two seeming exceptions to consider (nn.31, 33).
22 There is, of course, no validity to Brunt's claim, (1988) p. 261, that this phenomenon is post 49.
23 Plut.*Sulla* 8, *Mar.*35 with Keaveney (2005b) pp. 49–52. Interestingly stones were often the favoured weapon of mutineers. See next section.
24 Pompeius Rufus: Keaveney (2005b) pp. 61–2: Cinna: App.*BC.*1.66; Vell.Pat.2.20.4. The episode is treated in greater detail in 3(a). I cannot agree with Gabba (1967) p. 185 that this is a personal oath. See below.
25 Caes.*BC.*1.15–23, 2.28–32.
26 App.*BC.*4.62.
27 App.*Mith.*60. See further (b) below. I see no reason to follow Harmand (1967) p. 302 in supposing there might be something wrong with the original oath the men had sworn. What was really wrong was that Fimbria had murdered his commander.
28 Caes.*BC.*1.74–6.
29 Campbell (1984) p. 22 plausibly suggests this is the oath Caesar accused mutineers at Placentia of violating (App.*BC.*2.47). He is quite specific about the breaches they have made. They have failed to remain with him until the end of the campaign and they have refused to obey their officers' commands. For the length of service see Keppie (1983) pp. 35–6.
30 Plut.*Sulla* 27 with Keaveney (2005b) pp. 106–7. Treatment of this by commentators has been, I feel, uncertain. See Holden (1886) p. 146; Valgiglio (1960) p. 126; Ghilli (2001) p. 438 n.611. Piccirilli (1997) p. 376 observes that their subsequent behaviour shows they observed their oath.

31　I have a little more to say about this below.

32　App.*BC*.3.46; Dio 45.13.5. Syme (1939) p. 288 compares it to Octavians's oath for *tota Italia*. See further below n.70.

33　See Botermann (1968) pp. 48–9 and 5(c).

34　Dio 46.42.3, cf. 46.52.1.

35　(1984) pp. 20–1.

36　We may recall Gabba on this specimen. His judgement was similar. See n.24.

37　Yet Campbell (1984) pp. 21–2 teeters on the brink of contradiction by admitting this is still the *sacramentum* as it always had been. See below for some futher remarks.

38　Campbell (1984) p. 20 observes, 'if Servius is right' the soldiers had sworn to defend the state. But we saw above that it might not be advisable to invoke Servius' evidence here, nor do I see any reason to follow him (p. 21) in claiming the oaths in Caes.*BC*.1.23, 2.32 are oaths to Caesar personally rather than to Caesar as commander.

39　On Caesar's settlement see 4(b).

40　A point made by Gruen (1995) p. 373.

41　There is more on the theme in 3(c) when we examine the war between Caesar and Pompey.

42　Keaveney (2005b) p. 53.

43　See 3 for the details of this.

44　(1984) pp. 22–3. Cf. Harmand (1967) p. 301.

45　For the details of these switches in allegiance see 5(c). We may recall here, however, that Antony (n.31) perverted the *sacramentum* at Tibur by getting civilians to swear to it, while Octavian (n.33) seems to have been unsure of its force and felt it necessary to add another sanction. For the rest it must be said that, however much it might be falling into disrepute, the evidence shows it was still invoked.

46　(1937) pp. 22–32, 73–4. His views were accepted by Syme (1939) p. viii and Gabba (1976) pp. 26–7 but questioned by Rouland (1974) pp. 354–7, in my view rightly.

47　See, for instance, n.49.

48　See 2(d).

49　Suet.*Div.Jul*.23.

50　Diod.Sic.38.11 with Keaveney (2005a) pp. 95 n.54, 98 n.77. Von Premerstein (1937) pp. 27–30 doubts the authenticity of certain features of the oath, notably some of the deities invoked. He also connects it with the conspiracies in Liv.ep.71, assuming they were to aid Drusus. I prefer to assume they were those conspiracies out of which the confederacy was born: Keaveney (2005a) pp. 117–21. We can, however, agree that the oath had a partisan objective and envisaged clientage as was feared at the time. See Keaveney (2005a) p. 92 and note my qualificatory remarks in n.16 above where I point out that the intent and purpose of this clause differed from that which bound the swearer to the state of Rome.

51　So, for instance, Badian (1958) p. 207.

52　App.*BC*.1.29–32; Plut.*Mar*.29 with Gabba (1967) pp. 103–4; Lintott (1968) pp. 139–40; Carney (1970) p. 41 n.198.

53　As von Premerstein (1937) p. 30 saw. There has, however, been some controversy on this point. See n.55.

54　Plut.*Sulla* 10 with Keaveney (2005b) pp. 59–61.

55　Set out in Keaveney (1983b) pp. 79–80.

56　See next paragraph.

57　On *renuntiatio* see Levick (1981) especially pp. 380–1, 387–8.

58　App.*BC*.2.106 with Gelzer (1968) p. 278. Cf. Lintott (2003) p. 63.

59　Cic.*ad Att*.14.21.3; Dio 47.18.3.

60　App.*BC*.2.135 where the political situation which forced this concession 'in the public interest' is described.

61 App.*BC*.2.106, 124, 130, 145; Suet.*Div.Jul*.84, 86. This is, I believe, to be bracketed with the prayers for Pompey (see below) rather than, as von Premerstein (1937) pp. 34–5 thought, with the oath to Drusus (see above).

62 Involving, of course, religious vows rather than oaths.

63 *De Vir.Illust*.66. We cannot absolutely refute the claim that Drusus faked it in order to buy time in a worsening political situation – see Keaveney (2005a) pp. 91–2 – but the detail that it was induced by drinking goat's blood is as fictitious as the similar story about Themistocles and bull's blood, cf. Keaveney (2003b) pp. 95–8.

64 Seager (2002) pp. 145–6. The separate question of how this may have coloured his outlook in what was to follow is treated in 5(c).

65 Sall.Cat.22. Dio 37.30.3 says a child was sacrificed and the conspirators tasted of the entrails after pronouncing the oath. For a twentieth-century comment on these stories see McGushin (1977) pp. 151–3. If true this detail would, self-evidently, support von Premerstein (1937) p. 31 in his contention that the oath was private. For other human sacrifices see 2(a).

66 App.*BC*.3.77 who says that Bassus was coerced into swearing. There are variants in our account. See the fuller discussion in 5(d).

67 App.*BC*.5.20–21. Gabba (1970) p. 47 connects the oath here with the report of Dio 48.11.1–2 where it is said Octavian, realising he had inferior forces, wanted an agreement to give him time to augment and that when it failed he could blame others for this. On the officers involved see Gabba (1970) p. xxv.

68 *Res Gestae* 1. Discussions in Holmes (1928) pp. 144–5, 247–51; Syme (1939) pp. 284–9; Rouland (1979) pp. 505–6. He will also have heard, I am sure, of how Varro made Further Spain swear an oath of allegience at the start of the Second Civil War (Caes.*BC*.2.18).

69 As Caesar's had been.

70 For all that, it was unofficial – see Holmes (1928) p. 249. The simultaneous swearing in of provinces recalls those oaths and guarantees we saw the Romans extract from foreigners. The further political significance of the oath is discussed in 3(c).

71 See nn. 31, 33, 44. In the case of Bassus (n.65) the *sacramentum* is abandoned for a private oath.

72 (1984) p. 22.

73 But for the case of Octavian's oath see below.

74 And it may be said too of the worthless one made to Caesar.

75 Although it is not strictly germane to our purposes I shall make a brief comment (see n. 9) on the mention of the emperor in the imperial oath which is discussed by Campbell (1984) pp. 23–32. If we except the doubtful evidence of Servius (n. 7) there seems to be little in anything we have seen thus far which either actually attests a mention of *respublica* under the republic or points towards something which might be taken as a starting point for an imperial development. So I would argue it arose as a matter of course out of the change in the nature of the state. A real republic without a head had become a show republic with a head who enjoyed the widest powers including that of commander in chief. For a man of Augustus' intelligence it would not be difficult to see the advantages of such a change, especially when he contemplated the success of the oath of 32.

76 And liable to be killed with impunity: Brand (1968) p. 91 n.33.

77 Gruen (1995) p. 373 n. 57.

78 Oros.15.18.22–3; Flor.1.17.2; Lic. p. 25 Cr.; Val.Max.9.7.3, 8.3; *de Vir.Illust*.69. For a later example see App.*BC*.4.104.

79 Cinna: App.*BC*.1.78. Cato: Keaveney (2005a) p. 143, 152.

80 Val.Max.9.7 ext.2 with Mueller (2002) p. 127. As a victim he resembles, one supposes, for example Hortensius (MRR2.361).

81 MRR2.37.

82 Liv.ep.75; Val.Max.9.8.3 with Keaveney (2005a) pp. 152–3.

83 Oros.5.18.22–3.

84 *De Vir.Illust.*69

85 App.*BC*.1.78; Liv.ep.83. For an example of *superbia* in a modern army and its consequences see Lussu (1945) pp. 56–68.

86 App.*Mith*.51; Dio fr.104. 2–3. Cf. Keaveney (2005b) p.77.

87 Lic. p. 25 Cr.; Val.Max.9.7.3.

88 To judge by his comments Chrissanthos (2001) p. 68 has not appreciated this point. See next note.

89 Plut.*Sulla* 6; Front.*Strat*.1.9.2 which, despite Harmand's expression of agnosticism, (1967) p. 420, refers to this incident. The ulterior motive ascribed to Sulla by Plutarch, accepted by Harmand (1967) p. 276 and more recently by Amidani (1994), is anachronistic, cf. Keaveney (2005b) p. 43. We may compare Sulla's action with what Lussu (1945) pp. 172–84 tells us of a mutiny in the Italian army in the First World War. The ringleaders were condemned but then sent to the front to redeem themselves.

90 Keaveney (2005a) pp. 137–8. Some such parley also seems to have occurred between Sextus Pompey (uncle of Pompey the Great) and Vettius Scato of the Marsi: Keaveney (2005a) p. 151.

91 Plut.*Pomp*.10.11. I take these stories more seriously than Heftner (1995) pp. 109, 111–12 but less so than Nicolet (1980) p. 133.

92 Plut.*Pomp*.14; Front.*Strat*.4.5.1. Inconsistency: Seager (2002) p. 198 n.40. Frontinus' account (*Strat*.1.9.3) of how Pompey managed to punish those responsible for massacre and yet avoid a mutiny is further testimony to his skill in these matters.

93 Seager (2002) p. 22.

94 For these views see Badian (1958) p. 228 n.7 and Carney (1970) p. 60.

95 Plut.*Pomp*.3. Doubts in Badian (1958) p. 239 n.16; Seager (2002) p. 4 n.32.

96 For the background see Bennett (1923) pp. 15–19.

97 Plut.*Pomp*.3; Lic. p. 17 Cr. with Keaveney (1982c) pp. 112–13. Pompey's display reminds us histrionics were in fashion – see 3(a). Interestingly Licinianus says Strabo recovered slightly when Cassius arrived. One suspects the stimulus was the fear of losing power rather than the joy of receiving a successor. It is intriguing to speculate what might have happened to Cassius had Strabo recovered completely.

98 Plut.*Pomp*.3 with Heftner (1995) p. 75.

99 Plut.*Pomp*.5 with Keaveney (1982c) pp. 114–17. For doubts see Seager (2002) pp. 25–6.

100 Keaveney (2005a) p. 152.

101 App.*Mith*.52. See 3(a).

102 App.*BC*.1.91.

103 Keaveney (2005a) p. 134.

104 App.*Mith*.59–60, BC1.85–6; Plut.*Sulla* 25, 28, *Pomp*.7. Cf. Keaveney (1982c) pp. 119–20.

105 App.*BC*.1.87–8, 90–1. Auxiliaries too fell away – see Keaveney (2005b) p. 119.

106 Compare the tally for the period 509–134 in Messer (1920) pp. 162–69.

107 Origin of troops: App.*BC*1.82. Sulla and Norbanus: Keaveney (2005b) p. 111. Brunt (1988) p. 254 wondered if Appian had not 'garbled a contrast between troops drawn from old and new citizens'. As will emerge from the analysis of the situation below, it may be Brunt rather than Appian who has misunderstood.

108 See 3(a) where the possibility that money helped them make up their minds is discussed.

109 Keaveney (2005b) p. 77. This instinct can be seen also in the case of those who surrendered at Nola (n.27) in the Social War.

110 Keaveney (2005a) pp. 105–7.

111 App.*Mith*.59.

112 On all of this see Keaveney (2005b) pp. 108–9.

113 Dio fr.100 with Keaveney (2005a) p. 149 n.47. There is nothing to support Harmand (1967) p. 276 who supposes such political interference was a regular occurrence.

114 And punishments were becoming lighter. See Keaveney (1984) pp. 357–67. If we believe Plut.*Sulla* 6 Sulla must have found the situation frustrating.

115 Keaveney (2005a) pp. 142–5; (2005b) pp. 114–15.

116 Gruen (1995) pp. 373–4; Goldsworthy (1996) p. 30, 113, 251; Evans (1988) pp. 126–7.

117 Thus, I believe Gruen (1995) p. 372 misunderstands the significance of Caes.*BC*.39–41. Compare the behaviour of Wellington's men in the Peninsular campaign: Longford (1992) pp. 197, 211.

118 1(b); Keaveney (2005b) pp. 77–80, 82–3.

119 Keaveney (2005b) pp. 56–7.

120 Keaveney (2005b) pp. 114–15.

121 App.*BC*.1.89. Note also his earlier remark about the lion and the fox (Plut.*Sulla* 28).

122 See 3(c).

123 Keaveney (1978).

124 Caes.*BC*.1.12.

125 Caes.*BC*.1.12–13 with Gelzer (1968) p. 199.

126 Caes.*BC*.1.15–16.

127 Caes.*BC*.1.16–23; Dio 41.11.1–3; App.*BC*.2.38.

128 Caes.*BC*.1.72–7, 84–7; App.*BC*.2.42; Lucan 4.174–262. For Petreius' *sacramentum* see (a) above. Since Caesar says none of the Pompeians who surrendered were to be compelled to take the *sacramentum* against their will, we may assume some did so willingly. See further below.

129 Caes.*BC*.2.27–35.

130 *BC*.2.27. Plainly these had originated with Ahenobarbus' army (n.127). Compare n.131 below.

131 On the clemency of Corfinium see Gelzer (1968) p. 200.

132 On all of this see also (a) above.

133 Caes.*BC*.3.31.

134 Suet.*Div.Jul*.69; Dio 41.26–35; App.*BC*.2.47. See Chrissanthos (2001) p. 68 who points out that this is one of the rare occasions in the late republic when a commander checked a mutiny directly but neglected to take account that, in his hatred of mutiny (Dio 42.55.2–3; Suet.*Div.Jul*.70), Caesar undoubtedly would have liked to have gone farther but could not because at this juncture he dared not risk a loss of manpower, see Gelzer (1968) p. 219. In effect he was as circumscribed as Sulla, who also hated mutiny (Plut.*Sulla* 6), and Pompey had been some forty years before. See (b) above.

135 Caes.*BC*.3.19; Dio 41.47; App.*BC*.2.56. Narrating the story of the desertion of some Allobroges from his camp before Pharsalus, Caesar *BC*.59–61 remarks that desertion from his side was unusual but not from Pompey's. He gives no details, but the kind of thing recorded for Spain in 48 and 46 respectively (Caes.*BC*.1.77; *Bell.Hisp*.11) must have found parallels now. This sort of activity will, in part at least, explain why the Pompeians were wary of parley. Cf. Suet.*Div.Jul*.68.

136 But not perhaps as serious as Chrissanthos (2001) would have us suppose. In particular his handling of Cicero's evidence (p. 65) seems unsatisfactory. Cicero's attitude can surely be taken to mean he did not regard it as that serious a matter.

137 Others had been broken too. See Chrissanthos (2001) p. 70. There had also been a promise of money to be disbursed in the coming African War (App.*BC*.2.92). See also Hatscher (2000) pp. 174–5.

138 App.*BC*.2.92–4; Plut.*Caes*.51; *Bell.Af*.19, 28, 54; Dio 42.52.1–55.3; Cic.*ad Att*.11, 21.2, 22.2. Chrissanthos (2001) p. 70 emphasises the financial motive – rightly in my view. His analysis clearly shows the soldiers' lack of financial reward and thus renders plausible Dio's explanation here, even though elsewhere (41.17.3) he can attribute to Caesar and Pompey motivation which is more appropriate maybe to the Triumvirs.

139 Cic.*ad Fam*.12.18.1; *Bell.Alex*.66; Dio 47.26.3–27.1; App.*BC*.3.77, 4.58. See MRR 2.289. The contradictory and repetitive narratives of Appian illustrate his occasional failure to

integrate source material successfully. Cf. Keaveney (2003a) p. 234 and Botermann (1968) pp. 99–101.

It may also be mentioned that it was around this time that Cassius Longinus died. Appointed governor of Further Spain in 49 by Caesar, his behaviour led first to mutiny and then to open warfare. See *Bell.Alex*.48–64 with Gelzer (1968) pp. 241–2.

140 Dio 43.5. Cf. Gelzer (1968) pp. 266–7.

141 See Cic.*ad Fam*.7.3.2. Caesar's own exclamation after Pharsalus, *hoc voluerunt* (Suet.*Div. Jul*.30) adequately sums up this point, I believe.

142 See the account of the parley at Apsus (n.139 above).

143 *Bell.Af*.85.

144 We have to remember, of course, that many who were conscripted had little choice in the matter.

145 Dio 41.53, 58; App.*BC*.2.77.

146 Brunt (1988) p. 263 exemplifies this attitude. The evidence will be found in my (2005b) pp. 91–116.

147 Uttered in respect of Ilerda (Caes.*BC*.1.72) but obviously informing all the other occasions of overture enumerated in Caes.*BC*.3.90. We saw above (n.135) that these were not always welcome. Here we may add the murder of a prisoner by C. Longus Considius who was bringing a letter from Caesar (*Bell.Af*.4).

148 nn. 134 and 138. We saw there how Dio thought demands for discharge were specious, being designed to extract further concessions from Caesar, and that this was acceptable even if it must be acknowledged that some genuinely sought and were entitled to release from service. See the discussion of Chrissanthos (2001) pp. 69–71.

149 See, for instance, 2(d).

150 *In Pis*.92–3.

151 The mutiny in Lucullus' army: Keaveney (1992) pp. 120–6, 176–80.

152 Chrissanthos (2001) p. 70. There is a fuller discussion of Caesar's finances in 3(b).

153 Chrissanthos (2001) p. 70. There is no basis to the assertion of Brunt (1988) p. 268 that the Fimbrians were looking for a greater share of the booty.

154 As the demand so often involves land we have already said something about this, in the chapter dedicated to land, and the reader is now referred to that.

155 I certainly believe something more is required than the one vague generalised sentence Brunt (1988) p. 257 accords the topic. Weigel (1992) p. 92 recognised its importance but his treatment is brief.

156 App.*BC*.3.4–5, cf. 3.9; Cic.*Phil*.1.27, *ad Fam*.12.23.2; Plut.*Ant*.16, *Brut*.23; Suet.*Div. Aug*.16; Vell.Pat.2.60.3. See Holmes (1928) pp. 27–8 n.1 and Botermann (1968) p. 34 who points out that the enrolling of a bodyguard should be seen not as an attempt by Antony to establish a tyranny in the classic Greek manner but rather as an indicator of how the senate then regarded him. She also suggests Octavian may have been trying to seduce some of Antony's troops – a not unlikely scenario in view of his subsequent career.

157 App.*BC*.3.45. This incident also tells us something about the soldier's attitude towards land See 4 (b).

158 App.*BC*.3.31 (cf. 39), 43–5; Dio 45.12.2, 13.1–4; Liv.ep.117; Cic.*Phil*.3.4, 6, 11, 31, 5.22–3, 13.19, 14.31. Cf. Holmes (1928) p. 28. In his account of this mutiny Dio does not mention the political motive of desire to avenge Caesar but, as in the case of the latter's mutinies (see previous section), concentrates on the theme of extortion.

159 Cic.*ad Fam*.10.8.3, 32.3. Cf. *Phil*.13.35. This episode is discussed by Botermann (1968) pp. 72–4.

160 Dio 46.36.1 with the discussion of Botermann (1968) p. 72.

161 App.*BC*.3.66, 80, 84. On Appian's story that Ventidius intended to capture Cicero see Holmes (1928) p. 21 n.45.

162 Vell.Pat.2.62.5; Dio 46.40.5–41.2.

163 App.*BC*.3.53. In *BC*.3.56 Appian puts a defence of Antony into the mouth of Calpurnius Piso. Plainly there could be both good and bad mutinies.

164 Although Holmes (1928) pp. 61–2 seems to think there may have been an element of collusion between the two commanders. The more recent detailed discussion of Weigel (1992) pp. 60–1 comes to a broadly similar conclusion.

165 App.*BC*.3.83–4. Plut.*Ant*.18 offers a more colourful account with envoys disguised as prostitutes and an unkempt Antony pleading before the ramparts. He also adds the detail that success brings success. Plancus now came over to Antony.

166 App.*BC*.3.97.

167 App.*BC*.3.92–3.

168 Plut.*Brut*.25.

169 App.*BC*.3.79; Plut.*Brut*.25–8; Dio 47.21.5–24.4. See MRR2.342.

170 See n.138.

171 Liv.ep.114; Cic.*ad Fam*.12.18.1; Dio 47.26.3–27.1; App.*BC*.3.77–8, 4.58–9. Appian tells us that Murcus and Crispus were friendly with Cassius and anyway felt themselves bound to obey him as governor. He also tells us Cassius managed to get hold of an army which A. Allienus had brought from Egypt.

172 App.*BC*.4.60–2; Dio 47. On Dolabella see Holmes (1928) pp. 13–16, 47–8.

173 Gathered in the east. See Botermann (1968) pp. 89–96, 101–7.

174 App.*BC*.4, 100, 116, 130, 135; Dio 47.49.3.

175 Dio 48.10.1.

176 Fully discussed in 4(b).

177 App.*BC*.5.16; Dio 48.8–9.3. Octavian's reply here recalls Sulla's reaction to the murder of Albinus – see (b) above.

178 App.*BC*.5.30–1.

179 Dio 48.20.3.

180 App.*BC*.5.46–8. I describe this as 'play-acting' because it is difficult to imagine any Triumvir, let alone Octavian, passing up an opportunity to increase the size of his army merely to indulge a desire for revenge.

181 App.*BC*.5.50.

182 App.*BC*.5.65; Dio 48.25.2; Vell.Pat.2.78.1 with Holmes (1928) p. 80, 121 and Keaveney (2003a) p. 233.

183 App.*BC*.5.59.

184 One exception is Sextus Pompey who, in 42, disposed of his nominal colleague A. Pompeius Bithynicus: App.*BC*.5.70; Dio 48.19.1. Liv.ep.123. See Hadas (1930) p. 79 for an attempt to justify this.

185 App.*BC*.5.14, 66, 70; Vell.Pat.2.77.3. In his person Murcus sums up the flexibility of the age. Sent to Syria by Caesar, he joined Cassius and then threw in his lot with Sextus. See Holmes (1928) pp. 76, 89. According to Appian the latter found him to be too independent minded for his taste. Welch (2002) pp. 57 n.31 however finds Appian's story problematic.

186 App.*BC*.5.78, 96, 100–2; Dio 48.54.7, 49.1.4; Oros.6.18.25. Menas is called Menodorus by Appian: Holmes (1928) p. 109 n.1.

187 See the narrative of Holmes (1928) pp. 113–16 or Hadas (1930) pp. 123–47.

188 App.*BC*.5.123–9; Vell.Pat.2.81.1–2; Oros.6.18.33; Dio 49.13–14. See Keppie (1983) pp. 69–71 on the mutiny and Weigel (1992) pp. 88–93 on Octavian's takeover of Lepidus' army.

189 Here as above (nn.137, 147) Dio speaks of an ulterior motive. The soldiers, as on previous occasions, knew another war was coming. Octavian would have need of them and they proposed to maximise the profits to be extracted from the situation. See further n.73 for those wars.

190 See nn. 189 above and 194, 202 below.

191 Usually these decorations were more enthusiastically received. See Goldsworthy (1996) p. 276.

192 So Appian. For Dio's variant which is not of moment here see Keppie (1983) p. 70.

193 I agree with Keppie (1983) p. 73 that the incident in Dio 49.34.3–5 is only a minor local disturbance.

194 See n.190 and Holmes (1928) p. 119. Appian evidently concurs in the judgement as he finished his *Civil Wars* here – note his remark at *BC*.5.132.

195 Holmes (1928) pp. 130–5.

196 App.*BC*.5.17 and see my remarks on warlords in 2(d).

197 For the employment of slaves see 2(c).

198 Analysis tends to be somewhat sparse but compare the acute (Holmes (1928) pp. 84–5) with the vague (Brunt (1988) pp. 85–6). Of course excellence was not universal. For instance, of the ten legions Brutus led away from Mutina, four were experienced but affected by famine; the other six were mere raw recruits (App.*BC*.3.97)

199 Except where the infliction of archaic punishments was concerned, as Antony and Octavian, like Caesar before them, found out. Calvinus Domitius (Vell.Pat.2.78.3) seems to have been more successful here. He applied the *fustuarium* (beating to death with cudgels) in the case of a centurion whose flight in battle was held to be desertion.

    Incidents like that at Philippi when Brutus' men left off killing the enemy in order to plunder (App.*BC*.4.117) should not be cited as typical of the age but must be recognised as having a timeless quality. This one can be paralleled, for instance, in the campaigns of Lucullus. See Keaveney (1992) pp. 90–1 for the mule laden with gold which diverted his men from the pursuit of Mithridates.

200 The vague generalised declarations about unruly troops bringing down the republic, which are sometimes found in textbooks, must be scrupulously avoided. On the other hand the year 32 showed consuls and senators found it still easy to move: Holmes (1928) pp. 140–1.

201 Details in Holmes (1928) pp. 158–60, 171. By then, of course, his position was even stronger. See Syme (1939) pp. 305, 520–1.

202 Dio 49.13.2. Octavian took care to furnish concrete proof that he was putting things to rights: App.*BC*.5.130–2. Cf. n.190.

203 App.*BC*.5.15; Suet.*Div.Aug*.14.

204 See above.

205 We may remind ourselves that such seduction did not always succeed. Even Octavian failed on occasion.

206 This is amply illustrated, I think, by the Philippi campaign. See the careful analysis of Holmes (1928) pp. 80–8.

207 App.*BC*.3.78.

208 We may recall here our doubts about whether the *sacramentum* had a wider application or whether the soldier was bound by other oaths. See (a) above.

209 This outlook in its extreme form is captured perfectly in the classic passage of Appian (*BC*.5.17) where he says that, in the days of the Triumvirate, everybody claimed to be fighting for Rome and so switches of allegiance became easy and commonplace.

210 Though it will be recalled that Lucullus' problems presaged those of Caesar – see (c). Interestingly Clodius was never called to account for attempting to foment a mutiny in Lucullus' army – Keaveney (1992) pp. 122–4 – but two others, M. Atilius Bulbus and M. Alluis Staienus, were convicted of *maiestas* (treason) for fomenting mutiny respectively in the armies of C. Cascaius (propraet. 78) and Mam. Aemilius Lepidus (cos.77): Gruen (1995) pp. 524–5.

211 The connection between the Social and First Civil Wars is found in some ancient sources: Oros.5.12.1; Eutrop.6.9 – see the discussion in Keaveney (2005c) – which speak of them

as a ten years' war. Syme (1939) p. 17 also speaks of this but seems to be in ignorance of the source material. Strictly speaking the Social War was not, in itself, a civil war although it was fought against erstwhile allies and the issues in dispute became entangled in Roman politics and Rome's First Civil War. Further the similarities and differences in the behaviour of the troops over the period are instructive. Likewise, while we pass seamlessly from Caesar to the Triumvirate there are nevertheless differences and developments of which we must take account.

212 It was chiefly then that murderous subordinates flourished – see (b): a circumstance we have noted but can offer no explanation for. Indeed, in view of the bloodthirstiness of the Triumvirs it is surprising we do not hear more of it then.

213 See (b). One final observation may be made here. How far did reports of mutiny in one place inspire another elsewhere?

214 In the earlier period only Pompey's men, at his triumph, made protest about booty – see (b).

215 There were two legitimately constituted proconsuls involved here. The role of Metellus Pius is sometimes forgotten, cf. Keaveney (2005b) p. 111.

216 See 3(b) and (c).

217 We saw in our last section how Dio brought out this point. It has been remarked, cf. e.g. Holmes (1928) p. 128 n.1, that Dio can sometimes extrapolate a motive but here his deductions appear plausible and logical.

218 The concept of 'crisis without alternative' goes back, of course, to Meier (1966) pp. 201–5. I derive 'mutiny without alternative' ultimately from Dio 49.13.2. Speaking of Octavian's mutinous troops in 36, he says the latter, at first, paid them no heed because, with no enemy to face, he had no need of them. With this attitude and nowhere to desert to, the men naturally turned to mutiny. (Dio 49.13.3.)

219 (1939) p. 17.

220 Keaveney (2005b) p. 114.

6 The revolutionary army from Sulla to Augustus

1 Detailed annotation is not provided here as an acquaintance with the discussion which precedes is assumed.

2 This formulation is deliberate – see below on the exact moment when the army assumes a revolutionary guise.

3 And neither, I suggest, would want confusion to arise on that point.

4 However much he traded on the connection.

5 Two other passages reveal Plutarch's uncertain historical grasp. In *Mar*.9 he says Marius recruited slaves in 107 and in *Sulla* 6 accuses Sulla of loosening discipline in the Social War in order to have it as an instrument to use against Marius.

6 By way of comparison we may cite nineteenth-century Ireland. Dependence on one crop made ruin inevitable when blight attacked that crop.

7 And, as we know, formulated laws to see they did not re-appear.

8 We recognise that they come in a great variety. There is for instance the fatuous (tough on crime, tough on the causes of crime), the inspirational (Liberté, Egalité, Fraternité) and the sinister (ein Volk, ein Reich, ein Führer).

9 Keaveney (2005b) p. 43.

10 Although Cinna does not escape.

11 Sulla, of course, does not always receive credit for pursuing this latter objective.

12 In managerial patois they had become 'focussed'.

13 In two respects Cinna differed from Sulla. As Meier (1966) p. 230 emphasises, he had no comprehensive programme and like most of Sulla's imitators he came to a violent end.

14 The contrast with Sulla in 88 and Caesar in 49 is telling and instructive. Both relied on their armies and nothing else. Sulla enjoyed the absolute obedience of his; Caesar had to contend with mutiny.

15 We can see this from the march through Calabria and Apulia: Vell.Pat.2.25.1.

16 Conceding naturally that all revolutionary leaders did also have personal motives as well as public ones.

17 In fairness it should be said so too did Antony, but his schemes brought him to grief.

Appendix 1 The conspiracy of Catiline

1 Scholars have, of course, argued that Catiline was provoked by Cicero and also that what we dub a conspiracy was actually a number of separate plots which eventually coalesced, cf. Waters (1970); Seager (1973). For our purposes, however, we do not have to express an opinion on these theories. As will emerge, I hope, in our discussion it will suffice for us to recognise that a group of disgruntled nobles tried to capitalise on the grievances of others.

2 Plut.*Sulla* 32; Sall.*Cat*.47.2.

3 The known conspirators are tabulated and discussed by Gruen (1995) pp. 418–22.

4 Sall.*Cat*.21.1–2; Dio 37.30. Cf. Gruen (1995) p. 422.

5 Sall.*Cat*.20.14, 21.2.

6 Any hopes they might have had of the Roman populace vanished when the plebs discovered the Catilinarians proposed to fire the city. See Brunt (1988) p. 251.

7 Brunt (1988) p. 252.

8 Sall.*Cat*.28.

9 As Brunt (1988) p. 252 for instance noted.

10 1(b) and (d).

11 Although their economic plight should not be overlooked.

12 1(b).

13 See n.1.

BIBLIOGRAPHY

Aldrete, G. S. (1999) *Gestures and Acclamation in Ancient Rome*, Baltimore.

Amidani, C. (1994) 'L'assassinio di A. Postumio Albino e l'Assegnazione del comando Mithridatico a L. Cornelio Silla', *Aevum* 68: 89–94.

Angeli Bertinelli, M. G. (1993) in M. G. Angeli Bertinelli, C. Carena, M. Manfredini and L. Piccirilli, Plutarco: *Le Vite di Nicia e di Crasso*, Milan.

Astin, A. E. (1967) *Scipio Aemilianus*, Oxford.

Badian, E. (1958) *Foreign Clientelae* (264–70 B.C.), Oxford.

—— (1964) *Studies in Greek and Roman History*, Oxford.

Beard, M. and Crawford, M. (1999) *Rome in the Late Republic*, London, 2nd edn.

Beard, M., North, J. and Price, S. (1998) *Religions of Rome*, Cambridge, vol 1.

De Blois, L. (1987) *The Roman Army and Politics in the First Century B.C.*, Amsterdam.

Behrens, C. B. A. (1967) *The Ancien Régime*, London.

Bennet, H. A. (1923) *Cinna and His Times*, Menasha, WI.

Berry, D. (1996) *Cicero pro Sulla Oratio*, Cambridge.

Boatwright, M., Gargola, D. and Talbert, R. (2004) *The Romans from Village to Empire*, Oxford.

Botermann, H. (1968) *Die Soldaten und die römischen Politik in der Zeit von Caesars Tod bis zur Begründung des Zweiten Triumvirats*, Munich.

Brand, C. (1968) *Roman Military Law*, Austin, TX.

Bringman, K. (2002) *Geschichte der römischen Republik*, Munich.

Brunt, P. A. (1987) *Italian Manpower*, Oxford, 2nd edn.

—— (1988) *The Fall of the Roman Republic and Related Essays*, Oxford.

Butler, H. E. and Cary, M. (1927) *C. Suetoni Tranquilli Divus Julius*, Oxford.

Cairns, F. and Fantham, E. (2003) *Caesar Against Liberty,* Cambridge.

Campbell, J. R. (1984) *The Emperor and the Roman Army 31 BC–AD 235*, Oxford.

Carney, T. F. (1970) *A Biography of C. Marius*, Chicago, 2nd edn.

Chrissanthos, S. G. (2001) 'Caesar and the Mutiny of 47 B.C.', *Journal of Roman Studies* 91: 63–75.

Cobban, A. (1963) *A History of Modern France*, Harmondsworth, vol. 1.

Dandamaev, M. A. and Lukonin, V. G. (1989) *The Culture and Social Institutions of Ancient Iran*, Cambridge.

Defosse, P. (2003) *Hommages à Carl Deroux III: Histoire et épigraphie droit*, Brussels.

De Ligt, L. (2004) 'Poverty and Demography: The Base of the Gracchan Land Reforms', *Mnemosyne* 57: 725–57.

Deroux, C. (1983) *Studies in Roman History and Latin Literature III*, Brussels.

Drexler, H. (1935) 'Parerga caesariana', *Hermes* 70: 203–35.

Edwards, C. and Woolf, G. (2003) *Rome the Cosmopolis*, Cambridge.

Evans, J. K. (1988) 'Resistance at Rome: The Evasion of Military Service in Italy during the Second Century B.C.', in Yuge and Doi 1988, pp. 121–40.

Evans, R. J. (1994) *Gaius Marius – A Political Biography,* Pretoria.

—— (1999) 'Displaying Honourable Scars: A Roman Gimmick', *Acta Classica* 42: 77–94.

—— (2003) *Questioning Reputations: Essays on Nine Roman Republican Politicians*, Pretoria.

Fezzi, L. (2001) 'In Margine all' legislazione frumentaria di età republicana', *Cahiers Glotz* 12: 91–100.

Flower, H. J. (2004) *The Cambridge Companion to the Roman Republic*, Cambridge.

Foxhall, L. (1990) 'The Dependent Tenant: Land Leasing and Labour in Italy and Greece', *Journal of Roman Studies* 80: 97–114.

Frere, S. S. (1987) *Britannia*, London, 3rd edn.

Gabba, E. (1967) *Appiani Bellorum Civilium Liber Primus*, Florence, 2nd edn.

—— (1970) *Appiani Bellorum Civilium Liber Quintus,* Florence.

—— (1976) *Republican Rome: The Army and the Allies*, trans. P. J. Cuff, Oxford.

—— (2003) 'Caesar's Reforms' in Cairns and Fantham 2003, pp. 183–94.

Gargola, D. G. (1995) *Lands, Laws and Gods*, Chapel Hill, NC.

Garnsey, P. (1970) *Social Status and Legal Privilege in the Roman Empire*, Oxford.

Gelzer, M. (1968) *Caesar*, trans. P. Needham, Oxford.

—— (1969) *The Roman Nobility*, trans. R. Seager, Oxford.

Ghilli, L. (2001) in T. Muccioli and L. Ghilli, Plutarco: *Vite di Lisandro e di Silla*, Milan.

Goldsworthy, A. K. (1996) *The Roman Army at War*, Oxford.

Greenidge, A. H. J. (1904) *A History of Rome*, Oxford, vol. 1.

Gruen, E. S. (1984) 'Material Rewards and the Drive for Empire' in Harris 1984, pp. 59–82.

—— (1995) *The Last Generation of the Roman Republic*, Berkeley, 2nd edn.

Hadas, M. (1930) *Sextus Pompey*, New York.

Harmand, A. (1967) *L'Armée et le soldat à Rome de 107 à 50 avant notre ère*, Paris.

Harris, W. V. (1971) *War and Imperialism in Republican Rome*, Oxford.

—— (1984) *The Imperialism of Mid-Republican Rome*, Rome.

Hatscher, C. R. (2000) *Charisma und Respublica: Max Webers Herrschaftssoziologie und die römische Republik*, Stuttgart.

Heftner, H. (1995) *Plutarch und der Aufstieg des Pompeius: Ein historischer kommentar zu Plutarchs Pompeius vita Teil 1: Kap. 1–45*, Frankfurt-am-Main.

Hillman, T. P. (1988) 'Pompeius' *Imperium* in the War with Lepidus', *Klio* 80, pp. 91–110.

—— (1997) 'Pompeius in Africa and Sulla's order to demobilize', *Latomus* 56: 94–106.

Holden, H. (1886) *Plutarch's Life of Lucius Cornelius Sulla*, Cambridge.

—— (1900) *M. Tulli Ciceronis de Officiis Libri Tres*, Cambridge, 2nd edn.

Holmes, T. R. (1928) *The Architect of the Roman Empire*, Oxford, vol. 1.

Huzar, E. G. (1978) *Mark Antony: A Biography*, Minneapolis.

Jehne, M. (1987) *Der Staat des Dictators Caesar*, Cologne.

Jongmann, W. (2003) 'Slavery and the Growth of Rome. The Transformation of Italy in the Second and First Centuries BCE', in Edwards and Wolff 2003, pp. 100–22.

Kapuściński, R. (2001) *The Shadow of the Sun*, trans. K. Glowczenska, London.

Keaveney, A. (1978) Pompeius Strabo's Second Consulship', *Classical Quarterly* 28: 240–2.

—— (1982a) 'Sulla and Italy', *Critica Storica* 19: 499–544.

—— (1982b) 'Sulla Augur: Coins and Curiate Law', *American Journal of Ancient History* 7: 150–71.

—— (1982c) 'Young Pompey 106–79 B.C.', *L'Antiquité Classique* 51: 111–39.

—— (1983a) 'Sulla and the Gods', in Deroux 1983, pp. 44–79.

—— (1983b) 'What Happened in 88?', *Eirene* 20: 53–86.

—— (1984) 'Civis Romanus sum', *Critica Storica* 21: 345–72.

—— (1987) 'Vespasian's Gesture', *Giornale Italiano di Filogia* 39: 213–16.

—— (1992) *Lucullus – a Life*, London.

—— (1998) 'The 130's B.C.: Three Chronological Problems', *Klio* 80: 66–90.

—— (2003a) 'Cassius' Parthian Allies', in Defosse 2003, pp. 232–4.

—— (2003b) *The Life and Journey of Athenian Statesman Themistocles (524–460 B.C.) as a Refugee in Persia*, Lampeter.

—— (2005a) *Rome and the Unification of Italy*, Bristol, 2nd edn.

—— (2005b) *Sulla the Last Republican*, London, 2nd edn.

—— (2005c) 'The Terminal Date of Sulla's Dictatorship', *Athenaeum* 93: 423–39.

Keppie, L. (1983) *Colonisation and Veteran Settlement in Italy 47–14 B.C.*, London.

—— (1984) *The Making of the Roman Army from Republic to Empire*, London.

Konrad, C. F. (1994) *Plutarch's Sertorius: A Historical Commentary*, Chapel Hill, NC.

Leach, J. (1978) *Pompey the Great*, London.

Levick, B. (1981) 'Professio', *Athenaeum* 54: 378–88.

Lintott, A. W. (1968) *Violence in Republican Rome*, Oxford.

—— (2003) *The Constitution of the Roman Republic*, Oxford.

Lo Cascio, E. (1990) 'Ancora sui Censi minimi delle Classi Cinque Serviane', *Athenaeum* 76: 273–302.

Longford, E. (1992) *Wellington*, London.

Lough, J. (1960) *An Introduction to Eighteenth Century France*, London.

Lovano, M. (2002) *The Age of Cinna*, Stuttgart.

Lussu, E. (1945) *Un Anno sull' Altipiano*, Turin.

McGushin, P. (1977) *C. Sallustius Crispus, Bellum Catilinae, a Commentary*, Leiden.

—— (1992) *Sallust: The Histories*, Oxford, vol 1.

Mackay, C. S. (2004) *Ancient Rome: A Military and Political History*, Cambridge.

Marshall, B. (1972) 'The Lex Plotia Agraria', *Antichton* 6: 43–55.

Meier, C. (1966) *Respublica Amissa*, Wiesbaden.

—— (1996) *Caesar*, trans. D. McLintock, London.

Messer, W. S. (1920) 'Mutiny in the Roman Army', *Classical Philology* 15: 158–75.

Millar, F. (1998) *The Crowd in Rome in the Late Republic*, Michigan.

Morley, N. (2001) 'The Transformation of Italy, 225–28 B.C.', *Journal of Roman Studies* 91: 50–62.

Mouritsen, H. (2001) *Plebs and Politics in the Roman Republic*, Cambridge.

Mueller, H. F. (2002) *Roman Religion in Valerius Maximus*, London.

Nagle, D. B. (1976) 'The Etruscan Journey of Tiberius Gracchus', *Historia* 25: 487–9.

de Neeve, P. (1984) *Colonus*, Amsterdam.

Nicolet, C. (1977) *Rome et la conquête du monde méditerranéen*, Paris, vol 2.

—— (1980) *The World of the Citizen in Republican Rome*, trans. P. S. Falla, Berkeley.

Parker, M. D. (1958) *The Roman Legions*, Cambridge.

Paul, G. M. (1984) *A Historial Commentary on Sallust's Bellum Jugurthinum*, Liverpool.

Pelling, C. (1996) 'The Triumviral Period', in *Cambridge Ancient History*, Cambridge, vol. 10, 2nd edn, pp. 1–69.

Piccirilli, L. (1990) in C. Carena, M. Manfredini and L. Piccirilli, *Plutarco: Le Vite di Cimone e di Lucullo*, Milan.

—— (1997) in M. G. Angeli Bertinelli, M. Manfredini, L. Piccirilli and G. Pisani, *Plutarco: Le Vite di Lisandro e di Silla*, Milan.

Polverini, L. (1964) 'L'aspetto sociale del passagio della Republica a Principato', *Aevum* 38: 439–67.

Potter, D. (2004) 'The Roman Army and Navy', in Flower 2004, pp. 66–88.

Powell, A. (2002) '"An Island amid the Flame", the Strategy and Imagery of Sextus Pompius 43–36 B.C.', in Powell and Welch 2002, pp. 103–33.

Powell, A. and Welch, K. (2002) *Sextus Pompeius*, London.

Pina Polo, F. (1995) 'Procedures and Functions of Civil and Military *Contiones* in Rome', *Klio* 77: 203–16.

Pritchett, W. K. (2002) *Ancient Greek Battle Speeches and a Palfrey*, Amsterdam.

Rathbone, D. (1983) 'The Slave Mode of Production in Italy', *Journal of Roman Studies* 73: 160–8.

—— (1993) 'The Census Qualifications of the *Assidui* and the *prima classis*', in Sancisi Weerdenberg 1993, pp. 121–56.

Rawson, E. (1978) 'Caesar, Etruria and the *Disciplina Etruscia*', *Journal of Roman Studies* 68: 132–52.

—— (1994) 'The Aftermath of the Ides', in *Cambridge Ancient History*, Cambridge, vol. 9, 2nd edn, pp. 468–90.

Rich, J. W. (1983) 'The Supposed Roman Manpower Shortage of the Later Second Century B.C.', *Historia* 32: 287–331.

Rijhoek, K. G. (1992) *Studien zu Sertorius 123–83 v. Chr.*, Bonn.

Rosenstein, N. (2004) *Rome at War*, Chapel Hill, NC.

Rouland, N. (1977) *Les esclaves romains en temps de guerre*, Brussels.

—— (1979) *Pouvoir politique et dépendance personelle dans l'antiquité romaine*, Brussels.

Rudé, G. (1964) *Revolutionary Europe 1783–1815*, London.

Salmon, E. T. (1970) *Roman Colonisation under the Republic*, Ithaca, NY.

Sancisi-Weerdenberg, H. (1993) *De Agricultura: In Memoriam P. W. de Neeve*, Amsterdam.

de Sanctis, G. (1967) *Storia dei Romani*, Florence, vol. 3.1.

Sartori, F. (1973) 'Cinna e gli Schiavi', *Actes du Colloque 1971 sur l'esclage: Centre de recherches d'histoire ancienne VI Paris, Les Belles Lettres*, vol. 6, pp. 151–69.

Scullard, H. H. (1982) *From the Gracchi to Nero*, London, 5th edn.

Scheidel, W. (2004) 'Human Mobility in Roman Italy, I: The Free Population', *Journal of Roman Studies* 94: 1–26.

—— (2005) 'Human Mobility in Roman Italy, II: The Slave Population', *Journal of Roman Studies* 95: 66–79.

Schneider, H. C. (1977) *Das Problem der Veteranenversorgung in der späten römischen Republik*, Bonn.

Seager, R. (1973) 'Iusta Catilinae', *Historia* 22: 240–8.

—— (2002) *Pompey*, London, 2nd edn.

Smith, R. E. (1955) *The Failure of the Roman Republic*, Cambridge.

—— (1957) 'The Lex Plotia Agraria and Pompey's Spanish Veterans', *Classical Quarterly* 7: 82–5.

—— (1958) *Service in the Post-Marian Roman Army*, Manchester.

Spann, P. O. (1987) *Quintus Sertorius and the Legacy of Sulla*, Fayetteville, AR.

Stone, S. C. (2002) 'Sextus Pompeuis, Octavian and Sicily', in Powell and Welch 2002, pp. 134–65.

Syme, R. (1939) *The Roman Revolution*, Oxford.

—— (1979) *Roman Papers*, ed. E. Badian, Oxford, vol. 1.

Talbert, R. J. (1989) 'The Role of the Helots in the Class Struggle at Sparta', *Historia* 37: 22–40.

Taylor, L. R. (1962) 'The Forerunners of the Gracchi', *Journal of Roman Studies* 52: 19–27.

Terrenato, N. (1998) 'Tam firmum municipium: The Romanization of Volaterrae and Its Cultural Implications', *Journal of Roman Studies* 88: 94–114.

Valgiglio, E. (1956) Plutarco: *Vita di Mario*, Florence.

—— (1960) *Vita di Silla*, Turin.

Virlouvet, C. (1985) *Famines et émeutes à Rome des origines de la république à la mort de Néron*, Rome.

Von Premerstein, A. (1937) *Vom Werden und Wesen des Prinzipats*, Munich.

Ward, A. M. (1977) *Marcus Crassus and the Late Roman Republic*, London.

Wardle, D. (1998) *Valerius Maximus: Memorable Deeds and Sayings Book I*, Oxford.

Waters, K. H. (1970) 'Cicero, Sallust and Catiline', *Historia* 19: 195–215.

Weigel, R. (1992) *Lepidus the Tarnished Triumvir*, London.

Weinstock, S. (1971) *Divus Julius*, Oxford.

Welch, K. (2002) 'Sextus Pompeius and the *Respublica* in 42–39 B.C.', in Powell and Welch 2002, pp. 31–63.

Westermann, L. (1955) *The Slave Systems of Greek and Roman Antiquity*, Philadelphia.

Whitehead, D. (1986) 'The Measure of a Millionaire: What Crassus Really Said', *Liverpool Classical Monthly* 11: 71–4.

Wiehn, E. (1926) *Die illegalen Heereskommanden in Rom bis auf Caesar*, Marburg.

Wiseman, T. P. (1998) *Roman Drama and Roman History*, Exeter.

—— (2002) 'Roman History and the Ideological Vacuum', in T. P. Wiseman (ed.), *Classics in Progress*, Oxford, pp. 285–310.

Wistrand, E. (1987) *Felicitas Imperatoria*, Göteborg.

Woodham Smith, C. (1962) *The Great Hunger*, London.

Young, A. (1929) *Travels in France during the Years 1787, 1788 and 1789*, ed. C. Maxwell, Cambridge.

Yuge, T. and Doi, M. (1988) *Forms of Control and Subordination in Antiquity*, Leiden.

INDEX